A

SMARTER

CHARTER

A
SMARTER
CHARTER

Finding What Works
for Charter Schools
and Public Education

Richard D. Kahlenberg and Halley Potter

Teachers College, Columbia University
New York and London

Published by Teachers College Press, 1234 Amsterdam Avenue, New York, NY 10027

Library of Congress Cataloging-in-Publication Data

Kahlenberg, Richard D.
  A smarter charter : finding what works for charter schools and public education / Richard D. Kahlenberg, Halley Potter.
  pages cm
  Includes bibliographical references and index.
  ISBN 978-0-8077-5579-2 (pbk.)—ISBN 978-0-8077-5580-8 (case)—ISBN 978-0-8077-7325-3 (ebook)
  1. Charter schools—United States. 2. School choice—United States. 3. Public schools—United States. 4. Educational change—United States. I. Potter, Halley. II. Title.
  LB2806.36.K35 2014
  371.05—dc23

                                                                      2014018445

ISBN 978-0-8077-5579-2 (paper)
ISBN 978-0-8077-5580-8 (hardcover)
ISBN 978-0-8077-7325-3 (ebook)

Printed on acid-free paper
Manufactured in the United States of America

21 20 19 18 17 16 15 14   8 7 6 5 4 3 2 1

Contents

Acknowledgments

T HIS BOOK IS THE RESULT of several years of work and the help of many people. We are grateful for the support that The Century Foundation gave in encouraging and supporting this research, and particularly for the guidance and leadership of Janice Nittoli and Greg Anrig. We are also especially grateful to our wonderful interns Tara Dunderdale, Denise Jones, and Michael Steudeman, who helped conduct interviews and contributed significant research for this project.

A number of experts in the field gave us advice, answered research questions, and provided feedback on drafts. Their wisdom was influential as this book took shape. We would like to thank all those who helped, including Saba Bireda, Cindy Brown, Leo Casey, Christina Collins, Maria Ferguson, Erica Frankenberg, Mary Futrell, Jewell Gould, Joe Graba, Jonathan Gyurko, Frederick Hess, Ted Kolderie, Robin Lake, Michael Petrilli, Mitch Price, Bella Rosenberg, Marsha Silverberg, Louise Sundin, Bob Tate, Phil Tegeler, and Nancy Van Meter.

In addition, we are indebted to the educators and families who shared their experiences for this book. Teachers, administrators, parents, and students at charter schools were incredibly generous with their time in granting us interviews and allowing us to visit their schools and classrooms, often using precious planning time or evenings to assist with our research. This book would not have been possible without their assistance and their stories. Thanks to Vasthi Acosta, Jennifer Antolino, Sarah Apt, Carrie Bakken, Mike Chalupa, Jeremy Chiappetta, Jeff Cooper, Deborah Crockett, Ben Daley, Tracey Dann, Bill Day, Cristina de Jesus, John Delich, Josh Densen, Jeff Desserich, Karen Dresden, Sarah Fine, Aaron Forbes, Peter French, Alexandra Fuentes, Nicole Nash Gales, Peggy Gladden, Connie Goodly-LaCour, Edith Ibarra, Brian C. Johnson, Salina Joiner, Joan Jones, Allison Keil, Hope Kennell, Neerav Kingsland, Bill Kurtz, Geetha Lakshminarayanan, Kristin Leguizamon, Ana León, Stacey Lopaz, Bobbi Macdonald, Kathleen Maher, Biz Manning, Kathleen McCann, Celeste Mims-Covington, Jon Moscow, Jennifer Niles, Tiana Nobile, Monica O'Gara, Chris O'Neill, Cris Parr, Tracy Pendred, Patricia Perkins, Rich Pohlman, Peter Redgrave, Rob Riordan, Jeff Robin, Sahba Rohani, Larry Rosenstock, Mary Ann Rupcich, Gretchen Sage-Martinson, Tracy Schloemer, Kate Seidl, Bobby Shaddox, Rowan Shafer, Terri

Smyth-Riding, Jennifer Sonkin, Sarah Strong, Dee Thomas, Francina Yaw, and Arielle Zurzolo.

Lastly, we are grateful for the family and friends who helped and encouraged us throughout the project, especially Halley's husband, Nathan Taylor; and Rick's wife, Rebecca, and daughters Cindy, Jessica, Caroline, and Amanda.

Introduction

IN 1988, EDUCATION REFORMER and teacher union leader Albert Shanker proposed a new kind of public school—"charter schools"—which would allow teachers to experiment with innovative approaches to educating students. Publicly funded but independently managed, these schools would be given a charter to try their fresh approaches for a set period of time and be renewed only if they succeeded.

Freed from bureaucratic constraints, teachers would be empowered to draw on their expertise to create educational laboratories from which the traditional public schools would learn. And liberated from traditional school boundaries, Shanker and other early charter advocates suggested, charters could do a better job than the regular public schools of helping children of different racial, ethnic, economic, and religious backgrounds come together to learn from one another.

In the past 2 decades, charter schools have grown by leaps and bounds, from a single school in Minnesota in 1992 to more than 6,400 charter schools today, serving over 2.5 million students in 42 states. Between the 2012–2013 and 2013–2014 school years, enrollment grew by 13%, and seven districts now have more than 30% of public school students enrolled in charters (National Alliance for Public Charter Schools [NAPCS], 2013a, 2014).

But somewhere along the way, charter schools went in a very different direction from the one Shanker originally envisioned. Many charter school founders empowered management, not teachers, and adopted antiunion sentiments. Today, just 12% of charter schools are unionized, and teacher retention rates—one possible measure of professional satisfaction—are much lower than in traditional public schools (NAPCS, 2011; Stuit & Smith, 2012). Moreover, most charter schools largely discarded the goal of student integration. Today, charters are actually more economically and racially segregated than traditional public schools. The purpose of charter schools also evolved. Originally conceived as laboratories with which traditional public schools would collaborate, charters became a force for competition, with some suggesting they replace district schools.

All in all, the change was quite dramatic. Proposed to empower teachers, desegregate students, and allow innovation from which the tra-

1

ditional public schools could learn, many charter schools instead prized management control, reduced teacher voice, further segregated students, and became competitors, rather than allies, of regular public schools.

The reduced teacher voice and increased segregation might seem defensible if charter schools were clearly providing a superior form of education to students systemwide. But the best evidence suggests that is not the case. While there are excellent charter schools and there are also terrible ones, on average, charter students perform about the same as those in traditional public schools (see, e.g., Cremata et al., 2013; Gleason, Clark, Tuttle, & Dwoyer, 2010). In our view, the charter school movement, once brimming with tremendous promise, has lost its way.

The good news is that within the varied charter school world, there are a small but growing number of leaders and institutions that are resurrecting the original idea behind charters. In this book we profile 15 exciting charter schools that promote teacher voice or economic and racial diversity, or—in a few cases—do both. To us, these charter schools offer the right approach because, according to extensive research, students have a better chance of building deep knowledge and honing critical thinking skills in schools where teachers have voice and student bodies are integrated.

Moreover, the schools we profile offer a sensible way out of the charter school wars by rejecting competing visions in which charter schools are either to be vanquished or completely victorious. On the one hand, we disagree with charter school opponents, who would simply abandon the experiment entirely. Because of their freedom and flexibility, charters have the potential to provide excellent learning environments for students—and many do. Moreover, as a practical matter, even fierce critics such as Diane Ravitch (2013) note that charter schools are "here to stay" (p. 252). Public support for charters has continued to grow, from 43% in 2002 to 68% in 2013, according to annual Phi Delta Kappa/Gallup polls (Bushaw & Lopez, 2013; Rose & Gallup, 2003).

On the other hand, we disagree with some charter school enthusiasts who argue that charters should try to completely replace the traditional public schools. Despite their enormous growth, charters still educate only about 5% of public school students. The abiding purpose of charters must be not only to educate the students under their own roofs but also to bring lessons to the traditional public schools, which will educate the vast majority of American students for the foreseeable future.

The relevant question today is no longer whether charter schools are good or bad as a group. Rather we ask, can charter schools be taken in a better direction—one that finds inspiration in the original vision of charters as laboratories for student success that bring together children from different backgrounds and tap into the expertise of highly talented teachers?

OVERVIEW OF THIS BOOK

This book begins by presenting in Chapter 1 the changing face of charter schools, tracing the evolution of the idea from Shanker's original notion to a more conservative vision. Whereas Shanker had imagined teacher leadership and union support, others saw in charter schools the chance to circumvent teacher unions. Likewise, rather than emphasizing student diversity, charter schools began targeting specific student subgroups.

In Chapter 2 we conclude that the charter school movement took a wrong turn when it placed a heavy bet on the importance of maximizing administrator control and reducing the voice of teachers. In Chapter 3 we examine the evidence regarding the wisdom of the second major turn in the charter school movement: from a tool to integrate students to a mechanism for serving niche markets defined by race, ethnicity, and income, resulting in segregation levels even higher than in the traditional public schools.

Some charter proponents respond that while school integration and teacher voice might be nice things to have, what really matters is academic quality and charters produce superior results. But in Chapter 4 we review the research, which suggests that while charter schools were meant to serve as models for the regular public schools, on the whole, charters perform no better or worse than district schools.

The second half of the book discusses the exciting efforts of a growing number of charter schools to resurrect the early vision of schools that empower teachers and integrate students. In Chapter 5 we profile eight charter schools that empower teachers through unionization, by employing a co-op organizational structure, or by creating an intentionally nonhierarchical culture. In Chapter 6 we profile eight schools that buck the national charter trend in another way: they intentionally integrate students of different economic, racial, and ethnic backgrounds. And in Chapter 7 we profile three schools that prize both teacher voice and student diversity. Taking up these two threads of Shanker's vision and tying them together, these schools offer a powerful alternative to the dominant charter school narrative.

Unfortunately, schools that prize teacher voice and student diversity remain outliers in the charter school landscape, so in Chapter 8 we detail ways in which public policies and philanthropic priorities might be adjusted to revive the Shanker model.

A CALL TO ACTION

What are the prospects that Shanker's original vision of integrated charter schools that empower teachers will be revived in the future? No one knows for sure, but looking forward, some critical trends may guide the charter school movement in that direction.

First, in the long run, hostility toward teacher voice and teacher unions is a self-defeating strategy. Inhibiting teacher voice means charter schools are missing out on the ideas of lots of talented teachers, and it is generating an unsustainable level of teacher turnover that is both expensive and bad for children. Moreover, as a practical political matter, if charter schools wish to expand their reach beyond a small fraction of students, charter school leaders need to come to an accommodation with teacher unions. Starting in 2009, the competitive Race to the Top grant program provided a one-time offer of federal stimulus dollars to states to encourage and support the Obama administration's education reform priorities, including expanding charter schools. From 2010 to 2013, lawmakers in 18 states lifted caps on the number of charter schools allowed, many motivated by the hope of cashing in on these funds (Ackerman, 2013). But that leverage is coming to an end as Race to the Top money dries up. As long as charters are seen by unions as an explicitly antiunion vehicle, charter schools will face strong political opposition from very well-organized and powerful groups. Even where unions don't shut down expansion, they can push to limit funding for charters, which in turn may reduce the effectiveness of the enterprise (Gyurko, 2008). Finally, to the extent that charter school leaders wish to be exemplars for the entire public school system, rather than just create a boutique experience for relatively small numbers of students, leaders should be open to creating the type of labor–management relations that will make lessons more easily transferable.

Second, demographic trends raise the importance of charter schools serving as laboratories of integration. We are fast becoming a "majority-minority" nation, and that reality is hitting the school-aged population first. This development places a premium on schools that can demonstrate the best ways to educate a diverse population under one roof. Increasingly, educating children from different racial, ethnic, and economic groups in separate enclaves will leave them all unprepared for succeeding in a diverse workforce. Meanwhile, growing economic segregation of American neighborhoods, and the growing divide between rich and poor, will increase the need for schools to develop creative ways to give all children a chance to succeed. Existing efforts to make separate schools for rich and poor equitable have proven highly frustrating. Charters could show the way on how to create—and enable students to fully benefit from—diverse learning environments.

Finally, if charter schools continue down their current academic path, they are likely to lose momentum. Having only pockets of success coupled with an equal number of failures will give policymakers little reason to continue to invest in the enterprise.

That would be an enormous shame. As small, decentralized institutions, charter schools have the chance to innovate and be more democratic than traditional public schools. The handful of schools we profile in this book offer a way to capitalize on that democratic vision, by giving teachers more say and giving students a chance to interact with classmates of different backgrounds. Charter schools have tremendous potential to fulfill the great democratic mission of American public education, at once promoting social mobility and social cohesion. In the pages that follow, we describe the students, teachers, and principals who are working each day to help realize those goals.

1

The Dramatic Evolution of the Charter School Idea

AT 6'4", WITH A BRILLIANT MIND and a blunt, New York style, Albert Shanker, president of the American Federation of Teachers (AFT), cut an imposing figure. Although Shanker was head of the smaller of the nation's two leading teacher unions, he was more often than not the one invited to speak at education gatherings of business leaders and government officials because Shanker was known to advance provocative and creative ideas about how to improve public education. A former PhD candidate in Columbia University's Philosophy Department, Shanker was a font of ideas, which he articulated in a weekly column purchased by the teacher union in the Sunday *New York Times* beginning in the early 1970s. "The impact was extraordinary," Senator Daniel Patrick Moynihan said. "Union leaders in those days rarely wrote essays, still less felicitous, thoughtful analyses of public policy" (quoted in Kahlenberg, 2007b, p. 2). Shanker was at once a founding father of modern teacher unionism and a leading education reformer, supporting national education standards, a tough entrance exam for teachers, and plans to reward excellent educators and remove inadequate ones. In the last 2 decades of the 20th century, wrote educator E. D. Hirsch, Jr., "Albert Shanker made himself the most important figure in American education" (quoted in Kahlenberg, 2007b, p. 7).

So expectations were high on March 31, 1988, when Shanker rose to address the National Press Club in Washington, DC. He did not disappoint, shaking the education world with an extraordinary speech in which he proposed the creation of "a new type of school," which he later referred to as "charter schools" (Shanker, 1988b, p. 11).

THE ORIGINAL VISION BEHIND CHARTER SCHOOLS

Shanker was frustrated by the way education was being delivered in traditional public schools. Schools were run like factories, he said, in which students moved at the sound of a bell from class to class, where teachers lectured to them for hours on end, and where students with different learning styles were expected to learn in the same way at the same pace. This system worked fine for about 20% of students, said Shanker. But for the 80% of students who didn't learn well under that regime, he thought different approaches were needed. "Can we come up with a plan for a school which doesn't require kids to do something that most adults can't do, which is to sit still for 5 or 6 hours a day listening to somebody talk?" (Shanker, 1988b, p. 14).

Laboratory Schools

In his speech Shanker proposed a new mechanism by which a small group of teachers—between 6 and 12—could come together with parents and propose the creation of a different type of school. These teachers would say, "We've got an idea. We've got a way of doing something very different. We've got a way of reaching the kids that are now not being reached by what the school is doing" (Shanker, 1988b, p. 12).

These schools might experiment with team teaching; greater time set aside for teachers to share ideas; teachers as coaches, rather than lecturers; programs that allow students to learn at their own pace; and cooperative learning in which "kids can sit around a table and help each other just as the kids help each other on a basketball team" (Shanker, 1988b, p. 15)—ideas that, in those days, were pushing the envelope.

These schools wouldn't proclaim to have all the answers. In fact, Shanker suggested that they should admit this outright—"that we really do not know just how to reach the 80% of these kids . . . and that therefore we are engaged in a search" (Shanker, 1988b, p. 16). But through experimentation, the new charter laboratory schools might produce breakthrough lessons about curriculum or pedagogy, which could then be applied broadly to traditional public schools. Shanker suggested creating a national data bank in which charter school teachers could share experiences about what worked well for students. Small-scale experimentation was critical to the concept's potential success, Shanker said. While it is virtually impossible to change an entire school system at once, smaller groups of teachers could make inroads with charter schools and create new methods that could serve as examples for the larger system.

Under Shanker's program, proposals for charter schools would be reviewed, evaluated, and approved or rejected by panels that included union representatives, school board members, and outsiders. Charters would be schools of choice—no student or teacher would be compelled to be part of one. And Shanker proposed that the schools be given independence for a 5–10-year period to prove themselves, because new education ideas need time to be nurtured and cultivated. In order to make these new schools successful, he outlined two critical conditions: that schools provide teachers with strong voice; and that the schools educate kids from all walks of life.

Teacher Voice

In Shanker's vision, innovation in charter schools would come from giving teachers greater voice than in regular public schools. Not only would union representatives be part of the authorizing board of charter schools, charter school teachers would be represented by unions, and charter school proposals would include "a plan for faculty decision making" (Shanker, 1988b, p. 13). Rather than having a principal walk into a teacher's classroom once a year and provide an evaluation, for example, groups of teachers would work with one another in teams, and if some weren't doing their part, the others would hold them accountable. The idea was consistent with Shanker's support for peer assistance and review plans in traditional public schools, where expert teachers would try to assist struggling colleagues, and if unsuccessful, recommend termination (Kahlenberg, 2007b).

In charter schools certain union-negotiated rules could be bent to encourage innovation. For example, Shanker said, class size requirement might be waived in order to merge two classes to allow for team teaching (Fiske, 1989). But the basic union structures and protections should remain in place, he argued. Shanker noted that traditional school districts that were the most innovative provided such an environment. "You don't see these creative things happening where teachers don't have any voice or power or influence." Only when teachers feel protected from the whims of administrators are they willing to take risks (Shanker, 1988b, p. 9).

Shanker knew personally what it was like to be a teacher in New York City prior to collective bargaining, when teacher unions were weak, pay was poor, and principals were autocratic. Those experiences galvanized him in the early 1960s to work with other educators to form the United Federation of Teachers, which would become one of the largest and most powerful unions in the country. Unions brought greater dignity, security, and influence for teachers; and Shanker did not want to give up those gains in the new schools he proposed.

Indeed, with charter schools Shanker saw the possibility of taking teacher voice to a new level. Charter schools were part of his larger vision for moving teaching from a mere occupation to a genuinely respected profession, in which teachers took significant responsibility for the running of schools. In Shanker's vision, as Peter Cookson and Kristina

Berger (2002) note, teachers "would be recognized as experts and, given the freedom to follow their own educational visions, would surely make schools better places for teachers to teach and more effective environments for students to learn" (p. 33).

Economically and Racially Integrated Schools

In his proposal Shanker also emphasized the importance of ensuring that charter schools avoid de facto segregation by race, ethnicity, class, or ability: "We are not talking about a school where all the advantaged kids or all the White kids or any other group is segregated to one group. The school would have to reflect the whole group" (Shanker, 1988b, p. 15).

Shanker, who had marched with Martin Luther King, Jr., in the 1960s, had always been a strong integrationist. He despised segregation—whether imposed by White advocates of Jim Crow or Black separatists who championed "community control" of schools in New York City's Ocean Hill–Brownsville neighborhood. And he was an early supporter of the magnet school model that emerged as a desegregation strategy during the 1960s. Whereas the hallmark of charter schools was to be their unique governance model that offered increased flexibility for a finite period in exchange for increased accountability come time for the charter's renewal, magnet schools were set apart by specialized curricular or pedagogical themes and diverse enrollment. Magnets would advance racial and socioeconomic integration by drawing students from across an area, unconstrained by traditional attendance zones or district boundaries (Kahlenberg, 2007b).

Shanker had long favored integrated schools as a way of promoting both social mobility and social cohesion. Research found, Shanker noted, "that children from socioeconomically deprived families do better academically when they are integrated with children of higher socioeconomic status and better-educated families." He observed, "when children converse, they learn from each other. Placing a child with a large vocabulary next to one with a smaller vocabulary can provide a gain to one without a loss to the other" (quoted in Kahlenberg, 2007b, pp. 84–85).

Moreover, Shanker argued, segregation undercuts one of the central purposes of public education: to serve as the glue that holds American society together. "Without public education, there would be no America as we know it." Given that the United States draws upon immigrants from all over the world, with different religions, languages, races, and customs, public schools are uniquely important in this country. "The public schools, more than any other institution in our society . . . have brought together different groups—groups which in other societies would always be at war with each other—and taught them to respect and work with each other. . . . It is no exaggeration to say that the public schools helped to bring about a political, social and cultural miracle" (Shanker, quoted in Kahlenberg, 2007b, p. 236).

While in practice too many public schools remained racially and economically segregated in 1988, Shanker envisioned charters with the potential to be more integrated. As schools of choice, charters, like magnet schools, could be accessible to students from across a geographic area, rather than limiting enrollment based on what neighborhood a child's family could afford to live in, the way many traditional public schools do. Moreover, charters could draw students from more than one school district, thereby providing an opportunity to address interdistrict segregation. By severing the strong connection between residential segregation by race and class and segregation in schooling, charters could extend the use of choice—long the province of wealthy students who could attend private school—to allow students of all backgrounds to attend economically and racially integrated public charter schools.

The use of choice to promote integration had been advanced for years by liberal advocates of private school vouchers such as Theodore Sizer and Christopher Jencks. As James Forman, Jr. (2005), notes, "Race and class integration were central to Sizer's and Jencks's vision" (p. 1315). So too, with respect to charter schools, integrationist Amy Stuart Wells (1993) argued that charter schools plans could include "a 'diversity component' that would facilitate the creation of racially balanced student populations at each charter school" (p. 126).

Shanker was particularly intrigued by the possibility of new schools that could combine these two critical elements—enhanced teacher voice and school integration. His National Press Club speech proposing charter schools was based in part on a formative October 1987 visit to an innovative teacher-led middle and high school educating a diverse population in Cologne, Germany. The Holweide Comprehensive School staff was divided into teams of 6–8 teachers who were given enormous latitude on what subjects would be taught, when, and by whom, so long as students were prepared to meet common standards. The school's student body of 2,000 was highly diverse, with Turkish and Moroccan immigrant pupils learning alongside native Germans. Unlike most other German schools, where students were rigidly tracked, the Holweide school employed mixed-ability groupings, where "peer influence is used to promote learning." Cooperative learning trumped lectures. "The results," Shanker wrote in one column "are impressive," with unexpectedly large numbers of students going on to college (Shanker, 1988a).

REACTION TO SHANKER'S CHARTER SCHOOL IDEA

Four months after his National Press Club speech, Shanker's idea won the endorsement of the 3,000 delegates to the American Federation of Teachers convention in San Francisco (Kahlenberg, 2007b). In the Press Club address, Shanker didn't actually employ the term "charter school," but in a July 1988 column (Shanker, 1988c), he formally gave the name to his proposal. Drawing upon educator Ray Budde's (1988) report *Education by Charter: Restructuring School Districts,* Shanker said "charter" was an appropriate term, noting that "explorers got charters to seek new lands and resources." Invoking Budde's thinking, Shanker fleshed out the analogy: Discoverers such as Henry Hudson were people "with a vision or a plan" who were granted charters to explore "unknown territory" for a defined length of time, and involving "a degree of risk." Likewise, teams of teachers with "visions of how to construct and implement more relevant educational programs" would be granted charters to run schools for 3–5 years, testing out ideas "with no guarantee" of success (Shanker, 1988c).

Conservatives were initially unenthusiastic about Shanker's idea of diverse, teacher-led schools that would engage in broad experimentation. William Kristol, then chief of staff to Ronald Reagan's Secretary of Education William Bennett, said that while the department "didn't have problems" with the proposal, "we think there is lots of evidence that traditional methods are working" (quoted in Kahlenberg, 2007b, p. 312). Assistant Secretary of Education Chester Finn attacked the charter school proposal, saying it suggested that we did not already know what works in education (Kahlenberg, 2007b).

But if there was skepticism from the Reagan administration in Washington, policy leaders and influential educators in the state of Minnesota, including Ted Kolderie and Joe Nathan, were intrigued (Kahlenberg, 2007b). In October 1988 Shanker spoke at the Minneapolis Foundation's Itasca Seminar about the charter school idea, and among those in attendance was Democrat-Farmer-Labor (DFL) State Senator Ember Reichgott (later Reichgott Junge), a member of the Education Committee. She said she had never heard of charter schools but was taken by Shanker's "visionary" idea to create new schools and empower teachers. Reichgott Junge (2012) wrote later that Shanker had "asked two questions: How could teachers be part of a consistent way to make innovation an ongoing and valued part of the school community? And how could the system partner with teachers to encourage risk taking and change?" (p. 35).

Reichgott Junge (2005), who would go on to author the nation's first charter school legislation, was excited by the idea of making teachers feel more invested in schools. She noted that "many teachers were frustrated with their work and were leaving the profession. I wanted to give them more ownership" (p. 9). At the time, 8% of teachers were leaving the profession or retiring every year (Ingersoll, 2001b). Reichgott Junge (2012) recalls, "For me, chartering was all about empowering teachers—giving them the authority to take leadership as professionals by spearheading and forming new chartered schools. I felt it was an option for entrepreneurial teachers to break away from the system—the status quo—and try something new" (p. 113).

The idea of charter schools received another boost in November 1988, when the Citizens League, a community policy organization in Minnesota, issued an influential report *Chartered Schools = Choices for Educators + Quality for All Students* (School Structure Committee, 1988). Like Shanker, the committee that authored the report argued that charter schools should be guided by two central tenets: empowering teachers and promoting diversity. The report called first for "Providing Cooperative Management of Schools," giving teachers the chance to have greater say over how schools were run (p. 5). The second goal was "Building Additional Quality Through Diversity" (p. 9). The report specified that charter schools would enroll students of all races and achievement levels: "The committee's vision for chartered public schools is that they must, like any public school, serve all children" (p. 14). To promote diversity, the proposal called for charter schools to employ

> outreach programs to inform students, living both inside and outside the district, from a variety of income levels and races, about the school, . . . curricula designed to appeal to students who would make a diverse student enrollment, . . . programs and instructional approaches that encourage the interaction of students and promote integration, . . . [and] culturally- and racially-diverse staff. (p. 14)

The bottom line, the committee argued, was that "the school's student enrollment could not be segregated." Charter schools would be required to have "an affirmative plan for promoting integration by ability level and race," and failing to meet this requirement could be grounds for revoking the charter (p. 15).

But in a notable departure from Shanker's vision—and a hint of things to come—the report left the door open for minority-oriented schools. "Although these criteria would prohibit the establishment of schools designed for any single racial or ethnic group, the committee appreciates the complexity of this issue and suggests that the Legislature might wish to deal separately with voluntarily segregated schools established by minority groups" (p. 15). In addition, the report suggested that schools for academically at-risk students could be allowed as an exception to the policy that otherwise prohibits charters from screening students based on achievement level.

Overall, though, the report said that integrated schools should be the norm. "Rather than roll back the gains made by desegregation over the last generation, or settle for that achievement, we should expand the commitment to go further, to do more" (p. 17). And in a twist, the proposal also highlighted the importance of economic integration: "Although desegregation rules focus exclusively on students' race or ethnic background, family income levels better determine children's preparation for school and academic success." The committee suggested, therefore, that we should "be at least as concerned about segregation by income as segregation by race" (p. 18).

In 1990 the charter idea gained further prominence after the state legislature in neighboring Wisconsin passed the nation's first private school voucher law, providing public support for low-income Milwaukee students to attend private and parochial schools. The argument, advanced by Black Democratic legislator Polly Williams, was that low-income Black students deserved something better than the dysfunctional urban schools to which they were assigned. This development gave another reason for progressives to back charter schools: as an alternative to vouchers. Charters were a choice option that avoided the concerns posed by vouchers—entanglement of church and state and a lack of accountability for public dollars. Ted Kolderie, former director of the Citizens League in Minneapolis, Minnesota, and member of the committee that authored their *Chartered Schools* report, noted the news from Milwaukee. He argued in a November 1990 paper for the Progressive Policy Institute, a Washington, DC, think tank associated with the Democratic Leadership Council, that charters were a way to strengthen public education, not abandon it. Again, teacher empowerment was a core idea of the Progressive Policy Institute report. Kolderie wrote that charter schools could provide nothing less than "the opportunity for teachers to own and run the new schools" (p. 3).

As outlined by Shanker, Reichgott Junge, the Citizens League, and Kolderie, then, the original vision of charter schools rested on three pillars: (1) This new type of school should be allowed to experiment with desperately needed new approaches to reach students, approaches from which the traditional public schools could learn. (2) Charter schools would provide an enhanced level of teacher voice and teacher empowerment compared with the public schools, which saw large levels of teacher frustration and turnover. (3) Charters, by severing the tie between residential neighborhood segregation and school segregation, might help reinvent the old idea of the American common school, where students of different races, incomes, and religions could come and learn together under a single schoolhouse roof. These were the animating ideas behind the exciting new proposal for charter schools. But the question remained: Once the idea was written into legislation, how faithfully would these principles be honored in practice?

THE DEVELOPMENT OF A MORE CONSERVATIVE VISION OF CHARTER SCHOOLS

In 1991 Minnesota became the nation's first state to adopt charter school legislation—and, with it, came the first significant deviation from Al Shanker's original vision for charters. Over the years, Minnesota teachers had fought hard to ensure that educators, like lawyers, doctors, and architects, pass certification requirements in order to enter the profession. They also fought to ensure that teachers were supported and protected by democratically elected union representatives who could bargain collectively on their behalf. When Ember Reichgott Junge's charter school legislation was introduced in the Minnesota state legislature, however, it failed to include either universal teacher certification requirements or automatic collective bargaining rights for teachers. If enhancing teacher voice was a central tenet of the charter school idea, why, teachers asked, would the charter legislation strip teachers of the protections of the district contract? The Minnesota Federation of Teachers strongly opposed the legislation on licensure and collective bargaining grounds (Reichgott Junge, 2012).

In addition, Minnesota's charter law did nothing to prevent the creation of charter schools aimed at particular ethnic and racial minority groups, something Shanker found fundamentally at odds with the very idea of public education in America. Over time, Minnesota would come to host some 30 charter schools focused on students from specific ethnic or immigrant groups, such as Somali, Ethiopian, Hmong, or Latino populations (Rimer, 2009).

The new, more conservative, charter vision, which promoted neither teacher voice nor school integration, quickly swept the country. Democratic President Bill Clinton, elected in 1992, became a strong supporter of charter schools and pushed for federal seed money to promote them. Following Minnesota's adoption of the nation's first charter school law in 1991, state legislation was introduced and passed in capital after capital. By 2014, there were 6,400 charter schools in 42 states and the District of Columbia (NAPCS, 2014).

As states began enacting charter school legislation, the departure from Shanker's vision was repeated over and over again in the three critical areas: collaborating with traditional public schools, empowering teachers, and integrating students. As the original goals of charter schools were up-ended, conservatives like the Reagan administration's Chester Finn came to support charters. And, in a stunning reversal, Al Shanker, described variously as the "godfather," "de facto creator," and "initiator" of charter schools, came to oppose most of them (Ted Kolderie, Diane Ravitch, and Ruth Wattenberg, quoted in Kahlenberg, 2007b, p. 313). Below, we outline how this remarkable transformation occurred on those three criti-cal questions: (1) whether charters would cooperate with regular public schools or serve as competitors; (2) whether they would enhance teacher voice or increase management authority; and (3) whether they would promote diversity or cater to niche markets.

Cooperative Laboratories Versus Competitors

Whereas Shanker emphasized the way in which charter schools could serve as a laboratory for testing ideas that could improve public schools, many conservatives saw in charters the potential to inject greater com-petition with public schools, forcing them to improve. The model was similar to the argument advanced by conservative supporters of private school vouchers: that competitive pressures of charters would compel regular public schools to do better (Nathan, 1996). James Goenner, President and CEO of the National Charter Schools Institute, for ex-ample, suggested in 1996 that "charter schools are a vehicle for infusing competition and market forces into public education, a proven method for responsive change and improvement" (p. 32). As charter school leg-islation was passed in state after state, the competition rationale grew in strength. Indeed, in a 2013 examination of charter school laws, research-ers found the most popular purpose cited in state law for charter schools was to provide competition (Wohlstetter, Smith, & Farrell, 2013). The triumph of the market rationale over the laboratory theory also helps ex-plain why more than 80% of states with charter school laws allow public funds to go to private, for-profit charter operators (NAPCS, 2013b).

Some charter school advocates went further on the competition ques-tion and argued that charters should not merely serve as a spur to improve public schools but that in the long run the charter schools should replace the traditional public school system entirely. Hugh Price, president of the National Urban League, suggested in 1999 that we "charterize" all ur-ban schools. In 2009 Tom Vander Ark, former education director at the Bill and Melinda Gates Foundation, removed Price's urban qualifier to suggest, "All schools should be charter schools." And in 2013 U.S. Sena-tor Lamar Alexander (R-TN), the former U.S. Secretary of Education, said, "I still wonder why we, over time, don't make every public school a charter school." He continued, "You couldn't do it all overnight, but you could do it over 20, 25 years" (quoted in Zelinski, 2013). In New Orleans—where roughly 90% of public school students attended charter schools in 2013–2014, compared to less than 5% in 2004–2005 (Brinson, Boast, Hassel, & Kingsland, 2012)—U.S. Secretary of Education Arne Duncan was so enthusiastic that he called Hurricane Katrina "the best thing that happened to the education system in New Orleans" (quoted in N. Anderson, 2010a).

Along with the shift in goals, the public policy rhetoric changed from an emphasis on how charters could best serve as laboratory partners to public schools to whether charters as a group are "better" or "worse" than traditional public schools. Tellingly, a growing number of studies were conducted to determine not what lessons could be learned from charters but whether charters outperform or underperform traditional public schools (studies we will cite later in this volume).

Over time, the market metaphor came to replace the laboratory metaphor. As Peter Cookson and Kristina Berger observed in 2002, "Much of the charter movement is rooted in the same assumptions and philosophy that [voucher advocates John] Chubb and [Terry] Moe use to support their belief that the American public school system should be transformed into a market-based 'economy' that forces autonomous, publicly funded schools to compete for students" (p. 43). Meanwhile, given the adversarial and competitive environment in which charters and traditional public schools found themselves, there was precious little evidence that the two sets of institutions were actively cooperating to share best practices. As Scott D. Pearson of the U.S. Department of Education's charter school program noted in 2010, while "one of the promises of charter schools was they were going to be a source of innovation and be a benefit not only for the children attending charter schools, but [for] all public schools, . . . [in practice], . . . the collaboration is not as widespread as we would hope" (quoted in Zehr, 2010). Originally viewed as "isolated laboratories of innovation," charter schools came to be seen by many as a replacement for traditional public schools and "charter-school expansion as a solution itself" (Visser, 2013).

Enhancing Teacher Voice Versus Increasing Management Authority

The second dramatic shift in the charter school vision came in the critical area of teacher voice. In state after state, charter legislation followed the Minnesota model of failing to provide automatic collective bargaining rights for all charter school teachers similar to those enjoyed by regular public school teachers. (Just 5 of 42 states with charter school laws require charter school teachers to be covered by the district collective bargaining agreement [NAPCS, 2013b].) In theory, many state laws provided for the possibility of organizing charters on a school-school basis, but given the expense of unionizing a small number of teachers, few unionizing efforts have been made. Overall, teachers in just 12% of charter schools are unionized (NAPCS, 2011). By contrast, 60% of public school districts have an agreement with a union, and more than three-quarters of teachers nationwide are members of teacher unions (U.S. Department of Education, National Center for Education Statistics [NCES], 2008, 2012a). States did not offer a sensible middle ground, in which teachers would, upon the creation of a new charter school, have the automatic opportunity to vote on whether to form a union and create a contract that would be tailored to the individual needs of their school.

Over time, conservative charter school advocates argued that having a nonunion environment in charter schools was a key advantage—perhaps the defining advantage—over regular public schools. Finn, initially skeptical of the charter idea, came to champion them, arguing that "the single most important form of freedom for charter schools is to hire and fire employees as they like and pay them as they see fit" (quoted in "Unions Consider," 1996).

Union supporters responded that under collective bargaining agreements in traditional public schools, it is possible to fire teachers, so long as due process is provided; and many unions in district public school systems have embraced performance pay. But conservatives in the business world, politics, and the finance and philanthropic communities saw charters as an attractive vehicle for circumventing teacher unions, organizations they see as harmful to children. Republican Steve Forbes, for example, wrote an editorial in 2009 praising the results of New York City Charter Schools that are "not burdened with the mind-numbing, effectiveness-killing bureaucratic and union restrictions." In the same year, Jeanne Allen, then executive director of the Center for Education Reform, flatly argued, "A union contract is actually at odds with a charter school" (quoted in Greenhouse & Medina, 2009).

The antiunion sentiment of many charter schools and charter school supporters is underlined by the reaction to attempts to unionize or to assert union rights in the charter sphere. *The Washington Post* editorial page, for example, recounting a dispute in a unionized charter school in Baltimore, suggested, "Apparently not content with their part in stifling needed change in traditional schools, teachers unions are now setting their sights on undermining public charter schools" ("Undermining," 2009). Likewise, the Chicago Math and Science Academy, an Illinois charter school, was so opposed to recognizing a union created by teachers that it broke with the longstanding rhetoric of charter school supporters nationally and declared itself to be a "private" institution. The Academy said that even though the school receives more than 80% of its financial support from public sources—and even though charter schools nationally take pride in being "public" institutions—the Academy falls under federal labor law governing private institutions rather than the state law that governs public institutions. The National Labor Relations Board sided with the school, forcing teachers to go through a new unionization process (Woodard, 2013).

Promoting Diversity Versus Catering to Niche Markets

The third and final major evolution away from Albert Shanker's original vision of charter schools came in the realm of student diversity. Shanker believed having separate schools by race and class was inherently undemocratic, and he and some other early charter school backers saw charters as a way of breaking down segregation. That priority is evidenced in many early charter school laws, particularly those passed in the early to mid-1990s in states like Wisconsin, Hawaii, Kansas, and Rhode Island, which required all charter schools to take positive steps to promote diversity. According to a 2009 analysis by Erica Frankenberg and Genevieve Siegel-Hawley, 16 states had laws that permit or require charter schools to employ positive steps to bring about greater levels of racial and/or socioeconomic diversity.

But over time, concerns about diversity have often been eclipsed by efforts—well-meaning in nature, to be sure—that have the effect of concentrating minority and low-income students in racially and economically isolated charter schools. Rather than emphasizing diversity and the possibility for breaking down segregation, charter school supporters began advocating for schools to target minority and low-income group members, who are demonstrably in need of better schools. According to a 2010 study by the Civil Rights Project, for example, almost half of low-income students in charter schools attended schools where more than 75% of students are low-income, compared to about a third of low-income students in traditional public schools. In addition, 36% of all students in charter schools attended schools where 90% or more of students are from minority households, compared with 16% of all students in regular public schools (Frankenberg, Siegel-Hawley, & Wang, 2010; for further discussion, see Chapter 3).

How did a policy that began with the idea of promoting diversity end up exacerbating racial and economic concentrations? Fundamentally, charter school advocates suggested, integration and school quality are unrelated and distinct priorities, and quality matters more. When confronted by research finding higher levels of racial and economic segregation in charter schools, for example, Nelson Smith, then-president and chief executive of the National Alliance for Public Charter Schools (NAPCS), said, "We actually are very proud of the fact that charter schools enroll more low-income kids and more kids of color than do other public schools." He continued: "The real civil rights issue for many of these kids is being trapped in dysfunctional schools" (quoted in N. Anderson, 2010b).

Two arguments were advanced for targeting low-income, minority, and immigrant groups in racially and economically isolated charter schools: the need to maximize bang for the educational buck, and the belief that the special needs of these communities could be better addressed in concentrated settings.

Charter school operators, who are in the business because they believe they can do a better job of educating students than the regular public schools, by and large sought to bring the benefits of their schools to the students most in need. Under this view, the best way to help at-risk students and close the achievement gap is to prioritize low-income and minority students. Given scarce federal, state, and philanthropic dollars, funding a racially and economically integrated school that includes not only substantial numbers of low-income and minority students but also substantial numbers of middle-class and White students may be seen as diluting funding for at-risk students. Based on similar logic, charter school authorizers—the various state, local, or independent agencies charged with approving new charter schools, monitoring their progress, renewing charters for successful schools, and closing schools that fail to meet performance requirements—may favor high-poverty charter schools. Authorizers may choose to prioritize applications for schools located in the areas with fewest high-quality educational opportunities, which are often communities with concentrated poverty.

Advocates of low-income charter schools further suggest that disadvantaged students need a different set of pedagogical approaches than middle-class students. Highly routinized, "no excuses" schools set rigorous academic standards but also emphasize "noncognitive skills," such as self-discipline, and seek to develop an all-encompassing school climate to combat the culture of poverty from which their students come. Paul Tough (2006), author of a book about the Harlem Children's Zone, describes the philosophy behind "no excuses" secondary schools that target at-risk students: "The schools reject the notion that all that these struggling students need are high expectations; they do need those, of course, but they also need specific types and amounts of instruction, both in academics and attitude, to compensate for everything they did not receive in their first decade of life."

Journalist David Whitman (2008) suggests that highly effective high-poverty schools often employ a "paternalistic" approach specifically tailored to low-income students. He says they teach students

> not just how to think, but also how to act according to what are commonly termed traditional, middle-class values. These paternalistic schools go beyond just teaching values as abstractions: the schools tell students exactly how they are expected to behave, and their behavior is closely monitored, with real rewards for compliance and penalties for noncompliance. (p. 54)

Similar arguments are made on behalf of charter schools that cater to targeted immigrant populations. Educator Joe Nathan (2008), for example, supports the Twin City International Elementary and Middle Schools, which educate mostly Somali and Oromo students, because the schools provide a space where children can retain their home language and knowledge of their home culture. Likewise, Letitia Basford's (2010) qualitative study of Somali youth concluded that "attending a culturally specific charter school promotes positive intercultural competence in which students are able to build a good self-concept and find comfort in who they are as East African immigrants, as Muslims, and as American citizens" (p. 485). One student told Basford that in a charter school in which 100% of students are Muslim, she did not feel embarrassed running to the bathroom at prayer time the way she might have in an integrated school. Likewise, Jewish advocates have called for the creation of Hebrew language schools to "strengthen Jewish communal identity" (Michael Steinhardt, quoted in Weiss, 2008).

Proponents of charter schools that are self-segregated argue that they are qualitatively different from the segregated schools of the past because they are the product of acts of volition on the part of racial, ethnic, or religious minorities. Bill Wilson, an African American advocate who grew up attending segregated public schools in Indiana, notes, "We had no choice. I was forced to attend an inferior school, farther from home than nearby, better-funded 'Whites-only' schools. Higher Ground [a racially isolated charter school] is open to all. No one is forced to attend. Quite a difference" (quoted in Nathan, 2010).

Among the most influential actors in the charter school world—state legislators and philanthropists—the idea of catering to niche markets has, over time, generally trumped the original emphasis on creating schools that promote diversity and reinforce the American common school ideal. Laws in roughly a dozen states, including Illinois, North Carolina, and Virginia, prioritize charter school funding for at-risk or low-income students or, in Connecticut's case, students in districts in which members of racial or ethnic minorities constitute 75% or more of enrolled students.

Other state laws restrict attendance zones for charter schools, making it more difficult for charters to attract a diverse population from a wide geographic area (Education Commission of the States, 2013). And even state laws that require charter schools to mirror local demographics could end up concentrating poverty. For example, a 2010 New York State charter school law requiring charter schools to mimic the demographics of the surrounding neighborhood—implemented to address gaps in English language learner (ELL) and special education enrollment at charter schools—might mean, if enforced, that a school in Upper Manhattan District 6 would need to enroll a student population in which 98% are eligible for free or reduced-price lunch, a commonly used measure of low-income status (Cromida, 2012).

Likewise, the other key players in funding charter schools—philanthropists—often prioritize education projects in high-poverty locations, providing incentives for charter school creators to maximize the proportion of low-income students in a school in order to gain funding. The Walton Family Foundation (2013a), for example, focuses specifically on selected "Market Share Demonstration Sites," which are all districts with high concentrations of low-income students, and the Broad Foundation (n.d.) focuses generally on urban school districts. Some of the charter school chains that have received the most generous philanthropic support pride themselves on their ability to educate pupils in schools with high concentrations of low-income and/or minority students. KIPP schools, for example, boast that "more than 86 percent of our students are from low-income families and eligible for the federal free and reduced-price meals program, and 95 percent are African American or Latino" (KIPP, 2013).

Rick Hess of the conservative American Enterprise Institute notes the trend among foundations to support charter schools "that have the highest octane mix of poor and minority kids" and outlines how that priority can work at cross-purposes with integration. He wrote in 2011, "The upshot is that it is terribly difficult to generate interest in nurturing racially or socioeconomically integrated schools, even though just about every observer thinks that more such schools would be good for kids, communities, and the country" (pp. 127–128).

SHANKER'S REACTION TO THE CHANGING VISION OF CHARTER SCHOOLS

Before his death in 1997, Albert Shanker watched with growing dismay as the charter school idea he proposed at the National Press Club in 1988 morphed into something quite different. To begin with, Shanker was disturbed that the market-driven charter school rationale led some states to allow private for-profit corporations to enter the charter school business. For-profit companies, he warned, would inevitably put shareholder interests before educating children, and "vouchers, charter schools, for-profit management schemes are all quick fixes that won't fix anything" (Shanker, 1993). Shanker worried that while some charter school operators were well-intentioned, "there are other supporters of charter schools whose real aim is to smash the public schools" (Shanker, 1994).

Shanker was also furious that his charter school proposal had been turned into an antiunion vehicle for conservatives. In a private February 1996 American Federation of Teachers Executive Council meeting, Shanker complained that across the nation, from Pennsylvania to Washington, DC, to California, the charter school movement was being used in a way "designed to undermine unions and collective bargaining, to destroy them." He expressed annoyance that "it is almost impossible for us to get President Clinton to stop endorsing them in all of his speeches" (quoted in Kahlenberg, 2007b, p. 316). Just 30 years after teacher unions had begun collective bargaining, Shanker saw charters as a serious setback (Gyurko, 2008).

While charter school advocates said the union-free environment allowed for greater flexibility to fire bad teachers and hire good ones, Shanker argued that, on net, unions were a strong plus for both teachers and students, fighting for adequate teacher pay and benefits (to attract stronger candidates), reduced class size, more professional development, and strong discipline. The right-wing utopia, "where teachers have neither collective bargaining rights nor due process and school boards and principals can pretty much do what they like[,] already exists. It's called the American South." And those schools were hardly lighting the education world on fire (Shanker, 1996).

Moreover, as a practical matter, Shanker warned, as charters became an explicitly antiunion movement, their growth was naturally being opposed by unions. As a result, the lessons learned were being resisted by teachers in the unionized sector, undercutting a chief rationale for experimentation in the first place (Kahlenberg, 2007b).

Shanker also worried that charters were becoming a balkanizing force in education, undercutting a principal rationale for public funding of schools. For one thing, he worried about charter laws that allowed for "creaming." For example, he criticized a charter law in California that allowed schools to use contracts with parents to skim the most motivated families and exclude others. Contracts, which required parents to volunteer in school and attend meetings or be subject to fines, discriminated against students based on their parents' actions. "The parent contract serves as a kind of sorting device," he said, in which "children whose parents are scared off by the contract's tone, or don't have the time to volunteer, or can't read, or don't understand what is being asked, won't be enrolling in one of these schools" (Shanker, 1995).

Shanker also worried that some private religious schools were being closed and reopened in somewhat different form as charter schools, with taxpayer funds. Shanker (1994) wrote about a Michigan charter school, Noah Webster Academy, which received public funds to establish a computer network to educate a group of Christian home-schooled students. "The students will continue to study at home the way they do now, but every family will get a taxpayer-paid computer, printer and modem, and there will be an optional curriculum that teaches creationism alongside biology."

Finally, Shanker worried that some ethnically based charter schools were sowing racial disunity. In 1996 Shanker reprinted in his paid "Where We Stand" column an article by Michael Kelly from *The New Republic*, which described an incident at Washington, D.C.'s Afrocentric Marcus Garvey Public Charter School—which has since closed—in which a White reporter was assaulted and told to get her "White ass out of this school." Kelly (1996) wrote: "Public money is shared money, and it is to be used for the furtherance of shared values, in the interests of *e pluribus unum*. Charter schools and their like are definitionally antithetical to this American promise. They take from the *pluribus* to destroy the *unum*."

At base, Shanker suggested, the charter school experiment was not working. In a meeting sponsored by the Pew Forum in 1996, he suggested, "In the charter schools we now have, there is no record with respect to achievement or meeting standards." But Shanker wasn't willing to throw in the towel entirely. In the 1996 AFT Executive Council meeting, he suggested it was time to separate the wheat from the chaff. He said the AFT should "put out a careful analysis of the range of types of charter schools and what's good and what's bad about different provisions in them and how they work." Such an analysis "could have a tremendous impact on influencing good legislation and getting rid of lousy legislation" (quoted in Kahlenberg, 2007b, p. 318).

CONCLUSION

In the years since Shanker's death, most of the charter school movement has continued to move away from his original vision outlined in 1988. So the question becomes: Who had the stronger vision for charter schools? Albert Shanker, who wanted to increase teacher voice and promote integration as a way of improving schools for kids? Or free-market education supporters, who see teacher unions as a destructive force in education and say integration is unrelated to school quality? These are the issues addressed, in turn, in the next two chapters.

2

Reduced Teacher Voice

THE LOGO FOR CESAR CHAVEZ Public Charter Schools for Public Policy (n.d.) bears the face of their namesake, looking pensively into the distance behind the dome of the U.S. Capitol. The legacy of Cesar Chavez, famous labor organizer of farmworkers and community activist, lies at the heart of the mission of the Chavez Schools, which strive "to prepare scholars to succeed in competitive colleges and to empower them to use public policy to create a more just, free, and equal world." Chavez believed in the power of education, and particularly good teachers, to arm students with the academic skills and moral compass needed to be agents of change in the world. It was a great surprise to many, therefore, that when Chavez teachers attempted to organize in 2009, administrators met their efforts with hostility, provoking a tense conflict over the role of teacher voice at the school.

Founded in 1998, the Chavez Schools have grown from a single school serving 60 high school freshmen in the basement of a Safeway grocery store to a network of four middle and high schools spread throughout Washington, D.C., serving over 1,400 students. As one of the oldest charter school networks in the city, the Chavez Schools played an important role in the development of Washington, D.C.'s charter school sector, which now serves 43% of all public school students in the city (Brown, 2013). In March 2000 Irasema Salcido, the school's founder, spoke before the House Committee on Education and the Workforce about her experiences launching a charter school and encouraged lawmakers to support legislation to expand charter schools. Salcido (2000) highlighted the advantages that charter schools offer, including the ability to make decisions tailored to a specific school and freedom from bureaucracy. She also spoke about the power of teamwork. "I do not think that I ever knew what teamwork really was until I opened the Chavez School. . . . This is hard work and it requires people to work together and to trust and respect one another."

Following Salcido's House testimony, the profile of the Chavez School began to grow. A group of Chavez students had been invited to attend a speech by President Clinton the same year, and the following year Salcido received national recognition for her work with the school through a Use Your Life Award from Oprah's Angel Network. Sarah Fine (2009), a teacher at the founding Chavez campus in Capitol Hill from 2005 to 2009, described Chavez as a school that was "very interested in reaching students who otherwise would have fallen through the cracks and really energizing them around what it meant to learn and [be] given very meaningful work." Fine was attracted to the school by this energy, and because "the community of teachers was just fantastic" (personal communication, April 18, 2013). Jennifer Sonkin, who also came to Chavez's Capitol Hill campus in 2005, felt happy and supported during her first years at Chavez. The school gave her freedom to innovate and supported her graduate work (personal communication, May 24, 2013).

The Chavez network added two new schools in 2005 and another in 2007. But as the network grew, the spirit of teamwork, which Salcido had praised so highly in front of Congress, was in jeopardy. A new home office, created around that time to run the expanding network of schools, began making decisions that seemed to teachers to be sudden and arbitrary. The vacation schedule was changed after teachers had already signed contracts. Time for end-of-year capstone projects—a central way that the school fulfilled its mission of preparing students to enact social change—was cut short. Changes to curriculum and pedagogy came in rapid succession. Some teachers thought this whiplash was understandable, if not wise. "When you have students that are struggling, you feel a sense of urgency to do programmatic things that you think are going to help them. And you don't necessarily have the patience to see those things build momentum," explained former Chavez teacher Bill Day (personal communication, May 2, 2013). Sarah Fine said that teachers felt "barraged by this seemingly arbitrary set of requirements that kept getting piled on top of us at random times" (personal communication, April 18, 2013).

By 2008–2009, teacher morale at the Capitol Hill campus was low, and trust between teachers and administrators had been eroded by the erratic changes in programs and increasing teaching demands. A group of teachers, led by mentor teacher David Krakow, began meeting at coffee shops to organize and develop a list of discussion points to push back against the home office. Teachers wrote a letter to administrators asking for smaller class sizes, adequate prep time, limited yearly calendars, a transparent pay scale, and a collaborative structure of teacher representation (Smith, 2010).

It is perhaps not surprising that teachers at a school named for Cesar Chavez sought to organize. "You get a certain type of teacher here because we focus on public policy," observed teacher Jennifer Sonkin (personal communication, May 24, 2013). But the home office did not respond well to teachers' requests to be included in the decision-making process. Shortly after the teachers' letter reached administrators' desks, Krakow was informed that his contract would not be renewed the next year, despite the fact that he had recently been promoted to the position of mentor teacher. Krakow told the *Washington City Paper* that his principal had said to him, "You're not a good fit for the school," and that the director of human resources had explained that the school was opposed to unions (quoted in Smith, 2010).

Krakow filed a complaint with the National Labor Relations Board (NLRB), which in an independent investigation found merit behind some of his allegations. The NLRB issued a complaint of unfair labor practices against administrators at the school. Although the school denied organizing as the cause for his dismissal, citing budgetary reasons instead, Krakow settled with the school for three times the amount he would have been eligible for under NLRB guidelines. Furthermore, the school agreed to post a notice informing employees that they have the right to form a union and bargain collectively, along with a pledge that they would not attempt to discourage employees from organizing (Smith, 2010).

Krakow was not the only teacher to leave Chavez that year. Bill Day left to go to graduate school, basing the timing of his decision in part on administrative changes to the mentor teacher role which he had recently assumed. In a cost-cutting measure, the school combined the mentor teacher and department chair position, making mentor teachers now responsible for evaluating as well as coaching teachers. "I didn't want to be an evaluative leader," Day said (personal communication, May 2, 2013).

Sarah Fine (2009) left as well, describing her frustrations with the school in an op-ed for the *Washington Post:* "Over the course of 4 years, my school's administration steadily expanded the workload and workday while barely adjusting salaries. More and more major decisions were made behind closed doors, and more and more teachers felt micromanaged rather than supported." Fine came to Chavez to help empower students to make change, and yet she increasingly found herself lacking the power and input needed to succeed in that mission.

Joaquin Tamayo (2009), a new coprincipal at Chavez's Capitol Hill campus, responded to Fine's piece with a letter to the editor, stressing the need for teachers to embrace selfless public service. "No amount of praise showered on teachers will ever produce the kind of dramatic results we need to close the achievement gap—because, at its core, teaching is never about the teacher." Discounting concerns about tough working conditions and lack of support that led many Chavez teachers to depart, he continued: "An important lesson that we will teach our students is that the best service is done without regard to reward or remuneration." To make real educational reform, Tamayo argued, we will need "citizens more interested in serving others than in garnering praise for themselves."

Tamayo had lots of new "citizens" to work with in his teaching staff that fall. All told, almost half of all teachers in the Chavez Schools network left at the end of the 2008–2009 school year (Smith, 2010). While the Chavez Schools have made some progress in encouraging and facilitating teacher input since then—as we will discuss at the end of this chapter—teacher voice and teacher turnover remain areas of concern for both teachers and administrators. The school is still not unionized.

Most charter schools, like the Chavez Schools, have no teacher union. As noted earlier, more than three-quarters of all public school teachers nationally are members of teacher unions (U.S. Department of Education, NCES, 2008), but only 12% of charter schools are unionized (NAPCS, 2011). Most of the charter schools that do have unions are unionized by law; some states require all charter schools or certain types of charter schools (often conversion schools) to follow their district's collective bargaining agreement. Only 4% of all charter schools are unionized by choice, as the result of a teacher vote or as part of the design of the school. And 88% of charter schools have no teacher union at all (M. Price, 2011).

Although a far cry from Albert Shanker's original vision for charter schools, the dearth of teacher unions in charter schools is perhaps unsurprising. Workplace voice in general has certainly declined since labor's heyday. In a country where only 11.3% of workers are unionized, and a good portion of those jobs are in blue-collar professions (U.S. Department of Labor, Bureau of Labor Statistics, 2012), many recent college graduates would not recognize a union card if they saw one. Charter school teachers are on average younger than their district counterparts (Goldring, Gray, Bitterman, & Broughman, 2013), and young professionals may not expect to have voice in the workplace. "We think of that as normal because so many industries—and particularly so many professional industries—don't have unions," explained Sarah Apt, a 3rd-year teacher at a Philadelphia charter school (personal communication, September 7, 2013). Furthermore, managerial freedom is now a frequently touted benefit of the charter school model. In her Congressional testimony, Irasema Salcido (2000) highlighted the fact that "charter schools offer their founders the freedom to make decisions about curriculum, hiring, and budget. This freedom is very powerful because it allows administrators to take full responsibility of their decisions."

Still, the low rates of unionization in charter schools are a cause for concern. Evidence shows that teacher unions have a positive effect on student achievement, on average. Unions could be a tool for improving performance at charter schools, rather than the menace that some charter operators paint them to be. An atmosphere of hostility toward unions has also created an unnecessarily toxic political climate; charter schools have picked a fight with a powerful enemy. Most important, the lack of union representation is part of a bigger problem in charter schools—a lack of teacher voice—that has harmful consequences for students.

TEACHER UNIONS AND STUDENT ACHIEVEMENT

Republicans and even some Democrats have spoken out against teacher unions in recent years. Republican Chris Christie, governor of New Jersey, called the state's teacher union "a group of political thugs" (Blackburn, 2011). Democrat Joel Klein (2010), former chancellor of the New York City schools, said the "number one reason" for charter schools' success was "because they are not bound by legions of micro-managing regulations, including those contained in today's typical teachers' union contract." But is this popular narrative—that teacher unions depress achievement by defending ineffective teachers and opposing reforms— backed by research? First, we look at research evidence on the overall effect of teacher unions on student achievement, to the extent that this can be measured. Second, we consider conceptual arguments about how teacher unions influence educational outcomes.

Empirical Evidence

Before examining the evidence on teacher unions and student achievement, it is important to keep in mind several caveats. In general, there is relatively little empirical research examining the effect of teacher unions on educational outcomes. While it is not uncommon to find hundreds of studies examining a single factor in educational outcomes, a 2002 review of research by sociologist Robert Carini identified just 17 widely cited studies looking at the link between teacher unions and student achievement. Furthermore, isolating the effects of teacher unions on academic outcomes is difficult. Because collective bargaining may be correlated with any number of other school or district characteristics—and there are no randomized experiments to draw on—researchers have to control for a large number of other variables. Although student-level data are ideal, it is not often available, and many studies look at state or district averages instead. In addition, it can be difficult to find accurate information on whether and when teachers in a school or district unionized, and when a contract reflecting collective bargaining took effect.

The research that we do have, however, has generally found that teacher unions have small positive effects or no effects on the academic achievement of most students. Carini's (2002) literature review showed that 12 of 17 identified studies found increased student achievement in unionized schools. These studies were also more methodologically rigorous than the five studies that found negative effects: The 12 studies were more likely to look at achievement at the student level (rather than using state or district averages) and to control for more variables. A 2009 study found that unionization had no effect on dropout rates in the states studied (Lovenheim, 2009). And in 2008 Carini looked at student-level data from the National Education Longitudinal Study (NELS) and found that collective bargaining had no statistically significant effect on student test score gains between grades 8 and 10 in reading, math, history, or science.

Taken together, this research suggests that unions might be a tool for improving student achievement, or their effect might be neutral. However, the research does not paint a picture of unions as an enemy to student achievement.

Conceptual Arguments

Setting aside empirical tests, there is also a conceptual argument for why teacher unions might improve student outcomes. Teacher unions push for better working conditions for teachers, which in turn create a better learning environment for students. As Leo Casey (2006) explains, "The working conditions of teachers are, in significant measure, the learning conditions of students, and so improvements in the work lives of teachers generally translate into improvements in the education of students" (p. 181). The higher teacher salaries that unions bargain, for example, may help attract more qualified candidates to fill teaching positions. And when unions push for smaller class sizes and more professional development for teachers, they are advocating for policies that may increase student achievement (Carini, 2002). Higher pay and better working conditions may in turn lower teacher turnover and the negative effects it can have on student learning. In their seminal work *What Do Unions Do?* Richard Freeman and James Medoff (1984) found that, in the private sector, unionized workplaces had lower turnover than nonunionized workplaces, largely because unions gave workers a way to voice concerns and take action in response to workplace challenges that might otherwise have pushed them to leave. As we discuss later in this chapter, charter schools have much higher overall rates of teacher turnover than traditional public schools, and there is evidence that suggests union status may be a significant factor in explaining this difference.

Critics of teacher unions counter with the argument that unions also use their bargaining and political power for ill. In *Special Interest*, Terry Moe (2011) paints a scathing portrait of teacher unions as defenders of self-interested policies such as tenure and opponents of reforms such as merit pay that would benefit children. He concludes, "When all is said and done, the power of the unions to block change is the single most important thing that anyone needs to know about the politics of American education" (p. 277).

But this portrait is an exaggerated and outdated one. In recent years, teacher unions have taken a middle-ground position on many educational reforms. The New Haven Federation of Teachers, for example, approved a new teacher evaluation system in 2009 and a plan for merit-based raises in 2013. Teacher unions in Pittsburgh and Baltimore have brokered similar compromises. While it is true—as we will see in the following section—that unions are often one of multiple players in antagonistic education policy debates, there is a strong argument to be made that most of the things for which unions fight are good for teachers *and* good for kids.

A HOSTILE ATMOSPHERE

The story at Cesar Chavez Public Charter School in Washington, D.C., is just one example that raises questions about charter schools' openness to their employees' right to unionize. There is evidence of other charter schools taking an explicitly hostile stance toward unionization. From a labor perspective, this antiunion attitude is troubling as it threatens to curtail teachers' free speech and right to unionize. From a political perspective, it further polarizes an unproductive opposition between charter school advocates and teacher unions.

In Chicago, the charter management organization (CMO) Youth Connections Charter School announced the closure of one of its campuses the day after teachers at the school voted to unionize. The CMO's recommendation to close the school came after school management had already sent letters to the school's staff indicating intent to rehire them for the following year (Ormsby, 2012). At another Chicago charter school, administrators fired a teacher leading an organizing movement, despite having recently recognized her for exemplary performance with a salary raise and renewing her contract. Ronda Hartwell, who was 8 months pregnant when she was fired from her teaching job at the Chicago Math and Science Academy, said that she felt the school was trying to send a signal: "They are using me as a scapegoat to send a chilling message to the rest of the teachers" (quoted in Russo, 2010b).

At ASPIRA Olney Charter High School in Philadelphia, the management's opposition to unionization has taken the form of multiple delay tactics. In 2011 ASPIRA of Pennsylvania, part of a national nonprofit network, took over two struggling public high schools in Philadelphia and reopened them as Olney Charter High School. The mission of ASPIRA (n.d.), which runs a variety of educational and community-building programs, is "to empower our community through advocacy, and the education and leadership development of our youth." But, as at the Chavez Schools in Washington, D.C., teachers who were attracted to the school for its focus on community impact soon grew frustrated with sudden changes to the academic program made without teacher input.

Sarah Apt, who teaches ESL (English as a second language) at Olney, came to the school "because of the social-justice aspect" and saw unionization as compatible with this mission. "I wanted to be at a school where ESL was valued, where my students were valued. The union is a tool for that" (quoted in Blumgart, 2013). However, when a majority of teachers signed union authorization cards and a petition for union recognition, the school's principal refused to recognize the petition. Discussions about the union were postponed from one board meeting to the next, and teachers found antiunion materials in their mailboxes. When the local AFT union that had been working with the school filed two NLRB complaints against the management, ASPIRA countered by challenging the NLRB'S jurisdiction (Blumgart, 2013).

Olney teachers continued to fight for union recognition, holding a community rally at the start of the 2013–2014 school year. Teachers acted out a "Back to School Drive," filling a box labeled "Resources Our Students Need" with oversized props symbolizing the issues the union would fight for. One teacher put in a paper megaphone labeled "teacher voice." Another added a window made of cardboard and plastic wrap, symbolizing transparency. A tin can and string "telephone" for better communication, a clock to represent teachers' time, and joined puzzle pieces to symbolize unity and collaboration followed. Another teacher added a giant bag of money to the pile. "We do not have enough resources to spend on antiunion lawyers!" she yelled. "We need every resource that we can get for our classrooms, for our students, for our supplies." The last item added was a giant poster labeled "ASPIRA Union Contract." "All these things are great," a teacher announced, "but what we need is a union contract" (ASPIRA VOCES, 2013). As of that fall, teachers at Olney were still waiting for their union to be recognized by management and for contract negotiations to commence (Sarah Apt, personal communication, September 7, 2013).

When charter school administrators and managers hinder teachers' efforts to unionize, they are showing disrespect for teachers' right to free speech and to advocate for their students and themselves, and in some cases they are breaking the law. But charter school operators that are hostile toward unions also provide fuel for anticharter sentiment. Teacher unions are powerful political players, and they have pushed back with aggressive actions to slow the growth of charter schools.

Teacher unions have pushed for state caps on the number of charter schools that can be authorized and decreased funding for charter schools. In 2009 teacher unions in New York supported a budget that cut charter school funding, and in 2010 the UFT opposed legislation to lift the cap on charter schools in New York (which ultimately passed after some provisions were added to appease the union, including a ban on for-profit charter school operators).

In 2012 the National Education Association (NEA) and its state affiliate the Washington Education Association (WEA) together donated $450,000 to a campaign to defeat a ballot initiative that would allow charter schools in the state of Washington. That money paled in comparison to procharter donations in support of the initiative—which totaled more than $9 million—and the initiative passed by a small margin (Horne, 2012). But even after the election, the WEA has continued to be a thorn in the side of charter school supporters, filing a lawsuit challenging the initiative as unconstitutional.

In Washington State and elsewhere both charter school supporters and teacher unions will need to make concessions in order to work toward a more sensible and sustainable charter school policy. Charter school operators can help by reacting thoughtfully to teachers' efforts to unionize. Unions might be more open to expansion of charter schools if that sector were less hostile toward them.

NEGATIVE CONSEQUENCES OF REDUCED TEACHER VOICE

Union-busting allegations were only one part of the saga that resulted in high turnover and low teacher morale at the Chavez Schools. While forming a union might have improved the situation for teachers, and Krakow's firing almost certainly made the climate worse, the problems at Chavez were bigger than a union–management clash. That episode was the crescendo of multiple policies, decisions, and structures that left ers with little say in school decisions and little support in the class-room. Indeed, the greatest reason to be concerned about low unionization rates in charter schools is what this means for teacher voice more broadly.

Teacher voice can mean many things. When we use the term, we are referring to formal mechanisms in a school for teachers to participate in decisions about instruction, organizational issues, and workplace conditions. (We discuss our definition of *teacher voice* in Chapter 5.) From our perspective, unionization is neither a necessary nor a sufficient condition for having teacher voice in a school, but it can be a helpful tool for giving teachers a channel for participation. Teacher voice might be advanced in a nonunion environment where teachers function as both labor and management, running the school cooperatively or participating in multiple established channels for collaboration with administrators.

Teacher voice matters because when teachers have input in school decisions, there are positive effects on school culture and student achievement. Conversely, reducing teacher voice can have negative effects on schools and students. In the charter sector, there is strong evidence that low unionization rates are part of a bigger problem—a lack of teacher voice—that is hurting schools and students by producing high teacher turnover.

Why Teacher Voice Matters

Research shows that when teachers are engaged in school decisions and collaborate with administrators and each other, school climate improves. This promotes a better learning environment for students, which raises student achievement, and a better working environment for teachers, which reduces teacher turnover.

Stronger School Climate. Research finds a high level of teacher voice has positive effects on school climate. Richard Ingersoll (2003), an expert on teacher workplace issues, describes teachers as people "in the middle," "caught between the contradictory demands and needs of their superordinates—principals—and their subordinates—students" (p. 211). When teachers have the right amount of control, Ingersoll argues, they are able to do their job successfully, earning respect from principals, coworkers, and students.

Looking at data from the NCES Schools and Staffing Survey (SASS), Ingersoll (2003) found that as teacher control in "social decisions" (such as student discipline and teacher professional development policies) increases, the amount of conflict between students and staff, among teachers, and between teachers and the principal all decrease. As he summarized in a later article, "Schools in which teachers have more control over key schoolwide and classroom decisions have fewer problems with student misbehavior, show more collegiality and cooperation among teachers and administrators, have a more committed and engaged teaching staff, and do a better job of retaining their teachers" (Ingersoll, 2007, p. 24).

Increased Student Achievement. Not surprisingly, evidence suggests that having a strong teacher culture also improves student performance. Valerie Lee and Julia Smith (1996) measured the effects of teachers' work conditions and school climate on student achievement using longitudinal data tracking individual student learning gains from 8th to 10th grade. They found that, after controlling for student and school characteristics, student achievement is higher across all subjects when teachers take collective responsibility for student learning and when the staff is more cooperative. The study also showed that schools with high levels of collective responsibility and staff cooperation had more equitable distributions of student gains across socioeconomic status (SES)—lower-SES students in these schools tended to have gains on par with the gains of higher-SES students. Promoting collective responsibility and cooperation among teachers, then, may improve student outcomes and reduce achievement gaps.

Research on effective school organization also finds that collaboration, one manifestation of teacher voice, is an important component of school quality. One prominent recent example is the impressive 15-year longitudinal study produced by the Consortium on Chicago School Research. This study of hundreds of elementary schools in Chicago found that one of the organizational features that distinguished schools showing academic improvement from struggling schools was intense staff collaboration coupled with strong professional development. Furthermore, researchers found that building strong relational trust among teachers and administrators was crucial to school improvement (Bryk, Sebring, Allensworth, Luppescu, & Easton, 2010). Greg Anrig (2013) recently synthesized research on collaboration and school organization in his book *Beyond the Education Wars.* He found that "one of the most important ingredients in successful schools is the inverse of conflict: intensive collaboration among administrators and teachers, built on a shared sense of mission and focused on improved student learning" (p. 2).

Reduced Teacher Turnover. Schools with high levels of teacher voice also have less teacher turnover. Ingersoll (2003) found that higher levels of teacher control in social and instructional issues are associated with lov

teacher turnover rates. Schools with low levels of teacher control in social issues had an average turnover rate of 19%, compared to just 4% for
those with a high level of teacher control in social issues. A smaller, but
still significant, difference in turnover rates was associated with control
in instructional issues: The turnover rate for schools with a low level of
teacher control in instructional issues was 11%, compared to 7% for those
with a high level of teacher control in that area.

Controlling teacher turnover matters because excessive turnover con-
sumes financial resources, disrupts students' learning, and reduces the
number of highly effective experienced teachers. Each time a teacher
leaves and must be replaced, schools face financial costs associated with
advertising and recruitment, special incentives for new hires, administrative processing, and training for new employees. A 2007 study of five
districts found that the costs of turnover varied widely—from around
$4,000 per teacher leaving the district in Jemez Valley Public Schools,
New Mexico, to almost $18,000 per teacher who left Chicago Public
Schools (Barnes, Crowe, & Schaefer, 2007). Based on these estimates
and a national average teacher turnover rate of 12.5%, the National Commission on Teaching and America's Future (2007) estimates that the
overall cost of teacher turnover in the United States is $7.34 billion per
year. In an average urban district, these costs break down to $70,000 per
school per year to cover the costs of teachers leaving that school, plus an
additional $8,750 spent to replace each teacher leaving the district

Teacher turnover also disrupts the school community and hurts
student achievement. Research shows that more effective teachers are
more likely to stay in teaching (Hanushek & Rivkin, 2010), so teacher
turnover could theoretically improve student achievement if less effective teachers are replaced with more effective ones. However, research
on the effects of actual turnover show that it can have the opposite effect on student learning. A study of 4th- and 5th-grade students in New
York City found that students performed worse when teacher turnover
within their grade-level team was higher (Ronfeldt, Lankford, Loeb,
& Wyckoff, 2011). The effects were most pronounced for students in
grades where all of the teachers were new to the school, but there were
also smaller effects observed for students in grades where some of the
teachers were new hires. Notably, the harmful effects of teacher turnover were two to four times greater in schools with greater proportions
of Black students and low-achieving students. In low-achieving schools,
even students with teachers who had stayed at the school were harmed
by having turnover among other teachers in the school. This finding
suggests that teacher turnover can have negative schoolwide effects that
extend beyond individual classrooms.

Excessive staff turnover can be harmful in many types of organizations, but schools may be especially sensitive to these adverse effects. Research on employee turnover finds that excessive attrition is particularly disruptive in organizations where daily activities require employees to think creatively, adapt to new situations, and work cooperatively (Ingersoll, 2001a). Effective teachers need to know their students' backgrounds, understand community dynamics, be able to call on their colleagues for support, and create a consistent school culture across classrooms. Not only are these demands difficult for teachers new to a school, but they become more challenging for veteran teachers as the number of colleagues unfamiliar with the school's culture increases. To the extent that teacher voice increases teacher retention at a school, it is a strong organizational advantage.

Furthermore, high teacher turnover is problematic to the extent that teachers not only leave a school but exit the teaching profession. Research shows that teachers become more effective with experience, particularly during the first few years on the job (Chingos & Peterson, 2011). Thus, one of the benefits of strong teacher voice is that it can encourage teachers to stick with the profession, increasing the number of highly effective experienced educators. This could be particularly important in charter schools, which employ a greater percentage of inexperienced teachers. More than a quarter of charter school teachers have less than 4 years of teaching experience, compared to one-tenth of traditional public school teachers (Goldring et al., 2013).

Evidence That Charter School Teachers Lack Voice

How much voice do charter school teachers actually have? Are charter schools living up to Shanker's vision, creating an environment with high levels of teacher input and capitalizing on the benefits that has for school culture and student achievement? Difficult working conditions and high teacher turnover suggest that many charter schools are offering teachers little voice and suffering the consequences.

Tough Working Conditions. Charter school teachers on average face worse working conditions than teachers in traditional public schools. Employee benefits are one area in which the contrast is particularly sharp. Traditional public schools spend an average of $2,064 per pupil on employee benefits, compared to $847 per pupil at charter schools (Miron & Urschel, 2010). According to research from the Thomas B. Fordham Institute, in about 40% of states with charter school laws, participation in the state teacher pension plan is optional. When charter schools opt out of the state pension plans, most offer 401(K) or 403(B) plans, but some charter schools—including 20% of charter schools in Arizona—offer no retirement benefits. So while many charter school teachers have retirement plans comparable to those of traditional public school teachers in their state, others have no employer-sponsored plan whatsoever (Oldberg & Podgursky, 2011).

Charter school teachers also work more hours, on average, than traditional public school teachers. The 2011–2012 federal Schools and Staffing Survey shows that charter school teachers are required to work an average of 39.4 hours per week, compared to 37.8 hours per week for traditional public school teachers (Goldring et al., 2013). Press reports note that some charter schools require teachers to be on call for student questions until 9 p.m. (Rich, 2013).

This commitment of charter school teachers to working long hours is on one level a strength of the sector, but even strong advocates of charter schools realize that it can lead to burnout. In his book *Class Warfare: Inside the Fight to Fix America's Schools*—a generally optimistic account of passionate, hardworking, antiunion education reformers—journalist Steven Brill (2011) follows an assistant principal at New York City's Harlem Success Academy who went from dedication to burnout in just one year: "This wasn't a sustainable life," she said (p. 424). Brill concludes that the education reform movement must rein in grueling workloads and include unions if it is to be sustainable: "Unions are the organizational link to enable school improvement to expand beyond the ability of the extraordinary people to work extraordinary hours" (p. 425).

In some cases, charter school teachers also earn less than their district counterparts. Studies comparing pay for teachers in charter schools versus traditional public schools have mixed findings. National studies on charter school teacher pay have mostly shown that charter schools offer salaries competitive with those of traditional public schools (Malloy & Wohlstetter, 2003); however, there may be less room for salary growth at charter schools. Burian-Fitzgerald (2005) found that beginning teaching salaries are similar in charter schools and traditional public schools, after controlling for experience and qualifications. However, charter school teachers with several years of experience earn less than their public school counterparts. The average pay increase per year of experience for all teachers was $1,300, but for teachers in charter schools it was only $1,000.

These disparities in teacher pay are particularly glaring when contrasted with the high salaries earned by some executives at nonunionized charter schools. In 2011–2012, at least 16 charter school executives in New York City were paid more than the New York City Schools chancellor, who earned roughly $212,000. These charter schools and networks are all nonprofit, as New York state law bans for-profit charter operators, but their executive pay hardly reflects that fact. The highest paid charter executive in the city, Deborah Kenny of Harlem Village Academies, earned just under $500,000 (Monahan, 2013).

High Teacher Turnover. Charter school teachers have much higher rates of turnover than teachers in traditional public schools. According to an analysis of federal data for a nationally representative sample of teachers by David Stuit and Thomas Smith (2012), average teacher turnover is 24.2% in charter schools versus 11.9% in traditional public schools. This means that, nationwide, one in four charter school teachers switches schools or leaves the teaching profession each year, compared to one in eight traditional public school teachers. Teachers at charter schools are 170% more likely than public school teachers to leave the teaching profession and 50% more likely to switch to another school. (For more information on why turnover is so much higher at charter schools, see Sidebar 2.1.)

Some charter school supporters have suggested that high teacher turnover in the sector might be a result of charter schools removing ineffective teachers more efficiently than traditional public schools (Podgursky & Ballou, 2001). But data on teacher turnover generally do not back up this claim. First, differences in involuntary turnover (which includes firings as well as layoffs) are not sufficient to explain the gap in overall turnover rates. Based on Stuit and Smith's (2012) research, we calculate that a slightly higher percentage of all charter school teachers (3.1%) versus traditional public school teachers (1.5%) move to other schools or leave the teaching profession involuntarily. This difference, however, stems largely from the fact that many more charter school teachers are moving to other schools or leaving the profession *for any reason.* The proportion of all teacher turnover that is involuntary is roughly the same in charter schools and traditional public schools. Overall, the difference in involuntary turnover explains just 1.6 percentage points out of the 12.3 percentage point gap in turnover rates at charter schools versus traditional public schools.

Second, evidence does not support the theory that higher turnover in charter schools serves to remove ineffective teachers—voluntarily or involuntarily—more efficiently. A study of teacher turnover in Florida used value-added scores to measure the effectiveness of teachers leaving the profession or moving out of Florida public schools. At both charter schools and traditional public schools, lower-performing teachers are more likely to exit the profession. However, the relationship between effectiveness and likelihood of exiting was the same in both sectors—char-

---

SIDEBAR 2.1. HOW TEACHER AND SCHOOL CHARACTERISTICS AFFECT
TURNOVER IN CHARTER SCHOOLS

Compared to traditional public school teachers, charter school teachers are younger, less likely to be certified, more likely to be part-time, and less likely to have an education degree (Burian-Fitzgerald & Harris, 2004; Goldring et al., 2013; Miron & Applegate, 2007; Stuit & Smith, 2012). In addition, charter schools are more likely to have high concentrations of low-income and minority students, to be located in cities, and to be small (Frankenberg, Siegel-Hawley, & Wang, 2010; Snyder & Dillow, 2010). Many of these teacher and school characteristics have been associated with higher teacher turnover, independent of a school's charter status (Guarino, Santibañez, Daley, & Brewer, 2004).

Factoring in differences in teacher and school characteristics reduces the difference between the teacher turnover rates in each sector, but a sizable gap remains. Stuit and Smith (2012) found that controlling for teacher characteristics (such as age, experience, certification, and college selectivity) and school characteristics (such as racial/ethnic demographics, socioeconomic balance, urban versus nonurban location, and student absenteeism) accounted for 43% of the gap in teacher turnover rates between charter schools and traditional public schools; however, 57% of the gap remained even after considering these factors. That is a considerable difference in turnover—equal to 7 percentage points—that is not explained by teacher and school characteristics. In other words, restricting the comparison to teachers with similar characteristics in schools with similar characteristics, the charter sector still loses an additional 7 out of every 100 teachers per year, as compared to traditional public schools. A study of teachers in Los Angeles similarly found that differences in turnover rates in charter versus traditional public schools could not be explained by teacher and school characteristics (Newton, Rivero, Fuller, & Dauter, 2011).

Other teacher characteristics could account for some of the remaining gap in turnover rates. For example, charter school teachers are as much as 70% more likely than traditional public school teachers to have graduated from highly selective colleges (Cannata, 2008). (Stuit & Smith, 2012, accounted for college selectivity in their analysis, while Newton et al., 2011, did not.) They are also more likely to be interested in education reform and to have prioritized finding a school with a mission that matches their own philosophy (Brewer & Ahn, 2010). This may mean that charter school teachers have more career options outside of teaching than their traditional public school counterparts, or that they are interested in pursuing education reform outside the classroom, and that they are leaving teaching to pursue another option. However, if it is the case that high turnover is partly

---

SIDEBOX 2.1. *Continued*

---

due to attrition of idealistic graduates from top colleges, then charter schools need to consider what they can do to encourage more of these teachers to stay at their school. The best methods of meeting this challenge—increasing the professionalism of teaching jobs, improving working conditions, and boosting salary and benefits—could be achieved by introducing more teacher voice.

---

ter schools did not do a better job of making sure that the teachers who were exiting were the lower performers (Cowen & Winters, 2013).

We do know that charter school teachers who leave are more dissatisfied with their working conditions than teachers leaving public schools. Stuit and Smith's (2012) analysis and a study by Betheny Gross and Michael DeArmond (2010) found that charter school teachers are more likely than public school teachers to list concerns about job security, workplace conditions, and job responsibilities as reasons for leaving their school. Gross and DeArmond's (2010) study showed that exiting charter school teachers were less satisfied than teachers leaving public schools with all but one measured school characteristic. (These included rewards and tenure; workplace safety; student, parent, and community culture; professional culture and development; and materials and equipment—with no statistically significant difference in satisfaction with teaching assignments.) According to Stuit and Smith's (2012) research, the most common reason among charter school teachers for leaving the teaching profession was dissatisfaction with the school; 19% of charter school teachers listed this as the main reason for leaving teaching, compared to just 7% of public school teachers. Among charter teachers who moved to other schools, the most common reasons for moving were dissatisfaction with administrator support and dissatisfaction with workplace conditions. Furthermore, 13% of charter school teachers who moved to other schools wanted a better salary or benefits package, compared to only 6% of traditional public school teachers.

While it is difficult to prove a direct link, this survey data suggest that dissatisfaction with working conditions, which may be tied to a lack of teacher voice, is a major factor in charter schools' turnover epidemic. Further evidence that insufficient teacher voice is a factor in turnover comes from looking at the role of unionization. Stuit and Smith (2012) found that the largest factor in explaining the difference in teacher turnover rates between traditional public schools and charters schools was teachers' union status, accounting for 18.7% of the gap.

Teachers at charter schools cite dissatisfaction with their working conditions as reasons for leaving, and unionized teachers are less likely to leave. Connecting the dots, it is reasonable to hypothesize that if charter school teachers had more voice in decisions at their schools, they would be happier with their working conditions, and they would be less likely to leave.

CONCLUSION

Rather than being laboratories for teacher leadership and experimentation, as Albert Shanker envisioned, charter schools have instead prioritized managerial freedom, contributing to a number of troubling trends at the sector and school levels. Low unionization rates and hostility toward teachers' efforts to organize have created a toxic political climate that pits charter schools against teacher unions. Furthermore, a more systemic lack of teacher voice in charter schools likely contributes to high teacher turnover in the sector and poses risks for school climate and student achievement.

Some schools, including the Chavez Schools in Washington, D.C., appear to have recognized the downside to limiting teacher voice and have begun to shift policies. The Chavez Schools have made some progress over the past few years in granting teachers more voice. Jennifer Sonkin, an art teacher who weathered the storm of 2008–2009—a period she called "the dark years"—said that Chavez has a new principal who actively solicits teacher feedback and responds to teachers' concerns. "She's really trying to create less fear," Sonkin said of the new principal, "whereas I feel like in the past here, teachers were afraid to speak up in fear of confrontation" (personal communication, May 24, 2013).

Sonkin has also felt more support in recent years for teacher innovation and public policy programs at the school. In 2007–2008, Sonkin started New Orleans and Back, a community service capstone project that teaches Chavez students about the continuing impact of Hurricane Katrina on New Orleans and involves them in service projects that culminate with a visit to the city itself. In the beginning, Sonkin had to find her own outside funding for the program, and she spent countless extra weekend hours to pull it off. But Chavez Schools recently agreed to provide budgetary support to help make the program sustainable. Perhaps even more important, the school also started paying teachers a stipend for running extracurricular activities and gave Sonkin an extra planning period to help with the program, which she describes as a "huge" benefit (personal communication, May 24, 2013).

Alexandra Fuentes, a biology teacher who came to Chavez's Capitol

Hill campus in 2009, has also seen teacher voice gradually improve during her time at the school, although she notes that teacher turnover is still high. Fuentes started at Chavez right after Krakow, Fine, Day, and almost half of all teachers in the network left. She struggled with some of the same issues that frustrated her predecessors, including frequent policy changes and decisions made without teacher input. Fuentes almost left Chavez early in her time at the school after a new professional development model was implemented without teacher input. But the principal convinced Fuentes to stay and engaged in many conversations about teacher voice. School leaders now meet regularly with teacher leaders, and in the summer of 2013 teachers were invited to help revamp the school grading system. Fuentes, like Sonkin, has found the school supportive of her efforts to create innovative experiences for her students. The principal "was immediately on board" when Fuentes presented an idea in 2010 to take five students to present their research on HIV transmission at a conference hosted by Global HIV Vaccine Enterprise in Atlanta (personal communication, May 2, 2013).

Fuentes feels passionately about reducing teacher turnover by boosting teacher voice at her school and other charter schools. "Students need to have the same top teachers in the classroom year after year. They don't need teachers leaving, and having to start from scratch, over and over again. They need the strong relationships; they need that expertise. And you won't have that unless teachers have a voice in the working conditions of the school" (personal communication, May 2, 2013). Fuentes is working on tackling these issues at Chavez and beyond by engaging her school's administration in conversations about teacher retention, completing a yearlong fellowship to develop policy ideas with other teachers through TeachPlus, and writing about these issues for a broader audience. Fuentes (2012) wrote an editorial in the *Huffington Post* discussing some of the school's struggles with teacher turnover, and school leadership supported her in this work. Fuentes recalls Irasema Salcido reassuring and affirming her, saying, "I want your voice to be heard. This is something I know we need to work on, and I trust that what you write will do us justice" (personal communication, May 2, 2013).

Likewise, current administrators in the Chavez home office say that they are mindful of teacher turnover and have also increased channels for teacher voice. "We have explicit goals around the percentage of teachers that return year to year, especially focusing on teachers that are already effective or distinguished," explained Jeff Cooper, the network's Chief Operating Officer (personal communication, September 9, 2013). Cooper said that, as of 2013, most Chavez Schools retained 70–75% of teachers— a marked improvement over 2009 data; the network hopes to increase this figure closer to 80%. Terri Smyth-Riding, Director of HR at Chavez Schools, explained that the school has also bolstered outlets for teacher voice in the past few years. She described the HR department as "more of a vehicle to capture teacher voice" than in the past: teachers know that they can approach her with concerns, that "they have a person who's going to have an empathetic ear" (personal communication, September 9, 2013). In addition, the network has organized more focus groups to solicit teacher feedback and incorporate teacher voice into school decisions.

These stories show movement in the right direction, but that progress is fragile. Most of the strides in teacher input at the Chavez Schools have come from a more communicative and responsive administration. There is still no teacher union or other means of guaranteed teacher participation at Chavez, and without structural changes, the gains in teacher input may not last. With a new principal, new testing requirements, or budgetary changes, teacher voice might no longer be a priority. Sarah Apt, reflecting on the struggles to unionize at Olney Charter High School in Philadelphia, explained why a union in particular—not just a more receptive administration—was important to her and other teachers at that school: "If we don't have a voice that's legal, we don't have a voice that speaks" (personal communication, September 7, 2013).

Fuentes, likewise, would like to see a more formal system for teacher feedback at Chavez Schools. "My vision is for schools to have structured and meaningful ways for all stakeholders—families, students, teachers, and school leadership—to shape the policies and culture of the school." She also envisions a role for a union:

> As a school for public policy that is named for Cesar Chavez, a man who organized a union, we should address the role that unions ought to have in schools. Students deserve to have *effective* teachers in every classroom, and effective teachers need to be able to make the profession sustainable in order to remain in the classroom. We need a body that engages, empowers, and amplifies the voices of *effective* teachers to make the changes our students need. Cesar Chavez Public Charter Schools should take the lead to make that happen. (personal communication, November 22, 2013)

Teacher voice, for Fuentes (2012), is about giving teachers the power and support they need to do their jobs effectively. "When teachers are not empowered to make changes in schools that would enable us to better serve our students," she wrote in the *Huffington Post*, "teachers leave and students lose out."

3

Increased
Student Segregation

EDITH IBARRA'S QUEST to find a good school for her children involved trying three public schools in the area around Central Falls, Rhode Island, where she lives with her husband and four children. One of the most striking differences among the schools—and a deciding factor in where to send her children—was demographics: Racially and economically isolated schools provided a lower quality education than a diverse school.

Ibarra moved to the United States from Mexico in 2001. Her husband makes a living doing seasonal landscaping jobs, and their family gets extra support through the free lunch program at school. The family places a priority on finding educational opportunities for their children. "I am from a poor background, and I want something better for my kids," Edith Ibarra explained. "I don't want them to struggle like we did in the past, so I think education is the best thing for them" (personal communication, October 9, 2013).

Ibarra's eldest daughter, Yedmy, started kindergarten at Veterans Memorial Elementary, their local district school, in 2008. Ibarra soon became concerned about the quality of the education Yedmy was receiving. Ibarra, who describes her own English skills as "not 100%," was worried because the school placed her daughter in a special ESL class where instructional quality was poor and she was falling behind. In 2013, Veterans Memorial Elementary was labeled a "focus" school—the second lowest out of six categories—in school rankings by the Rhode Island Department of Education (2013b). Enrollment at the school was roughly 76% Hispanic, 22% White, and 2% other races/ethnicities. Ninety-five percent of students were eligible for free or reduced-price lunch (U.S. Department of Education, NCES, 2012b).

With her second child, Sergio, set to start kindergarten the following year, Ibarra worried how he would do at Veterans Memorial. So when she heard a story on a Spanish radio station about a new charter school forming, Ibarra jumped at the opportunity and put in an application for her son.

In 2009 Sergio enrolled at Democracy Prep Blackstone Valley (later renamed Blackstone Valley Prep Mayoral Academy), a charter elementary school, and the difference was apparent immediately. The school had a number of special academic features, including a longer school day, and the student body was much more diverse than at Veterans Memorial: 43% of students were White, 42% were Hispanic, 13% were Black, and 1% were other races/ethnicities. Sixty-one per cent of students were eligible for free or reduced-price lunch, and 39% were too wealthy to qualify or did not apply (NAPCS, 2013c).

Academic results at the school were a huge contrast with what Ibarra had seen at Veterans Memorial. A few months into the school year, Ibarra observed, "my son was reading, my son was writing, my son was talking English. And the first day he went to school, he didn't speak [English] at all." Sergio was also learning math that his older sister had yet to study. "I was amazed about it," Ibarra recalled (personal communication, October 9, 2013).

And the diversity of the student body at Blackstone Valley Prep also introduced social benefits. Ibarra liked that Sergio could interact with students from different cultural backgrounds. After the negative experience at Veterans Memorial Elementary, Yedmy attended the Learning Community Charter School in Central Falls, which is high-achieving, high-poverty, and predominantly Hispanic. But even though the Learning Community has a reputation for good academics, Ibarra eventually moved Yedmy to Blackstone Valley Prep as well, feeling that the more diverse school had a stronger program.

If the general shift in the charter school model from teacher empowerment to weakening unions had negative consequences, the change from charters as a force for desegregation to "niche" schools that try to meet the needs of narrow "markets" of students by race, ethnicity, income, and religion is even more troubling: It is at odds with the central goals of public education. Fundamentally, public schools are aimed at promoting social mobility in the private economy and social cohesion in our democratic society. That is, schools are meant to give all children, no matter their parents' income, a chance to rise; and, at the same time, to teach children of all walks of life what they have in common as Americans.

The increasing focus of charters on segmenting markets into narrowly defined chunks—at-risk students, particular immigrant groups, or racial groups—profoundly undercuts both goals. Because separate schools for rich and poor are rarely equal, the explicit targeting of at-risk students in economically segregated schools weakens the potential of charters to promote social mobility. And the racial and ethnic balkanization of students in many charter schools undermines the critical aim of fostering social cohesion and good citizenship.

As noted in Chapter 1, whereas Albert Shanker envisioned charter schools as institutions that would educate a broad cross-section of American students, and many early supporters held out the hope that charters could be more racially and economically integrated than regular public schools, today charters are more segregated by race, class, and ethnicity. And much of this is by design. The education policy and philanthropy communities, to date, have placed a premium on funding charter schools that have high concentrations of poverty and large numbers of minority students, oddly boasting about high levels of racial and economic segregation. Other charter schools consciously seek to serve particular immigrant or religious groups.

On one level, this approach is understandable. Immigrant groups and members of religious denominations may find solace in being educated among people of similar backgrounds. Likewise, focusing on efforts to maximize the number of at-risk children served in charter schools would seem to yield the greatest bang for the buck when such schools are high-performing. Yet, while high-performing, high-poverty charter schools do exist and receive considerable media attention, large numbers of high-poverty charter schools struggle academically. And separate schools for immigrant students and those of particular faiths raise serious questions about the role of public schools in promoting American identity. Moreover, charter schools catering to "White flight" in places like Minnesota and North Carolina, and charter schools that exclude special education students, are even harder to defend.

In this chapter, we examine the evidence suggesting (1) that charter schools are even more economically and racially segregated than traditional public schools; (2) that many charter schools are more segregated by design in order, supporters say, to meet the special needs of at-risk students, immigrant groups, religious groups, or racial groups; (3) that some charter schools are havens for White flight, exclude special education students, and "cream" the most motivated families; and (4) that a charter strategy of "niche" schools, which exacerbate economic and racial segregation, is a mistake, because it both undercuts the role of public education in promoting e pluribus unum and often reduces outcomes for students.

ECONOMIC AND RACIAL SEGREGATION IN CHARTER SCHOOLS

Research has generally shown that charter schools are even more economically and racially segregated than traditional public schools, both on average nationally and in a number of regions across the country.

National Studies

The seminal study on charter schools and school segregation was conducted by Erica Frankenberg, Genevieve Siegel-Hawley, and Jia Wang and published by the Civil Rights Project in 2010. (For more details on the data in this study, see Sidebar 3.1.) The researchers found that the nation's charter schools were more likely than traditional public schools to be urban; majority low-income (51–100% of students receiving free or reduced-price lunch); extremely high poverty (76–100% free or reduced-price lunch); and/or racially isolated for minorities (90–100% of students are racial minorities).

The findings from the Civil Rights Project revealed that a majority (56%) of the nation's charter school students attended schools that are located in cities, compared to 30% of traditional public school students. Using the above definitions, 54% of charter school students were in majority–low-income schools compared with 39% of public school students. In fact, 28% of charter school students were in extremely high-poverty schools, compared with 16% of traditional public school students. Similarly, 36% of charter school students are enrolled in schools where at least 90% of students are racial minorities, compared to 16% of traditional public school students (Frankenberg, Siegel-Hawley, & Wang, 2010).

Using data from the Civil Rights Project, we further calculate that 47% of low-income charter school students attended schools where more than 75% of the student body is low-income, compared to 32% of low-income students in traditional public schools. Likewise, Frankenberg and her colleagues found an astonishing 43% of Black charter school students attend schools where 99–100% of students are minorities, compared to 15% of Black students in traditional public schools (Frankenberg, Siegel-Hawley, & Wang, 2010).

Charter school advocates strenuously objected to the Civil Rights Project study because it used an absolute definition of segregation (such as 90–100% minority) as opposed to a comparative analysis of charter schools and nearby public schools or the district average. Because charter schools are more likely to be located in urban areas, it is unsurprising that they have higher levels of poverty and racial isolation, these advocates noted, just as urban schools generally do (Ritter, Jensen, Kisida, & McGee, 2010). This criticism, however, ignores the fact that charter schools, unlike the traditional system of public schools, have considerable leeway on where to locate; after all, some charter schools (discussed later in this book) intentionally locate in mixed-income neighborhoods or on the border between economically distinct neighborhoods, as a way of promoting socioeconomic diversity in the student body. Likewise, some

---

**SIDEBAR 3.1. THE NATURE OF THE DATA
IN THE CIVIL RIGHTS PROJECT STUDY**

Frankenberg, Siegel-Hawley, and Wang (2010) used the federal Common Core of Data from the 2007–2008 school year involving 48 million traditional public school students and 1.2 million students in charter schools. The research is the most comprehensive study to date on the issue and sheds considerable light on the topic, although the data were not flawless. As the authors note, one in four charter schools failed to report free and reduced-price lunch figures. There was no way to tell how many of these schools were simply failing to report versus how many did not participate in the program, but data from a smaller sample of schools suggested that many charter schools indeed were not providing free lunch programs at all. However, the most recent data show that the proportion of charter schools missing free and reduced-price lunch data has shrunk dramatically, from 21.3% in 2007–2008 to 8.6% in 2009–2010 (Aud et al., 2012).

"inter-district" charter schools are, by design, meant to draw on suburban and urban populations simultaneously (Frankenberg, Siegel-Hawley, & Orfield, 2010). To restrict a charter school target population to a single district is a conscious policy choice, not an inevitable fact of life.

In our view, charter schools should not mechanically mirror the background residential segregation in neighborhoods but instead should aspire in most cases to reflect the socioeconomic and racial makeup of a metropolitan region. Of course, the possibility of integration is constrained by logistical barriers; some schools may not be able to create an integrated environment because residential segregation makes driving distances too onerous. But research from educators Ann Mantil, Anne G. Perkins, and Stephanie Aberger (2012), seeking to estimate the viability of socioeconomic school integration, concludes that "dramatic reductions in the number of high-poverty schools across the United States are within reach" (p. 156). Nationally, several metropolitan-wide public school choice programs—in places such as St. Louis, Milwaukee, Boston, Omaha, Hartford, Rochester, and Minneapolis—suggest that in considering the possibilities of integration, the metropolitan region, not the local school district, is the relevant basis for comparison (Holme & Wells, 2008).

But for the sake of argument, assume the critics of the Civil Rights Project study are correct and the relevant basis of comparison for charters is a set of nearby public schools. Research using those parameters also suggests charters exacerbate segregation. The Civil Rights Project's study, for example, found that looking just at schools in cities, charter school students are still more likely to be in racially isolated schools: 52% of charter students in urban schools are in 90–100% minority schools, compared to 34% of their traditional public school counterparts (Frankenberg, Siegel-Hawley, & Wang, 2010). When refined even further to look at charter schools compared to other *central city* schools, charter students were still more likely than traditional public school students to attend hypersegregated minority schools (Ritter et al., 2010; see also Miron, Urschel, Mathis, & Tornquist, 2010).

Regional Studies

Regional studies—using a variety of comparative measures—also generally find that charter schools increase the segregation of students by both race and income. A 2012 study by the University of Minnesota's Institute on Race and Poverty found that in 2010–2011, only 18% of charter schools in Minnesota's Twin Cities were "integrated" by race (proportion of non-White students is between 20% and 60%), compared to 36% of traditional public schools (Institute on Race and Poverty, 2012). Likewise, the study found that Black, Hispanic, and Asian charter school students were each more likely than their counterparts in traditional public schools to attend racially isolated schools (where more than 60% of students were non-White). Conversely, White students in charter schools were also more likely than White students in traditional public schools to be in schools where more than 80% of students are White.

Studies from North Carolina have likewise shown that the state's charter schools are more likely than the traditional public schools to be "racially unbalanced" (Clotfelter, Ladd, & Vigdor, 2013, p. 8). In addition, when moving from a traditional public school to a charter school, Black students on average moved to schools where a greater proportion of their classmates were Black, while White students moved to schools with decreased Black representation (Bifulco & Ladd, 2007).

A 2008 study of charters in Arizona conducted by David Garcia similarly found that, on average, students left district elementary schools with high levels of racial/ethnic segregation to attend charter elementary schools that were even less diverse (increasing exposure to students of their own racial/ethnic background) than the traditional public schools that they were leaving.

One exception to this pattern was a 2009 RAND study of two states and five large urban school districts, which found that students generally transferred from segregated public schools to similarly segregated charter schools (Zimmer et al., 2009). But even the RAND study begs the question: Can charters, as schools of choice not constrained by residential segregation, do better?

SEGREGATION BY DESIGN FOR MARGINALIZED GROUPS

It is not surprising that students in charter schools are more economically and racially isolated than those in regular public schools given that many charter schools specifically target marginalized populations—at-risk and low-income students, immigrants, religious and racial minorities—as part of their explicit mission.

Charter school operators often boast of serving students in economically isolated settings. In a 2007 study, researchers Suzanne Eckes and Anne E. Trotter studied eight high-achieving charter schools in racially diverse rural and urban communities that were started by leaders devoted to social justice. The authors hypothesized that these schools would use state statutory language to achieve a diverse student body; however, they instead found that leaders of the selected schools focused on attracting the most underserved students. For instance, a school leader in San Antonio, Texas, described forming geographic boundaries for the school that intentionally excluded middle-class neighborhoods:

> We have one middle-class parent and the kid has done real well, but we haven't had too much of that; we set a geographic boundary of the inner loop of San Antonio, so to come to our school you have to live inside that loop, and there are two military bases inside that loop, and if you live on the bases, you cannot come and you live in [neighborhood name], which is old money, you can't come either. We did that so that we would not get the demographic that we don't want; we are not here to serve students who already have good schools. That's a way we can make sure we can stick to our target. (quoted in Eckes & Trotter, 2007, p. 77)

Similarly, many charter schools target marginalized ethnic or cultural groups that feel alienated from traditional public schools. Estimates of hard numbers of such schools are difficult to come by, though one of the few efforts to quantify the trend suggested that, in 2009, there were more than 100 charter schools nationally with themes tied to a particular cultural or ethnic group (Gootman, 2009). Minnesota, the birthplace of charter schools, has a particularly high concentration; 30 of its 138 charter schools (more than 20%) had a specific ethnic or immigrant focus as of 2009 (Rimer, 2009).

The types of ethnic or racial charter schools include Greek/Hellenic schools in Brooklyn, New York, and Wilmington, Delaware; ethnic Hawaiian schools; Hispanic/Latino-focused schools in Denver, Philadelphia, and Florida; and African American schools throughout the country (Mulvey, Cooper, & Maloney, 2010). Nationally, more than 200 Afrocentric charter schools were opened between 1996 and 2004 (Sykes, 2004).

Hmong immigrants from Laos were the target of at least seven charter schools in the Minneapolis–St. Paul area as of 2008 (Bailey, Harr, & Cooper, 2008). The Hope Community Academy (n.d.), for example, seeks "to educate students in an atmosphere enriched by shared Hmong and American values" and is 93% Asian/Pacific Islander (U.S. Department of Education, NCES, 2012b). It is important to note, however, that not every school with an ethnic theme or language educates a racially and ethnically isolated population. For instance, in Washington, D.C., the Latin American Montessori Bilingual Public Charter School (LAMB), with a Spanish-English dual immersion model, is 21.8% African American, 57.6% Hispanic/Latino, 20.2% Caucasian, and 0.4% Asian/Pacific Islander. The student body is 31.7% low-income (District of Columbia Public Charter School Board, 2012).

Charter schools aimed at particular religious communities also have sprouted up. Tarek ibn Ziyad Academy (TiZA), which had two Minnesota campuses, was founded in 2003 by Islamic Relief, USA, but closed in 2011 after the ACLU sued the school for violating the separation of church and state, citing practices such as locating in a religious facility and exposing students to religious iconography, having prayer during school hours, and requiring female students to wear a skirt or *jilbab* (Koumpilova, 2011; Mulvey et al., 2010). Christian groups that feel marginalized in the secular public schools have also started their own charter schools. To take one example, in Florida the private Palmetto Christian School converted to the public Palmetto Charter School, keeping the same staff and principal and gaining permission to hold special events in the church that is adjacent to the school (Mulvey et al., 2010). Jewish groups have also created Hebrew language charter schools in different parts of the country. For example, the Ben Gamla Charter School in Hollywood, Florida, was started in 2007 as "America's first English-Hebrew charter school" (Trotter, 2007). The school's first principal was an orthodox rabbi, and the school ran into trouble early on when the Broward County School Board rejected its curriculum because it was deemed to have religious elements. The school is 86% White, compared with a 47% White population in Broward County and 62% in the City of Hollywood, and, as of 2008, less than 1% of students at the school were Black, compared to 25.5% of students in Broward County and 12.7% of students in the City of Hollywood (Mulvey et al., 2010).

"CREAMING" AND FACILITATING WHITE FLIGHT

While most charters that segregate by design are aimed at marginalized groups in America, some charters also engage in old-style "creaming" by catering to White flight or shedding students who have learning disabilities.

In Minnesota, for example, the Institute of Metropolitan Opportunity at the University of Minnesota Law School has documented "a growing pattern" of predominantly White suburban charter schools that are less diverse than nearby public schools. Using 2012–2013 data, the Institute found that 67% of suburban charter schools had more than 80% of White students compared to just 44% of traditional public schools in the suburbs. The majority of these schools were located in attendance zones for more racially diverse traditional public schools (Orfield & Luce, 2013).

Some urban areas are experiencing the same phenomenon. For example, the Twin Cities German Immersion School, which follows a German and American curriculum, is located in a diverse neighborhood in St. Paul and has the potential to draw a diverse student body. (Until recently, a charter school focusing on East African culture was across the street.) Federal data, however, show that in 2010–2011, the school's student population was 98% White, and just 10% of students were eligible for free or reduced-price lunch (U.S. Department of Education, NCES, 2012b). Likewise, in Philadelphia, the Green Woods Charter School made applications available only for those who attended a one-day open house held at a private golf club in the suburbs (Ravitch, 2013). In a city where 14% of public school students are White, 77% of Green Woods Charter School students are White (NAPCS, 2013c). The school reports no data for free and reduced-price lunch because none is offered. According to the school's website, "At present, Green Woods does not have a breakfast or lunch program. Our families pack a lunch and a healthy snack for their children to eat each day" (Green Woods Charter School, 2013). The school indicated that it intends to begin serving lunch in 2014.

Fortunately, overwhelmingly White and wealthy charter schools have been less common than critics of charter schools originally feared (Garcia, 2010). But the fact that 8.6% of charter schools did not report data on the number of students eligible for free and reduced-price lunch in 2009–2010 is worrisome to the extent that some subset of these schools, like Green Woods Charter School, are not participating in the program, thereby ill-serving and potentially excluding low-income students (Aud et al., 2012).

Moreover, while charters do not generally cater to White and wealthy students, they are often less likely to educate special education students and English language learners. Federal law requires charter schools to provide special education services and prohibits schools from limiting enrollment of students with disabilities (Mead & Green, 2012); however, in practice, charter schools enroll a much smaller proportion of students with disabilities, on average. A 2012 report of the U.S. Government Accountability Office (2012) found that just 8% of charter students nationwide have disabilities, versus 11% of students in traditional public schools. A 2013 CREDO study had similar findings about enrollment of special education students and also revealed large gaps in serving ELLs. Nine percent of charter school students in the study's 27-state sample were ELLs, compared to 13% of students in feeder traditional public schools and 10% of students in all traditional public schools (Cremata et al., 2013). In a particularly egregious case, one Minneapolis charter school took over a regular public school and promptly requested that 40 autistic children leave the school (Ravitch, 2013).

Another form of "creaming" is more subtle and does not show up in hard data about race, income, and special education or ELL status. It involves the difference in parental attitudes and motivation levels between choosers and nonchoosers. Economists have long understood the issue of "self-selection bias"—that those who choose to participate in an activity (such as attending a charter school) may be different from those who do not apply, even after controlling for demographic characteristics. Imagine, for example, two low-income African American students attend an open house with their mothers for a charter school that has a strong "no excuses" program, including large amounts of homework and classes on Saturday. After hearing the description, neither student wishes to take on the extra work involved; one mother says fine and leaves, while the other tells her child, you are going to take on this challenge, and I will support you. There is a difference between these two families that will not show up on race or income data but could nevertheless prove important. (This difference will become significant in Chapter 4, when we discuss the outcomes in charter schools.)

THE HARMFUL EFFECTS OF SEGREGATION

Charter school advocates often say that whatever the level of segregation found in charter schools, it is defensible on two grounds. First, what matters more than whether schools are racially or economically integrated is whether students are learning and performing at high levels. Achievement trumps integration. Second, unlike the segregation of old, that was enforced by state and local policymakers, today's segregation is the result of choice—including choice by people of color—to attend particular schools. If parents want to choose racially and economically isolated schools, that is their right. Parental choice trumps integration.

In the pages below, we explain why we believe both arguments are wrong. The evidence suggests that economic school integration and school quality are not two separate (or competing) goals; they are deeply connected. While it is possible to create high-achieving, high-poverty charter schools or traditional public schools, they are exceedingly rare. Economic integration can powerfully improve school quality. Moreover, while parental choice is an important value in education, it is not the only one. We all pay taxes to support public schools—whether or not we have children in the system—because the schools have critical public purposes (preparing students to become productive contributors to the economy, instilling democratic values and American identity). These goals can, under certain circumstances, conflict with the private choice of parents. To take an extreme example, most people would agree that the parental right to choose a school should not extend to public support for a White supremacist school because using public funds to subsidize such an enterprise undercuts our democracy and the shared commitment to emphasizing what we have in common as Americans.

The Importance of Socioeconomic and Racial Integration to Democratic Citizenship

Separate schools for rich and poor and White and minority students undercut the primary lesson of democracy—that we are all social equals. American public schools—whether district schools or charter schools—are not only about raising academic achievement and promoting social mobility; they are also in the business of promoting an American identity, social cohesion, and democratic citizenship. In an increasingly diverse nation, public schools are the glue that reminds students what they have in common as Americans.

Research finds that segregation by race and class undercuts that goal by increasing the risk of students having discriminatory attitudes and prejudices. Children are at risk of developing stereotypes about racial groups if they live in and are educated in racially isolated settings. Diverse schools, by contrast, can help prevent bias and counter stereotypes (Pettigrew & Tropp, 2006). When school settings include students from multiple racial groups, students become more comfortable with people of other races, which leads to a dramatic decrease in discriminatory attitudes and prejudices (McGlothlin & Killen, 2005; Rutland, Cameron, Bennett, & Ferrell, 2005). Numerous studies have found that racial integration in public schools is important to producing tolerant adults and good citizens (see, e.g., Wells & Crain, 1994). As Justice Thurgood Marshall noted in one desegregation case, "Unless our children begin to learn together, then there is little hope that our people will ever learn to live together" (*Milliken v. Bradley*, 1974). Research confirms that students who attend racially diverse high schools are more likely to live in diverse neighborhoods 5 years after graduation (Phillips, Rodosky, Muñoz, & Larsen, 2009).

The rise of "niche" charter schools—Afrocentric schools; schools for Somali, Ethiopian, or Hmong immigrants; Hebrew language schools; or Islamic or Christian schools—is deeply problematic because it is at odds with these fundamental objectives. In some cases, these schools raise important questions about the separation of church and state, but beyond that, these specialty schools fail to remind students what they have in common as Americans. Our nation's diversity is one of its chief assets, and we should encourage families to instill in their children a pride in their ethnic or religious heritage. Public schools, however, should seek to cultivate parallel pride in our shared American identity as well as encourage respect and appreciation for our pluralistic society.

It is true that throughout American history public schools have often fallen short of the goal of full integration that emphasizes commonality while respecting cultural differences. On one hand, Horace Mann's common school model, which was widespread by the end of the 19th century, is an important ideal. It paved the way to free public education, ensured a well-educated citizenry, and helped to unite different immigrant groups together with a common American identity. On the other hand, at a time when the United States was experiencing an influx of Catholic immigrants, the common school was strongly influenced by dominant Protestant culture, and enthusiasm for the model was partly fueled by anti-Catholic sentiment (Mulvey et al., 2010). Public education in our country at first did not include children of color, and then served them in separate and inferior institutions. And the goal of forging a common American identity was at times taken too far in harsh efforts to assimilate immigrant groups and Native Americans (Provenzo & Mc-Closkey, 1981). Segregation and bias are problems that afflict American public schools to this day.

The marginalization of different racial, ethnic, and religious groups in public schools throughout American history partly explains the impulse to create charter schools catering to the specific needs and desires of previously excluded or mistreated populations. However, we think this is the wrong approach. This thinking ignores what Albert Shanker and others have identified as the fundamental purpose of education in the United States: to teach children what it means to be American. Instead of giving up on the possibility of integrated schools, we should constantly work toward the goal of creating public schools where all segments of American society are respected and included.

At their core, in free democratic societies, schools are meant to develop children who will grow up with critical minds to be tolerant, independent-thinking citizens and productive employees. But in America, given our diversity, Shanker believed that public schools should provide a common education to children from all backgrounds that teaches not only skills but also American history, culture, and democracy. Shanker argued, "If public schools become places where children learn that, fundamentally, they are not American, there will be no reason for taxpayers to continue supporting them. And there will be little to hold society together" (quoted in Kahlenberg, 2007a).

Educator Deborah Meier (2002) has also noted the role that schools need to play in American democracy. "Variety needs to be balanced by the acknowledgment that there exists a larger community—one we all have a stake in—a shared public," she has written. "For me the most important answer to the question 'Why save public education?' is this: It is in schools that we learn the art of living together as citizens, and it is in public schools that we are obliged to defend the idea of a public, not only a private, interest" (p. 176).

Ultimately, separate schools for disadvantaged communities, even when designed to empower those groups, rarely work well in practice. And the perpetuation of racial hierarchies in America is itself a threat to our democracy. "We must have integrated schools," Martin Luther King, Jr., argued in the 1950s. "That is when our race will gain full equality" (quoted in Marable, 2002, p. 125). More than a half century later, conditions have changed, but integration remains a democratic imperative. Sheryll Cashin (2004) addresses that issue:

> Despite the enormous challenges, I have come to the conclusion that cultivating race and class integration, especially of the institutions that define social mobility—like schools, universities, and the workplace—and building coalitions of enlightened self-interest across boundaries of homogeneity are the only route to creating the kind of full democratic society we imagine our very diverse country to be. (p. 291)

Segregated charter schools undermine that goal.

The Enduring Connection Between Integration and School Quality

In addition to offering important civic advantages, integrated schools—particularly those that bring together students of different socioeconomic backgrounds—produce stronger academic outcomes for students of all backgrounds. Almost 50 years ago the congressionally authorized Coleman Report found that the single most important predictor of academic achievement is the socioeconomic status of the family a child comes from, and the second most important predictor is the socioeconomic makeup of the school attended (Coleman et al., 1966). Students generally perform significantly better in schools with strong middle-class populations than they do in high-poverty schools. Virtually all of the characteristics and resources that educators talk about as desirable in a school—high standards and expectations, good teachers, active parents, a safe and orderly environment, a stable student and teacher population—are more likely to be found in economically mixed schools than in high-poverty schools. (While some contend that charter schools have severed the link between economic school segregation and quality schooling, our discussion in Chapter 4 questions that belief.)

The Effects of Segregation on Student Outcomes. Research suggests that while it is possible to make schools with high concentrations of poverty work—we all know of such individual schools—it is extremely uncommon. A study by Douglas Harris (2007), for example, found that middle-class schools (which he defines as those with fewer than 50% of students eligible for free or reduced-price lunch) are 22 times as likely to be consistently high performing as majority–low-income schools (those with 50% or more of students eligible for subsidized lunch).

Students in middle-class schools perform better in part because middle-class students on average receive more support at home (including better nutrition and health care) and come to school better prepared. But the vastly different educational environments typically found in middle-class as contrasted with high-poverty schools also appear to have a profound effect on achievement. On the 2011 National Assessment of Educational Progress (NAEP) given to 4th-graders in math, for example, low-income students attending more affluent schools scored substantially higher than low-income students in high-poverty schools. The gap in their average scores is roughly the equivalent of almost 2 years' learning (Lubienski & Lubienski, 2006). Moreover, low-income students given a chance to attend more affluent schools performed more than half a year better, on average, than middle-income students who attend high-poverty schools (National Assessment for Educational Progress [NAEP], 2011). (See Sidebar 3.2 for examples of further research.)

One of the most methodologically rigorous studies on the effects of socioeconomic integration is a lottery-based study by Heather Schwartz of the RAND Corporation. Schwartz's (2010) carefully controlled study examined students and families who were randomly assigned to public housing units in Montgomery County, Maryland, a diverse and high-achieving district outside Washington, D.C. This research took advantage of a rare opportunity to compare two education approaches. On the one hand, the Montgomery County school district has invested substantial extra resources (about $2,000 per pupil) in its lowest-income schools to employ a number of innovative educational approaches. On the other hand, the county also has a longstanding inclusionary housing policy that enables low-income students to live in middle- and upper-middle-class communities and attend fairly affluent schools. The study controlled for the fact that more motivated low-income families may scrimp and save to get their children into good schools by comparing students whose families were *assigned by lottery* into higher-poverty and lower-poverty schools.

Schwartz found very large positive effects on student learning as a result of living in lower-poverty neighborhoods and attending lower-poverty elementary schools even though students in higher-poverty schools received additional compensatory spending. Low-income students attending lower-poverty elementary schools (and living in lower-poverty neighborhoods) outperformed low-income elementary students who attend higher-poverty schools with state-of-the-art educational interventions by four-tenths of a standard deviation in math—which is considerably larger than the effects seen for many educational interventions. Furthermore, the study finds that roughly two-thirds of the benefit comes from the school, and one-third from the neighborhood. This suggests there may be considerable value in programs that integrate at the school level alone, though greater benefits clearly accrue from integration at both the neighborhood and school levels.

On the surface, Schwartz's study would seem to contradict results from a federal housing income integration program known as Moving to Opportunity (MTO), which saw few academic gains for children. But MTO involved students who moved to schools that were still mostly high-poverty schools, with an average free and reduced-price lunch population of 67.5% (compared to a control group attending schools with 73.9% of students receiving subsidized lunches) (Sanbonmatsu, Kling, Duncan, & Brooks-Gunn, 2006). By contrast, the vast majority of Montgomery County schools in Schwartz's sample had less than 60% of students receiving free or reduced-price lunch.

The Effects of Economic Integration on Middle-class and High-income Students. Research also suggests that economically diverse schools do not negatively affect the achievement of middle-class and high-income students and can, in fact, benefit the learning of middle-class students in important ways.

SIDEBAR 3.2. RESEARCH ON SOCIOECONOMIC SCHOOL EFFECTS

A number of local and international studies find that the socioeconomic status of the students in a school is linked to differing levels of student achievement even after controlling for the individual socioeconomic status of a student's family. To take a few examples:

» In 2002 researcher David Rusk's study of public schools in Madison-Dane County, Wisconsin, found that among 4th-grade students, for every 1% increase in middle-class classmates, low-income students improved 0.64 percentage points in reading and 0.72 percentage points in math.

» Data from the 2006 Programme for International Student Assessment (PISA) for fifteen-year-olds in science showed a "clear advantage" from attending a more affluent school, regardless of students' own socio-economic backgrounds (Organisation for Economic Co-operation and Development [OECD], 2007).

» In 2010, analyzing data from PISA, researchers concluded that the academic successes of nations like Finland and Canada appear to be related in part to their greater degrees of socioeconomic school integration (Perry & McConney, 2010; see also Willms, 2010).

» Also in 2010 a reanalysis of James Coleman's data using a more sophisticated statistical technique found that the social class of the school matters even more to student achievement than does the SES of the family (Borman & Dowling 2010).

» In a 2012 study examining achievement gaps on the National Assessment of Educational Progress for math and reading in 2007 and 2009, researchers found that Black and Latino students had smaller achievement gaps with White students when they were less likely to be stuck in high-poverty school environments (Mantil et al., 2012).

Of course, the studies cited above employ cross-sectional data and may reflect self-selection bias; that is, particularly motivated low-income families may work hard to ensure their children attend strong schools, so the superior performance may reflect at least in part a family effect rather than a school effect. But numerous studies that track student growth over time, and which carefully seek to control for self-selection bias, also find favorable outcomes for students who attend economically mixed rather than high-poverty schools:

SIDEBAR 3.2. *Continued*

» In 2005 Russell Rumberger and Gregory J. Palardy, examining a large data set, found that a school's socioeconomic status had as much impact on the achievement growth of high school students in math, science, reading, and history as a student's individual economic status.

» A 2010 review of 59 rigorous studies on the relationship between a school's socioeconomic makeup and outcomes in math found "consistent and unambiguous evidence" that higher school poverty concentrations are linked with less learning for students "irrespective of their age, race, or family SES" (Mickelson & Bottia, 2010).

» In a 2013 longitudinal study of the effect of poverty concentrations on attainment that controlled for a number of student and school factors, Gregory Palardy found that the socioeconomic composition of a school was highly related to high school graduation and college enrollment. Students at schools with high average socioeconomic status of students were 68% more likely to enroll at a 4-year college than their peers at schools with low average socioeconomic status. Peer influences were critical, the study found, which suggested "that integrating schools is likely necessary to fully addressing the negative consequences of attending a low SEC [socioeconomic composition] school" (p. 714).

Lottery-based studies provide among the best research on school effects by controlling for self-selection bias through random assignment. These studies compare outcomes of students randomly selected to attend a school and those who also entered the admissions lottery but were not selected. Because all students entered the same lottery and winners were chosen randomly, researchers can assume there are no systematic differences between winners and losers in factors such as family motivation. This lottery-based research also finds that economic integration can be a powerful driver of academic success:

» A 2009 lottery-based study of Connecticut's interdistrict magnet school program found that attending a socioeconomically and racially integrated magnet school had positive effects on student achievement at both the middle and high school levels (Bifulco, Cobb, & Bell, 2009).

» A 2010 study of students in Montgomery County, Maryland, found that students living in public housing randomly assigned to lower-poverty neighborhoods and schools outperformed those assigned to higher-poverty neighborhoods and schools (Schwartz, 2010; see more detailed discussion in this chapter).

While the research suggests that sprinkling a few middle-class students into a school of highly concentrated poverty may hurt their academic achievement, so long as a strong core of students are middle class (not eligible for free or reduced-price lunch), middle-class student achievement does not decline with the presence of low-income students. Studies find that integration is not a zero-sum game, in which gains for low-income students are offset by declines in middle-class achievement (Kahlenberg, 2001). The research on racial integration found similar results: Test scores of Black students increased and White scores did not decline (Crain & Mahard, 1977; Armor, 1995).

Research suggests that low-income students can benefit in economically mixed schools and middle-class students are not hurt academically for two central reasons. First, the numerical majority sets the tone in a school: The negative effects of concentrated poverty tend to kick in only where a clear majority of students are low-income (Kahlenberg, 2001). For example, a U.S. Department of Education study of 20,000 8th-grade students found that the negative effects of rising poverty levels in schools were not linear but rather were most pronounced in schools where 51–100% of students were eligible for free or reduced-price lunch (J. Anderson, Hollinger, & Conaty, 1992). For this reason, we recommend charter schools that are generally in the range of a 50% low-income and 50% middle-class population. (See Chapter 6, Sidebar 6.1 for a discussion of what ideally integrated charter schools would look like in terms of economic and racial demographics.)

The second reason why middle-class children are not negatively affected by attending economically diverse schools is that they are less sensitive to school influences (for good or ill) than low-income children. This "differential sensitivity" to school environment, one of the central findings of the 1966 Coleman Report, has been dubbed "Coleman's Law." The reason, Coleman explained, is that aspirations and achievement are more firmly rooted for those with stable family backgrounds, who might benefit from economic security, live in a two-parent household, or have resources for out-of-school educational enrichment; those with more unstable family backgrounds—who face food or housing insecurity, live in single-parent households, or spend less time under adult supervision, for example—are more open to the influence of peers. Other researchers have consistently confirmed this finding (Kahlenberg, 2001). Recent research from Caroline Hoxby (2000) and from Eric Hanushek, John Kain, and Steven Rivkin (2009) confirms that Black and Latino students have greater sensitivity to the negative effects of segregation than White students.

Moreover, students of all backgrounds, including those from middle-class families, benefit from learning in socioeconomically and racially diverse environments. In this way, the benefits of socioeconomic and racial integration flow both ways—to minority students and to Whites; to low-income students and to wealthier students. As a "Brief of 553 Social Scientists" in the *Parents Involved in Community Schools v. Seattle School District* (2007) school integration case noted, "learning in diverse classrooms, where students from different backgrounds communicate their different experiences and perspectives, encourages students to think in more complex ways" (App. 12). Research from K–12 settings shows that racial and economic integration is associated with academic achievement gains for students of all economic and racial/ethnic backgrounds (see, e.g., Berends & Peñaloza, 2010). And at the college level, students educated in diverse settings have been shown to develop higher-level critical thinking and cognitive skills (Antonio et al., 2004; Marin, 2000).

In addition, middle-class students benefit in integrated environments by learning to work with others unlike themselves—a 21st-century workplace skill highly valued by employers. Increasingly, business leaders are looking for employees who can work with others to come up with creative solutions. As one educator noted, "Einstein is dead. It's not the lone genius but the laboratory team that has produced most of the new thoughts and inventions in the last half century" (quoted in Mathews, 1998, p. 246).

Studies find that employees are much more likely to be fired for the inability to get along with others than for incompetence (D. W. Johnson & R. T. Johnson, 1994). As a result, one national survey of employers found that businesses are increasingly interested in entry-level employees who can "work in teams or participate in problem-solving groups" (Lynch, 2000, pp. 23–24). Not surprisingly, business groups have been strong supporters of socioeconomic integration plans in a number of communities. In La Crosse, Wisconsin, for example, business leaders advocated for socioeconomic integration of the schools because, they told teachers, "people have to be able to work together. . . . The number one problem in the workplace is not not knowing your job or not knowing the skills for your job. . . . It is people with skills not being able to get along with coworkers" (quoted in Kahlenberg, 2001, p. 235).

Why Socioeconomic Integration of Schools Affects Student Outcomes

Why does it matter to student achievement if a child attends a middle-class or high-poverty school? While money matters a great deal in education, people matter more. Consider the three main sets of actors in a school: students, parents, and teachers.

The Role of Peers. Research suggests that students learn a great deal from their peers, and it is an advantage, on average, to have a strong core of middle-class peers for a variety of reasons.

Low-income students attending economically diverse schools benefit from the larger vocabularies, greater knowledge, and more positive attitude toward learning found, on average, among their middle- and high-income peers. It is an advantage to have classmates who are academically engaged and aspire to go on to college. Peers in middle-income schools are more likely to do homework, attend class regularly, and graduate—all of which have been found to influence the behavior of classmates (Kahlenberg, 2001). It is also an advantage to have high-achieving peers, whose knowledge is shared informally with classmates all day long. By age 3, middle-class peers have more than twice the vocabulary of low-income children, for example, so any given child is more likely to expand his or her vocabulary in a middle-class school through informal interaction (Hart & Risley, 1995). In contrast, high-poverty schools are more likely to suffer from an environment where students miss school, skip classes, do not complete homework assignments, and create disorder in the classroom. Middle-class schools report disorder problems half as often as low-income schools, and low-income schools are about three times as likely to report the presence of street gangs as more affluent schools (Dinkes, Cataldi, & Lin-Kelly, 2007, 2008).

Middle-class schools also have a more stable student population. For example, data from the 1998 National Assessment of Educational Progress showed that 43% of 4th-graders who were eligible for free or reduced-price lunch changed schools at least once in the previous 2 years, compared to 26% of students who were not eligible (Rumberger, 2003). These differences in mobility are important not only at the student level but also at the school level. Students who move schools frequently suffer negative effects to their academic achievement. But excessive student mobility can also be detrimental to the learning of all students in a classroom, even those who stay put, because it requires teachers to divert time and effort from instruction to acclimating new students, slowing down the pace of learning for the class as a whole (U.S. Government Accountability Office, 2010, 2012).

The Role of Parents. Low-income students attending economically diverse schools also benefit from the greater involvement by middle- and high-income parents who volunteer in the classroom, have high standards, hold school officials accountable, apply political pressure to ensure adequate funding, and provide private financial support (Kahlenberg, 2001).

There is some evidence that charter schools have greater levels of parental involvement than traditional public schools with similar demographics, due to both institutional differences—such as smaller sizes—and a selection bias for parents with above-average participation (Bifulco & Ladd, 2006). However, numerous studies have shown that socioeconomic status is a primary predictor of parental involvement, and that middle-class parents are more likely to be involved in schools (see Kahlenberg, 2001). Middle-class parents are less likely to face some of the challenges that make school involvement difficult, such as inflexible work schedules, lack of transportation, or unreliable phone and Internet access.

Middle-class parents are also likely to have the political savvy to push for adequate financial resources and to defend a system in which property-rich areas have an easier time financing good public schools. Most studies find that low-income students need considerably more spent on their education than middle-class students do in order to produce high levels of achievement, yet affluent districts spend a cost-adjusted $938 more per pupil, compared to high-poverty districts (Arroyo, 2008). Within-district disparities also exist, generally to the disadvantage of low-income students (see Rothstein, 2000).

The Role of Teachers. High-poverty schools of all kinds have a hard time attracting and retaining quality teachers. While a subset of high-achieving charters have placed a premium on attracting excellent teachers with high expectations and have had considerable success in doing so, many charters continue to struggle in attracting and retaining high-quality teachers in high-poverty environments, just as traditional public schools do (Gross & DeArmond, 2010).

Teachers in middle-class schools are more likely to be licensed, to be teaching in their field of expertise, to have high teacher test scores, to have more teaching experience, and to have more formal education (Darling-Hammond, 1997; Jerald & Ingersoll, 2002). Likewise, metrics that consider the "value added" to tests scores by individual teachers have found that the most effective teachers teach disproportionately in higher-income schools (Isenberg et al., 2013). In Washington, D.C., for example, affluent Ward 3 in northwest Washington had 135 teachers across its 10 schools in 2011 who had highly effective ratings on the district's IMPACT evaluation, which has a large value-added component. Across the Anacostia River in the poorer section of the city, Wards 7 and 8 had just 71 highly effective teachers spread across 41 schools (Turque, 2011a, 2011b).

The evidence for value-added measures should be treated with caution. It may be that value-added measures such as IMPACT are biased toward higher-income schools, failing to adequately account for school and student factors outside teachers' control. However, it may also be the case that more effective teachers are more likely to choose to teach in predominantly middle-class schools. Teachers generally consider it a promotion to move from lower-income to middle-class schools, and many of the best teachers transfer into middle-income schools at the first opportunity (Kahlenberg, 2001). As Michael Petrilli (2012) of the Thomas B. Fordham Institute has noted, "Teachers practice on poor children, then take their improved skills to affluent children" (p. 22).

Sometimes, efforts are made to lure highly talented teachers to high-poverty schools by offering financial bonuses, but those efforts frequently fail. Research consistently finds that teachers care at least as much about work environment as they do about salary (Hanushek & Rivkin, 2007; Jacob, 2007). Teachers care about school safety, whether they will have to spend large portions of their time on classroom management and discipline issues, and whether parents will make sure kids do their homework.

Accordingly, it is very difficult to attract and keep great teachers in high-poverty schools, even when bonuses are offered. In other sectors (such as the military and health care), salary premiums of 10–30% are common in filling hard-to-staff positions (Kowal, Hassel, & Hassel, 2008). In education, Eric Hanushek, John Kain, and Steven Rivkin (2002) estimated that, in order to get nonminority female teachers to stay in urban schools, school officials would have to offer a salary premium of 25–43% for teachers with zero to 5 years' experience. Given the significance of labor costs in overall school spending, a 25–43% salary premium would require an extraordinary expenditure unlikely to be sustainable under current political and economic conditions.

A 2013 study of the federal Talent Transfer Initiative, which offered a $20,000 bonus to effective elementary school teachers who agreed to move to low-achieving schools within the same district and stay 2 years, found few teachers interested. The study of 10 school districts in 7 states found that effective teachers had a positive impact when they transferred to low-performing schools, but 78% didn't even fill out an application, despite the fact that the financial reward offered was far more sizeable than the typical merit aid award of a few thousand dollars or less. "It's a hard sell, even with $20,000 on the table," Steven Glazerman of Mathematica Policy Research, which conducted the study, told *Education Week* (quoted in Sawchuk, 2013; see also Glazerman, Protik, Teh, Bruch, & Max, 2013).

CONCLUSION

For myriad reasons, then, the shift in focus for most charter schools from a potential desegregation tool to a market-based niche model has been a great disappointment. While many well-intentioned charter school leaders are motivated by a desire to promote social justice and see education as a "civil rights issue," they are oddly blind to the profound lesson of *Brown v. Board of Education*: that in America, separate schools for Black and White and rich and poor are inherently unequal.

4

The Disappointing Results in Many Charter Schools

THE CONCERNS WE OUTLINED in the previous two chapters—that charter school teachers often lack representation and voice and that charter schools are often more racially and economically segregated—might be subject to the following response: Teacher voice and integration are nice things to have, but what really matters is bottom-line outcomes. Even though teachers often have less say in charters and such schools are generally less integrated, the argument runs, what matters far more is school quality, and charter schools produce superior results to those achieved in traditional public schools.

But does the best research evidence support this claim? Do charter schools routinely outperform traditional public schools, rendering concerns about increased segregation and reduced teacher voice distracting carping about secondary-level issues? The answer—from a growing body of research—is no. As the evidence in this chapter suggests, students in most charter schools perform about the same as—not significantly better than and not significantly worse than—students in comparable public schools.

A 2010 analysis by Peter C. Weitzel and Christopher A. Lubienski concludes, "The record on achievement is mixed, with most of the best evidence showing results similar to or somewhat below those of other public schools" (p. 222). A 2011 meta-analysis of the effects of charter schools conducted by Julian R. Betts and Emily Y. Tang is similarly inconclusive: "The overall tenor of our results is that charter schools are in some cases outperforming traditional public schools in terms of students' reading and math achievement, and in other cases performing similarly or worse" (p. 55). And a 2013 summary of research on charter school performance by Priscilla Wohlstetter, Joanna Smith, and Caitlin Farrell concludes "findings continue to be mixed" (p. 55).

To be sure, there are bright spots in the charter school constellation. In certain high-profile cities, such as New York and Boston, charters have shown stronger results, though it is not clear that this success can transfer to other less "hip" jurisdictions that may have a harder time attracting very well educated young teachers (Harris, 2014). Likewise, there is some evidence that low-income students gain more from attending charter schools than middle-class students, but issues of self-selection may influence these results.

Perhaps the central lesson of research on the performance of charter schools is that just being a *charter school* is not a guarantee of success any more than is being a *district school*. Student outcomes at individual charter schools—and at individual district schools—vary widely, and results depend on how specific schools are run. Unfortunately, as we discuss later in this chapter, some charter school networks that have been celebrated for their success have holes in their performance records, and education leaders may have drawn the wrong conclusions about the best direction for charter schools.

Below, we review the evidence from three sets of studies, each of which have their strengths and drawbacks: (1) national studies that have broad scope but do not always control for self-selection bias; (2) studies of individual cities that often employ randomized controlled experiments that control for self-selection bias but may not be generalizable to a broader population of charter schools; and (3) studies examining individual charter school chains that are considered highly successful, which have the potential to help reveal best practices but are sometimes exaggerated or misinterpreted.

NATIONAL STUDIES

Three national studies stand out as being among the most rigorous and widely cited examinations of student performance in charter schools: research by Stanford University's Center for Research on Education Outcomes (CREDO) in 2009 and 2013; by the Institute of Education Sciences (IES) within the U.S. Department of Education in 2010; and by the RAND Corporation in 2009.

CREDO Studies

The 2009 CREDO study examined data from 15 states and the District of Columbia, which together educated more than 70% of charter students in the United States. The researchers employed a "virtual twin" method in which they followed longitudinal data for individual charter school students and matched data based on students of similar demographics in traditional public schools to see which students performed better over time. The researchers compared students of the same feeder school, race, ethnicity, gender, eligibility for free or reduced-price lunch, ELL status, special education status, and prior test scores.

The study, which was supported by pro–charter school foundations, provided what Education Secretary Arne Duncan called a "wake-up call" for charters (quoted in "A Sobering," 2009). Looking at math gains, students in 17% of charter schools outperformed those in regular public schools, students in 37% of charter schools underperformed, and students in 46% showed no difference (CREDO, 2009). In other words, when comparing student math gains at charter schools to those of comparable students at regular public schools, more than twice as many charter schools underperformed as outperformed.

One bright spot was the 2009 study's finding that among low-income and ELL students, those in charter schools outperformed those in traditional district schools. The finding was clouded, however, by the possibility of self-selection bias. The virtual twin methodology was able to control for a variety of demographic factors, but the lack of a randomized controlled experiment meant the researchers could not discount the possibility that the low-income families who took advantage of the charter school opportunity might have been more motivated than those who, through active choice or default, remained in the traditional public schools. And there is good reason to believe that low-income families who choose charter schools may be more motivated than those do not, while the dynamic may even be reversed among middle-class families. As we saw in previous chapters, middle-class students in traditional middle-class public schools often have strong learning gains, so there may be less reason for the most motivated and educationally astute families to move to charter schools. By contrast, high-poverty public schools often provide a weak learning environment, increasing the chances that the most motivated and educationally savvy low-income families would have reason to seek the alternative environment found in charter schools. If self-selection bias entered in, low-income charter school students were not only more likely to come from more motivated families, they were also likely to benefit from having a more motivated *peer group* in charter schools.

In 2013, CREDO published an update of its 2009 study, this time looking at charter schools in 25 states and the District of Columbia, which together educate more than 95% of all charter school students in the country (Cremata et al., 2013). Researchers employed the same virtual twin methodology used in 2009. Looking at an update for just the 15 states plus D.C. studied in 2009, the charter schools studied performed about the same as they did in the previous study, but as a group they showed a slight increase in performance because of the closure of low-performing schools; some 8% of the 2009 sample had been closed by 2011. The schools showed increased performance relative to regular public schools, largely because regular public schools showed smaller learning gains in 2013 than in 2009, while charter impacts remained constant.

Among the new and expanded sample, students in 29% of charter schools performed significantly better than their virtual twins in traditional district schools in math, while students in 31% did significantly worse, and those in 40% showed no significant difference. In reading, students in 25% of charters outperformed those in regular public schools, while students in 19% performed worse and those in 56% showed no difference. As in the 2009 study, low-income and ELL students in charter schools did better than their virtual twins in regular public schools. In the 2013 study, Black and Hispanic students also did better in charter schools.

These results show an upward trend in charter school performance relative to regular school performance, but the differences between charter schools and regular public schools in the full sample are still very small: Charter schools had a small but statistically significant positive impact in reading, and the impact of charter schools on math was negative but statistically insignificant. Matt Di Carlo (2013) of the Albert Shanker Institute noted that the size of the overall impact of charter schools in reading and math in the 2013 CREDO study is about .01 standard deviations, which is roughly equal to "one percent of the typical test-based achievement gap between White and Black students."

IES Study

In 2010 the National Center for Education Evaluation and Regional Assistance of the Institute of Education Sciences within the U.S. Department of Education published the results of what *Education Week* called "the first large-scale randomized trial of the effectiveness of charter schools across several states and rural, suburban, and urban locales" (Maxwell, 2010). The study (Gleason et al., 2010) compared differences in outcomes between students admitted to charter middle schools and those not admitted in random lotteries at 36 charter schools from across the country. The study's main analysis looked at 1,400 students who were lottery winners (experimental group) and 930 students who lost the lottery (control group).

The lottery design is considered stronger than CREDO's virtual twin model because it compares children from similarly motivated families (all of whom entered the lottery). The downside, however, was that the IES sample size—36 schools—was substantially smaller than CREDO's. Moreover, because only charter schools that are oversubscribed are included in the study, the study compares what are likely to be typical public schools to more desirable charter schools, hardly an apples-to-apples comparison.

Despite the study's limitation to popular, oversubscribed charters, the researchers found that attending a charter school had no statistically significant impact, on average, on student achievement; however, like the CREDO studies, IES found a differential impact depending on student income. Among middle-class students (those not eligible for free or reduced-price lunch), the authors found that attending a charter school had a negative effect on reading and mathematics scores. By contrast, lower-income students saw a positive effect on mathematics scores from attending a charter school. Finally, the study concluded that, in mathematics, students in higher poverty charter schools made the greatest gains.

At first glance, the finding that students in higher poverty charter schools made the greatest math gains would seem to fly in the face of a great deal of research suggesting that concentrations of poverty have a negative effect on schooling. But the students who won the lottery to attend high-poverty charters are compared to lottery losers who are likely to attend high-poverty traditional public schools. Marsha Silverberg, project officer for the report, explained:

> What our study says is that charter schools that serve higher proportions of low-income students do better at educating students RELATIVE to the traditional public schools those kids would have attended, than do charter schools that serve lower proportions of low-income students. These differences in impacts could have more to do with the education students get in the traditional public schools than with the education they get in the charter schools. In other words, charter schools that serve higher income students are probably in neighborhoods that have, on average, reasonably good traditional public schools. Charter schools that serve a high proportion of lower-income students are probably in neighborhoods where, on average, the traditional public schools are not very good. (Personal communication, November 7, 2013)

In this way, the IES study may be consistent with the wide body of research suggesting that peers matter in education. While IES is able to control for self-selection bias at the individual family level, by comparing lottery winners and losers, the researchers do not control for the effect of peers. Charter school lottery winners are surrounded by classmates who also applied; lottery losers, by contrast, may come from motivated families but are then educated in traditional public schools with some other lottery losers but also substantial numbers of peers who (by choice or default) did not apply to a charter school.

RAND Study

The IES and CREDO study findings of mixed overall impact are consistent with a 2009 study conducted by RAND researchers. RAND's study of charter schools in eight states looked at longitudinal student-level data at charter middle and high schools, where students had baseline elementary test scores that could be used to measure growth (Zimmer et al., 2009). The researchers concluded that nonprimary charter schools in five of seven locations studied (San Diego, Philadelphia, Denver, Milwaukee, and Ohio) showed average achievement gains that were not substantially different from those of local traditional public schools. Charters in the other two locations (Chicago and Texas) had smaller gains than their local traditional public schools. The researchers did, however, find higher graduation and college attendance rates among charter students in the two locations where long-term attainment data were available.

STUDIES OF INDIVIDUAL CITIES

National studies suggest that there is considerable geographic variation of charter school performance, so it is important to look at charter school impacts in different locales (Cremata et al., 2013). In Ohio, for example, charters have performed poorly. In looking at the state's results in December 2007, Checker Finn, a strong supporter of charters, asked frankly: "Why are so many charter schools inadequate, even mediocre? What went wrong?" (quoted in Gyurko, 2008, p. 36). More attention has been paid to other jurisdictions in which high-profile studies have found success—such as Boston, New York City, and New Orleans. But a closer examination suggests there are sometimes gaps in these success stories.

New York City

In New York City, a 2009 study by researchers Caroline M. Hoxby, Sonali Murarka, and Jenny Kang received considerable attention for purporting to find that, for students who attended charter schools from kindergarten through 8th grade, these charter schools could close the "Scarsdale–Harlem gap"—the gap between affluent suburban Scarsdale and low-income Harlem students—by 66% in English and 86% in math. The study's design appeared to be very strong as it compared 30,000 winners and losers in charter school lotteries in New York City and covered nearly all charter schools in that jurisdiction. At the time, 94% of New York City charter school students entered through a lottery. If legitimate, the gains would have been truly stunning.

Critics noted, however, that the study relied on a set of methodologi-cally questionable assumptions which appears to have inflated the gains; the methodologically sound gains, by contrast, were substantially smaller than those reported. The problem is that the study did not follow a single cohort of students from the initial lottery before kindergarten through 8th grade. Instead, a majority of the students had been in charter schools for only 3 or 4 years (Basile, 2010). Hoxby and her colleagues then made certain methodologically troublesome assumptions that had the effect of magnifying the size of gains.

According to Sean Reardon (2009), the design of the Hoxby et al. study appropriately considered student gains from kindergarten through 3rd grade and found relatively modest improvement. But when they designed the comparison of students in charters and traditional public schools in grades 4 through 8, they controlled for the previous year's test scores—scores that were earned *after* the charter school lottery and could have been affected by the students' charter admission status—thereby eliminating the benefits of the random design (see Basile, 2010). Reardon also noted that they implicitly assumed in grades 4 through 8 that charter school students would continue to make the same size gains, when in fact experience suggests that a student who makes significant gains in a par-ticular year is not equally likely to make the same degree of progress in a subsequent year. The Hoxby et al. study showed some student success in New York City charters, Reardon said, but not anything like the dramatic claims made.

Boston

Boston charter schools have also been the subject of highly lauda-tory studies that do suggest legitimate success at some charter schools but less sweeping success than has been reported. In 2009 the Boston Foundation published a study by a group of highly respected researchers, including Harvard's Thomas Kane, which found that students who ap-plied for and won the lottery to attend charter schools in Boston signifi-cantly outperformed students who lost the lottery and attended regular public schools. The growth for charter school students (as compared to traditional public schools students) in math was equal to 0.54 standard deviations—which is "roughly half the size of the Black–White achieve-ment gap," or the same as moving from 50th to 69th percentile (Ab-dulkadiroglu et al., 2009, p. 9).

The Boston Foundation 2009 study, however, was subject to a dif-ferent criticism than that leveled at Hoxby's New York City study. Un-like the New York study, the Boston Foundation study only evaluated a small fraction of charter schools because only 7 of 29 charters were over-subscribed, necessitating the use of a lottery (Jennings, 2009). Because oversubscribed charter schools may be among the strongest schools, the Boston Foundation research might be characterized as finding—to no one's surprise—that the top quarter of charter schools outperform the general population of traditional public schools. If the reverse compari-son were made, between the top quarter of traditional public schools and the general charter school population, charter schools might not have come off looking so good.

The Boston Foundation updated its study in October 2013 and was able to address much of the criticism of its earlier study because the pro-portion of charter schools that were oversubscribed and employed lot-teries had increased significantly. The 2013 report covered a majority of schools (12) and 87% of charter school enrollment (Cohodes, Setren, Walters, Angrist, & Pathak, 2013). The study found that a year of atten-dance at a Boston charter school continued to have a very positive effect on student achievement, and the effect size remained large, though less than half the size of the earlier study: 0.25 standard deviations in math in both middle and high school.

Separately, Stanford's CREDO released a report in 2013 evaluating Massachusetts charter schools, including those in Boston, using the vir-tual twins methodology. The study found unprecedented achievement gains in Boston charter schools: "In fact, the average growth rate of Bos-ton charter students in math and reading is the largest CREDO has seen in any city or state thus far" (CREDO, 2013a, p. 7).

Why did charter school students perform so much better in Boston than elsewhere, under CREDO's analysis? And why does the gold-stan-dard randomized lottery research employed by the Boston Foundation find such strong gains? The studies do not say, but it is relevant to note that in Boston the student population in charter schools—and thus the classmates of lottery winners—was more advantaged than students in tra-ditional Boston public schools on several scores. In a reversal of what the national data suggest, a lottery winner's classmates in Boston charter schools are more economically advantaged than in the traditional public schools. At the middle school level, for example, 67.9% of Boston charter school students are eligible for subsidized lunch compared with 81.8% of those in traditional public schools (Cohodes et al., 2013).

Boston charter students also have higher levels of baseline proficiency in math and English Language Arts at both the middle school and high school levels. They are less likely to be special education students, and they are substantially less likely to be English language learners: At the middle school level, charter school students are 5.6 times less likely to be English language learners as students in the traditional Boston Public Schools, and at the high school level, they are 8.6 times less likely to be ELLs (Cohodes et al., 2013). These disparities have been longstanding in Boston public schools (Vaznis, 2009). (By contrast, Boston Pilot Schools, which have charter-like flexibility but are unionized—and were found to be less effective than charters—generally have low-income, special education, and ELL populations that look more like Boston's traditional public schools than charters [Abdulkadiroglu et al., 2009, p. 18, Table 4].)

On top of all this, students in Boston charter schools have suffered high levels of attrition—further advantaging the peer environment. A 2009 analysis by the Massachusetts Teachers Association's Center for Education Policy and Practice found that senior enrollment at Boston charter high schools was on average only 42% of freshman enrollment, compared to 82% at traditional public schools.

In sum, in explaining why the Boston charter schools are more successful for the students who attend and stay in these schools than charter schools nationally, the answer may well lie in the fact that students who win the charter school lottery in Boston are surrounded by classmates who are considerably more advantaged than the classmates of lottery losers. If that is true, the experience would reaffirm the very large body of research from traditional public schools suggesting students will perform better if they are surrounded by peers who are more, rather than less, advantaged (see Chapter 3). The big lesson of Boston charters, in other words, may underscore the benefits of socioeconomic school integration.

New Orleans

New Orleans charters are also widely seen as a success story. After Hurricane Katrina devastated the city, reformers transferred control over more than 100 of the city's lowest-performing schools to the state-run Recovery School District, which is now heavily weighted with charter schools, in order to create better opportunities for students. Education Secretary Arne Duncan says the school reform efforts in New Orleans are "stunning" ("Lessons from New Orleans," 2011). According to a report by CREDO (2013b), students in New Orleans charters learn the equivalent of 4 months more in reading and 5 months more in math compared with students in traditional public schools. Moreover, only 6% of New Orleans charter schools had lower reading scores than their feeder traditional public schools, and only 4% had lower math scores.

The comparative results are impressive, but critics note that besting the traditional public schools in New Orleans is not difficult. The regular schools were never strong, and, as of 2013–2014, they educated only about one-tenth of area public school students (Jindal, 2013; National Education Policy Center, 2013). Even with comparative success, the heavily charter-based Recovery School District ranked 69th of 70 districts in Louisiana in 2011 (Ravitch, 2011). In fact, as of 2013, 79% of Recovery School District charters were rated D or F by the Louisiana Department of Education ("The Great Charter Tryout," 2013).

STUDIES OF INDIVIDUAL CHARTER MANAGEMENT ORGANIZATIONS

If the national charter school research is generally mixed, and if the individual city success stories are sometimes less impressive than they seem— or, where valid, point to the benefits of socioeconomic integration—what about the research on high-flying, high-poverty charter management organizations? Do high-profile schools like the Harlem Children's Zone and KIPP demonstrate that Albert Shanker was wrong and the more conservative charter school vision is right? Do they suggest that poverty and segregation are just excuses and the key to success is eliminating the power of the teacher unions to obstruct good educational programs? We take each in turn.

Harlem Children's Zone

The Harlem Children's Zone charter network, the brainchild of charismatic educator Geoffrey Canada, embodies an intriguing mix of liberal and conservative theories. On the one hand, families in the Harlem Children's Zone receive substantial wraparound services—health and nutrition, parenting classes, and pre-K programs. On the other hand, the charter schools are hostile to unions, with Canada claiming that a union–management contract "kills innovation; it stops anything from changing" (quoted in Vasagar & Stratton, 2010).

The Harlem Children's Zone has received extravagant praise. In a 2009 *New York Times* column entitled "The Harlem Miracle," David Brooks discussed an evaluation of the program by Harvard's Will Dobbie and Roland G. Fryer, Jr. Brooks wrote that a Harlem Children's Zone charter middle school had, by the 8th grade, "eliminated the achievement gap between its Black students and the city average for White students."

But others were more skeptical. In a piece entitled "Just How Gullible is David Brooks?" Aaron Pallas (2009) noted that while Harlem Children's Zone charter schools performed at high levels on the New York State exam for which they were specifically prepared, these same students did poorly on the Iowa Test of Basic Skills, scoring in the 33rd percentile nationally. The Iowa tests are significant, Pallas noted, because "if proficiency in English and math are to mean anything, these skills have to be able to generalize to contexts other than a particular high-stakes test." Moreover, in 2010, an article by Sharon Otterman in the *New York Times* reported that the Harlem Children's Zone charter schools struggled when New York State increased the difficulty of its exams: Although the schools outperformed city schools in math, English scores at the schools were less impressive—below average at one campus and above-average but stagnant at another (Otterman, 2010b).

KIPP

In contrast to the Harlem Children's Zone charter schools, KIPP, the Knowledge is Power Program, educates a much larger number of students and has a robust and well-documented track record of success. KIPP now has 141 schools in 20 states and the District of Columbia serving 50,000 students. More than 86% of KIPP students are eligible for the federal free and reduced-price meals program, and 95% are African American or Latino (KIPP, 2013). The school program emphasizes "tough love": a longer school day and school year, more homework, and the explicit teaching of middle-class habits and norms.

To its credit, KIPP has commissioned a number of outside studies of outcomes at KIPP schools. These studies find that KIPP students show impressive average gains across subjects, on high-stakes standardized tests as well as low-stakes tests that include assessment of critical thinking (Tuttle et al., 2013). In his book on KIPP, Jay Mathews (2009b) reports that average scores of KIPP students have risen from the 34th percentile at the beginning of 5th grade to the 58th percentile at the end of 7th grade in reading, and from the 44th to the 83rd percentile in math. "Gains that great for that many low-income children in one program have never happened before" (p. 2).

To be sure, KIPP enrolls fewer special education and ELL students than surrounding districts. One study that KIPP commissioned, for example, found that 9% of KIPP students were in special education programs compared to 11% in nearby traditional public schools. Likewise, 7% of KIPP students had limited English proficiency compared with 13% of district students (Nichols-Barrer, Gill, Gleason, & Tuttle, 2012). Still, KIPP enrolls an overwhelmingly disadvantaged student population, and those students who stay in KIPP schools appear to benefit enormously.

What is far more controversial is the *meaning* of KIPP's success for traditional public schools. One interpretation of KIPP is that its success with low-income and minority students in highly segregated nonunion environments suggests that poverty and segregation are just "excuses" for low performance and that unions get in the way of allowing management the tools to create great schools (Thernstrom & Thernstrom, 2003). *The Houston Chronicle* editorialized in 2010, "The lesson, we think, is clear. If KIPP can do it, other schools can, too—and we should demand that. No excuses" ("KIPP's Good Work," 2010). Davis Guggenheim, director of the 2010 film *Waiting for Superman,* points to KIPP and concludes, "We've cracked the code" on how to educate low-income students (quoted in Giordano, 2010).

But on exploration, KIPP's success hardly means that poverty and segregation do not matter. Indeed, the KIPP model relies heavily on self-selection of students, considerable attrition, and low levels of replacement of students who leave. All of these features reinforce the idea that the peer environment in KIPP schools may matter a great deal. While KIPP's results are very impressive, they hardly suggest that regular public schools, which educate whoever happens to live in the neighborhood, can ignore concentrations of poverty.

To begin with, KIPP does not educate the typical low-income student, but rather a subset fortunate enough to have striving parents. To a certain degree, that is true of all choice and charter schools, but it may be particularly true of KIPP. The KIPP model—an extended day, week, and year; a large homework load; and contract of commitment that parents and students must sign—is likely to intimidate some students and families more than a typical charter school (Mathews, 2009b).

More important, KIPP cohorts of students shrink over time, leaving as peers only those students who have survived a demanding set of expectations. KIPP schools have high rates of attrition (as do many high-poverty schools) and (unlike most high-poverty schools) do not fully replace those who leave middle school with new 7th- and 8th-graders (Tuttle et al., 2013).

Taking account of both phenomena—a high attrition rate and a low replacement rate—a 2011 study by Gary Miron, Jessica Urschel, and Nicholas Saxton found that a typical KIPP grade cohort shrunk by about 30% between grades 6 and 8. A whopping 40% of African American male students left KIPP schools between those grades, according to the study.

Having few new entering students during grades 7 and 8 is an enormous advantage not only because low-scoring transfer students are kept out but also because in the later grades, KIPP students are surrounded by other self-selected peers who have made it through what is universally acknowledged to be a very rigorous and demanding program. In terms of peer values and norms, then, KIPP schools appear to more closely resemble economically mixed schools than traditional high-poverty schools.

(As we shall see in Chapter 6, Sidebar 6.3, on the one occasion when KIPP took over a regular high-poverty public school—and came close to having to serve a regular, rather than self-selected, student population—KIPP discontinued the program and got out of the business.)

Some KIPP supporters think the criticism about self-selection and skimming is unfair given that KIPP (and charters generally) are at the same time criticized for segregating low-income and minority students. Journalist Matthew Yglesias (2011), for example, wrote, "If KIPP's not condemned for skimming the easiest cases, it's condemned for promoting segregation by declining [through the use of "no excuses" pedagogy] to make itself appealing to the easiest cases." But in fact both criticisms are on point because KIPP attracts motivated students and yet is incorrectly pointed to by some supporters as proof that economic and racial segregation works just fine in American public schools.

If it is wrong to characterize KIPP as an example of segregation's success given the significant differences in the student makeup between KIPP and traditional high-poverty public schools, what about the second prong of the conservative argument: that KIPP's nonunion environment is critical to its success? Here, the examples of the successful and union-ized KIPP Ujima Village Academy and KIPP Harmony Academy schools in Baltimore are relevant. In these schools, which under Maryland law are part of the district's larger collective bargaining agreement, the union pushed KIPP management in 2009 to provide teachers more pay for working as many as 40% more hours. KIPP initially said it could not afford to and threatened to close the schools at the end of the year. But, eventually, the two parties worked out a 10-year agreement, the only one of its kind in the country (Bowie, 2011). Under the terms of the deal, KIPP teachers would be paid between 15% and 24% more than district teachers depending on KIPP's budget in a particular year (Jewell Gould, personal communication, June 19, 2013). Union and management were able to reconcile a valued part of KIPP's program (an extended day, week, and year) with union concerns that teachers be properly compensated for extra duties.

Indeed, the lack of teacher voice elsewhere in KIPP's network may hamper its potential in important ways by promoting churn among teach-ers. An SRI International study of five San Francisco–area KIPP schools, for example, found that nearly half of teachers who taught in the 2006–2007 school year had left before the beginning of the 2007–2008 school year (Woodworth, David, Guha, Wang, & Lopez-Torkos, 2008), and KIPP (2012a) reports 26% teacher turnover networkwide. This compares with a 20% turnover rate in high-poverty schools generally (Woodworth et al., 2008).

Likewise, the third conservative lesson—that poverty doesn't matter and is just an "excuse"—is not borne out by the KIPP experience. While KIPP certainly demonstrates that all kids can learn if given high expectations, good teachers, and a supportive peer environment, the scars of poverty are still evident among KIPP students. KIPP's predominantly low-income students do very well compared with other low-income students nationally, which is an important accomplishment, but the effects of poverty remain. As of 2012, 40% of the KIPP students who graduated 8th grade 10 or more years ago have earned a bachelor's degree, compared to 10% of low-income students and 33% of all students nationwide. However, KIPP's college completion rate is still a far cry from the average completion rate for high-income students (71%) and KIPP's own goal of 75% college completion, leading KIPP cofounder Mike Feinberg to conclude that there is much work left to do (KIPP, 2012b; Radcliffe, 2011).

We do not know of any research on employment outcomes for KIPP students, but we do know that one drawback to attending economically segregated schools—even ones in which students do well academically, such as KIPP—is that students are cut off from social networks that can be valuable in the job market. Scholarship confirms the adage that in seeking employment, whom you know matters as much as what you know. Researchers have found that 57% of job seekers use personal contacts to land their first job and half have done so in finding their most recent job. Studies also find that one of the greatest benefits to Black students of attending desegregated schools came when graduates were looking for jobs (cited in Kahlenberg, 2001). Indeed, researcher Claude Fischer and colleagues (1996) found that, even after *controlling* for individual ability and family home environment, attending an advantaged school reduced the chances of adult poverty to 4% compared to 14% for similar students attending a high-poverty school.

If the superficial lesson from KIPP is very wrong—that eliminating teacher voice allows schools to render poverty and segregation irrelevant—what does KIPP's success suggest? Two primary lessons emerge. First, peers matter a great deal. Providing hard-working, striving low-income students with an environment in which they are surrounded by peers who will support achievement—as occurs in KIPP's shrinking cohorts of students, and as occurs, routinely, in middle-class schools of any size—appears connected to positive outcomes.

Second, money spent wisely matters as well. One of KIPP's important innovations was the longer school day and school year, and having a set of highly dedicated teachers who are willing to put in long hours. Those things cost money, and KIPP spends considerably more than typical public schools. (This is consistent with research in the regular public school system, where smart investments can pay considerable dividends; see, e.g., Kirp, 2013.) To its credit, KIPP has won the backing of some of the richest individuals in the country. Private donations to KIPP totaled more than $90 million in 2007 alone (Lilly Family School of Philanthropy, 2013). Miron, Urschel, and Saxton (2011) concluded that KIPP schools had over 50% more revenue per pupil than local school districts (roughly $18,500 vs. $12,000). These data are derived from a time prior to federal awards to KIPP of $50 million in a federal i3 grant, plus $10 million in matching funds (Dillon, 2010).

CONCLUSION

The charter school experiment was launched with very high expectations. The original vision, for laboratory schools from which regular public schools would glean lessons, suggested a high standard. Charters would give teachers the chance to spread their wings and students the chance to interact with classmates from all walks of life.

When most charter schools moved in a very different direction—reducing teacher voice and increasing levels of economic and racial isolation—the argument was advanced that these trade-offs were tolerable because students would learn more. On the whole, the evidence in this chapter suggests, that has not happened. The group of schools that were supposed to be held up as exemplars, models for the traditional schools, in reality perform, on the whole, no better.

The idea of charter schools simply "staying the course" after 2 decades of unimpressive results is unappealing. Not only critics but also important players within the charter school movement have recognized the need for better quality control and oversight in the sector. In November 2012 the National Association of Charter School Authorizers (NACSA) launched a campaign to close low-performing charter schools and replace them with high-quality schools, declaring that "more failing schools must close for reform to fully succeed."

Ted Kolderie, one of the founders of the charter school movement, suggests that we need to get beyond the debate over whether charter schools are good or bad and instead home in on the question of *what types* of charter schools best serve students. "People want to know whether a charter school is better than a district school," Kolderie says, "which to me is essentially like asking whether eating out is better than eating at home. It depends. What is it we're eating?" (quoted in Hawkins, 2011).

So what direction should charter schools take in the future? The small subset of charter schools that do excel—such as the KIPP charter schools and the Boston charters—appear to do well in part because they allow motivated low-income students to be educated in an environment where they have peers who also support achievement. The KIPP schools in particular also provide considerable time and resources to those students. These successful schools do not support the conservative thesis that segregation works, poverty doesn't matter, and unions are the problem. To the contrary, as the evidence in this chapter suggests, schools like KIPP underline the truth that resources matter in education, and that peers matter too.

At this point in the history of charter schools, we need to broaden the public imagination of what charter schools look like. The exciting news is that throughout the country, a small but growing number of charter schools have already begun returning to the original vision. They are seeking to empower teachers and desegregate students. And as we shall see in the chapters to follow, they hold the potential to restore the original grand promise of the charter school movement to revolutionize the broader system of public schooling in America.

5

Charter Schools
That Empower Teachers

WHILE A LACK OF TEACHER VOICE is a problem in many charter schools, some charter schools are breaking the mold and providing explicit means for teachers to collaborate and participate in school decisions. These schools have balanced the goals of flexible management and teacher protection. They have given teachers a role in shaping the school while retaining a strong central vision and mission. They exhibit practices and models that other charter schools could emulate.

We interviewed staff members at eight charters schools or networks where teachers, founders, or administrators have taken steps to promote teacher voice:

- Amber Charter School (K–5 school), New York, NY
- Avalon School (7–12 school), St. Paul, MN
- City Neighbors (network), Baltimore, MD
- Green Dot Public Schools (network), Los Angeles, CA
- High Tech High (network), San Diego, CA
- IDEAL School (K–8 school), Milwaukee, WI
- Minnesota New Country School (6–12 school), Henderson, MN
- Springfield Ball Charter School (K–8 school), Springfield, IL

Profiles of the schools are provided in the Appendix. A ninth school with teacher voice, Morris Jeff Community School, which recently opened in New Orleans, is discussed in Chapter 7.

Our choice of schools was not a methodologically rigorous selection but rather an existence proof. We wanted to show that charter schools that empower teachers exist, tell some of their stories, and draw lessons for other schools. We found schools by combing news articles and following leads from educators and researchers. And, mindful of Shanker's idea that charter schools should be laboratories for developing promising practices to help all schools, we chose schools with evidence of success: where teachers report having voice in many key areas, where teacher retention and satisfaction are high, and where student outcomes are positive.

It is also worth noting that these nine charter schools are not the only public schools empowering teachers. Some of these schools are connected to coordinated efforts by groups such as Education Evolving, a Minnesota-based organization that promotes teacher leadership and autonomy, and the Teacher Union Reform Network, which brings together AFT and NEA local chapters to promote innovative roles for unions. While the role of teacher voice in charter schools and public schools more generally has been severely marginalized over the past 2 decades, a dedicated group of educators have continued to pursue this cause (see Farris-Berg & Dirkswager, 2013).

In defining teacher voice for our investigations, we wanted to know what types of voice empower teachers to be more effective in the classroom, to create a supportive and sustainable workplace, and to grow as professionals. After talking to teachers, administrators, and researchers, we saw common themes in their responses. We developed a definition of teacher voice based on a formal role for teachers to participate in decisions about a range of school issues: instruction and curriculum; organization, scheduling, and teaching assignments; hiring, evaluation, and dismissal; salaries and benefits; and teacher professional growth.

There are a number of factors that we purposely excluded from our definition. Agnostic on the question of *how* teachers achieve voice in various school issues, we see having a union as neither sufficient nor necessary for having teacher voice in a school. Similarly, we did not enumerate specific policies—such as the opportunity for tenure, a defined salary schedule that rewards teachers for experience or degrees, or clearly enumerated duties and set working hours—as required elements of teacher voice. The teachers we spoke to wanted voice in crafting specific policies for teachers at their school rather than having these one-size-fits-all protections.

We focused on the types of voice that most influence teachers' effectiveness at their school, both by applying their experiences to decisions about what is taught and how it is taught and by helping to shape a work environment that will support them in a sustainable and fulfilling career. We confined our definition to influence in school-level issues; teacher voice in state, local, and federal education policy decisions is also important, but it requires a separate system for guaranteeing teacher input that was outside the scope of our focus on school-level improvements. At the other end of the spectrum, we also excluded decisions about school operations (building issues, transportation, supplies, meals, and so on). Although teacher voice in these logistical issues also has value—and the teachers we interviewed at co-op schools are responsible for operational decisions—they again fall outside our core focus of empowering teachers in the classroom.

We were also intentional about what we included in the definition. It was important to us to specify that teachers have a "formal" role in decision making so that teachers and administrators both have clear expectations that can weather changes in school leadership. Having a sensitive and inclusive principal who seeks teacher input, without formal policies to ensure such input will continue when the principal moves on, was in our view insufficient. We included issues related to how the school runs as well as how teachers are compensated, since both influence teachers' effectiveness and commitment to the school. Teachers at schools with the strongest teacher voice were able to participate in all of our identified issue areas through formal means. Other schools included fewer issue areas or relied on informal mechanisms but still had strong voice overall.

With this definition of teacher voice in mind, we found that charter schools with strong teacher voice had a variety of mechanisms for ensuring teacher participation. We studied a number of unionized charter schools with strong teacher voice that came to have a union through various means—by teacher vote, by design of the founders, or by working with a district union. We also looked at co-op schools, where teachers assume all of the duties normally assigned to administrators, and at schools with collaborative cultures, where school-specific structures incorporate teachers into the decision-making process.

Rather than finding a single best model for teacher voice, we found strengths and weaknesses in each. Unionization, co-op models, and collaborative cultures are all promising ways for charter schools to increase teacher voice and reap benefits in the learning environment provided for students. Furthermore, combining the most promising aspects of different models could create the strongest systems for teacher voice.

We begin the chapter by highlighting schools that foster teacher voice through a union. We examine the different roles that unions play at each school in terms of addressing compensation and workplace concerns, helping build strong communication between teachers and administrators, and preserving a high level of teacher engagement even as a network grows. We then consider alternative structures for teacher voice—teacher co-ops and schools with collaborative cultures—evaluating the relative strengths and weaknesses of each. Finally, we look at evidence of student outcomes, demonstrating that robust teacher voice and strong student achievement can coexist in charter schools.

ACHIEVING VOICE THROUGH A UNION

For all the charters-versus-unions rhetoric in education debates, a small choir of supporters from both the charter world and the union world has continued to argue that charter schools and teacher unions can work together effectively. AFT President Randi Weingarten has been outspoken during her tenure about the need for unions and charter schools to adopt more open attitudes toward each other. "To get better schools we have to learn how to merge teachers' commitments to their daily work with the spirit of entrepreneurship," she said at a forum of charter school and teacher union leaders in 2006, back when she was president of the United Federation of Teachers (UFT), New York City's teacher union. "Today there is too little entrepreneurship within the school district structure and too little [teacher] professionalism in charter schools" (Weingarten, quoted in Hill, Rainey, & Rotherham, 2006, p. 2). Weingarten's successor at the UFT, Michael Mulgrew (2010), has also spoken out in support of a role for charter schools, as long as "they are run correctly and they help improve their communities."

The National Alliance for Public Charter Schools (2008) is opposed to state laws that require charter schools to be part of collective bargaining agreements; however, the alliance recognize that a portion of charter school teachers are union members, it has issued important data looking at unionization in charter schools, and it has stated a commitment to "embrace all public charter school teachers—those who are members of unions and those who are not" (p. 1). And despite the charter–union animosity created by the Race to the Top program, which rewarded states that lifted charter school caps, the Obama Administration has acknowledged common ground for unions and charters. U.S. Secretary of Education Arne Duncan has on multiple occasions reminded audiences of the charter school movement's roots with Albert Shanker and the AFT (see Duncan, 2009a, 2009b, 2009c). At the NAPCS Conference in 2009, Duncan (2009d) told the crowd of charter school leaders, teachers, and supporters: "Charters are not inherently antiunion. . . . Many charters today are unionized. What distinguishes great charters is not the absence of a labor agreement, but the presence of an education strategy built around commonsense ideas: More time on task, aligned curricula, high parent involvement, great teacher support, and strong leadership."

Union–charter cooperation is not a panacea, as the struggles of the UFT Charter School in New York have shown. In 2005 the UFT tried a new experiment, opening its own charter elementary school in Brooklyn, New York, and adding a secondary branch soon after. Then union president Randi Weingarten (2006) explained that they opened the school out of a desire "to see the debate over charter schools shift from politics back to best practices in education—just as Al Shanker intended." But rather than showing a union-run success story, the UFT Charter School, which drew on a racially and economically isolated group of students, has by almost all accounts been a failure. A 2013 review of the school's charter by the State University of New York (SUNY) Charter Schools Institute, the school's authorizer, cited multiple problems including high principal turnover, incidents of corporal punishment, underequipped classrooms, financial instability, low test scores, and violations of the Individuals with Disabilities in Education Act (Fertig, 2013). Although the school was unionized, it failed to create an environment where teachers are valued and parents are involved. The school's founding principal resigned after three years amidst accusations that she was unresponsive to teacher and parent concerns (E. Green, 2008). Based on the negative appraisal in the report, SUNY renewed the school's charter reluctantly, with the caveat that the school's middle grades, where achievement was particularly low, would have to be consolidated to operate in the same building as the elementary school (Cramer, 2013). The elementary and middle school grades at UFT Charter School earned an "F" on the city's 2013 school progress report, although the high school grades fared better, earning an "A" (Warerkar & Blau, 2013).

Still, in many cases unions could bring a missing and much needed perspective to charter schools. While unionization is not a guarantee of success, some unionized charters do extremely well. Indeed, the faltering performance of the UFT Charter School in Brooklyn stands in sharp contrast to a stellar record at another union-operated charter school, University Prep Charter High School in the Bronx, which was cofounded by the UFT and charter school entrepreneur Steve Barr (Warerkar & Blau, 2013). Furthermore, the stories of teachers at charter schools who feel shut out of the decision-making process, as well as data on teacher turnover and teacher dissatisfaction, show a mismatch between teachers' desire for voice and the reality of charter school management. Schools will not be effective learning environments unless these two visions are better aligned.

And charter schools also present an opportunity for teacher unions, which have seen little progress in the past decades in increasing the stature of the teaching profession. In 2011 Louise Sundin, the former long-time president of the Minneapolis Federation of Teachers and a national vice president of the AFT, testified in front of the Minnesota legislature about the frustrations she has had trying to increase the professionalism of teaching over the past 30 years. "Teaching has not become a true profession.

Why would the best and brightest come into teaching when it is not moving to become more professional but is under attack?" Sundin sought to create teacher-led schools, but district support had been hard to sustain. In order to find the flexibility needed for teacher leadership and autonomy, Sundin concluded, teachers may have to "risk reaching for that 'third rail' of the charter schools opportunity." She asked the legislature to approve a new union-created charter school authorizer to achieve this goal. Later that year, the Minnesota Guild, a nonprofit created by the Minneapolis Federation of Teachers, became the first union-backed charter school authorizer in the nation. The first Guild-approved school will open in 2014 (Louise Sundin, personal communication, January 28, 2014).

In the unionized schools that we investigated, having a teacher union helped teachers gain input in school decisions in several prominent ways. Salaries, benefits, and work schedules were central issues of concern for teachers, and unions helped teachers and administrators develop compromises. Having a union was also a tool for building a better relationship between teachers and administrators to work through smaller issues as they arise. In addition, as a charter network grows, a thoughtful teacher union can help preserve teacher voice in the face of new levels of bureaucracy.

Addressing Compensation and Workplace Concerns

The first and foremost role of teacher unions in the charter schools we investigated was to address issues of workplace conditions and compensation. Springfield Ball Charter School, a K–8 school in Springfield, Illinois, and Amber Charter School, a K–5 school in East Harlem, New York City, provide strong illustrations of this point. Most of the teachers we talked to at Ball and Amber were attracted to teaching in a charter school in part by the flexibility of a small school setting. Some had been frustrated by the bureaucracy in large districts. Jennifer Antolino, now a 3rd-grade teacher at Amber, did a Google search 10 years ago for jobs at charter schools after reaching a breaking point of frustration with "the huge bureaucracy" of New York City public schools, where even quitting her job was an exercise in red tape (personal communication, May 10, 2013). Others, like Ball teacher Hope Kennell, were just looking for "a change" and the freedom "to teach in my way" (personal communication, May 21, 2013). But teachers also wanted fair compensation and some stability. A union contract written specifically for their school helped provide the right mix of protection, compromise, and flexibility.

Fighting for Salary Transparency. Mary Ann Rupcich taught at Springfield Ball Charter School for 15 years, from its opening in 1999 to her retirement in 2013. Rupcich has had her hands in a number of school projects over the years, including running the school's garden. And for many of her years at Ball Charter, Rupcich hosted a Stone Soup celebration each October, inviting her past and present students to come eat "stone soup"—made, in the style of the old folk story, from a stone plus many vegetables from the school's garden—while reading books together.

This sort of multiage experience is central to the educational model at Ball, where students spend 2 years "looping" with the same teacher in a class combining students from two traditional grade levels. And a lesson that combines gardening and literacy is also a fitting combination for a school that was created with funding from the Ball Foundation (2012), a nonprofit created by a former CEO of a horticultural company with an interest in literacy and teacher professionalism.

Like most of the school's founding teachers, Rupcich was attracted to Ball Charter School by the innovative academic model started by the school's original principal, which included multiage classrooms and the use of a "literacy learning continuum," which tracks students' progress along a path of different stages of literacy, rather than a traditional system of letter grades (personal communication, June 11, 2013). As the first and still the only charter school in Springfield, Illinois, Ball attracted many teachers with district experience who were excited to teach in an innovative setting. But within a few years, teachers at Ball became frustrated with how they were being compensated for their work.

Ball Charter, a K–8 school, was founded with the idea of being innovative not only in its academic model but also in the calendar and compensation. Ball had a longer school day than the public schools, by about an hour, and a much longer school year. Teacher John Delich remembers working 24 days more than the district teachers during the early years at Ball (personal communication, June 6, 2013). At the same time, Ball followed an idiosyncratic and obscure system for salaries. School founders hoped to lure a few highly qualified teachers with competitive salaries, leveraging them as mentor teachers, while keeping salaries for most teachers lower (John Delich, personal communication, May 10, 2013). The board and administrators kept salary information secret from teachers, and teachers had little knowledge about what they could do to earn a raise. Delich described the old process of determining salaries: "Teachers were called in to the principal's office each year, and handed a tiny slip of paper folded in half. This was their salary for the next year, and they were told to keep it private" (personal communication, June 6, 2013). Kathleen Maher, who taught at Ball for 5 years and helped form the union, said that teachers were frustrated when they realized that they were earning much less than their district counterparts, despite working longer days and years, and that they had no clear path to a pay increase (personal communication, June 11, 2013).

Teachers approached the principal and the board but had their arguments silenced. They "shut us down," Rupcich recalled (personal communication, June 11, 2013). So teachers decided to unionize, in Delich's words, "to have a better understanding of the finances, and then to make sure that we were still attracting the best teachers we could. Because you know how news gets out—if you're not making as much as somebody else in the same town, you're probably not going to get the best teachers to come over" (personal communication, May 10, 2013). Rupcich said that the general outspokenness of the original staff members was a likely factor in the decision to challenge the pay policies and form a union: "I think because . . . we were encouraged [by the founding principal] to voice everything about everything, that laid the seeds for us to really fight to get union representation" (personal communication, June 11, 2013).

Teachers voted to unionize and marked nominations for union president on the back of a napkin at a local restaurant. John Delich was elected as one of the founding union presidents (personal communication, May 10, 2013). Initial negotiations with the board were tough. During the same time that teachers unionized, the school's founding principal left, and her successor was antagonistic toward the union. Kathleen Maher remembers talking so much as a member of the bargaining committee that she lost her voice (personal communication, June 11, 2013). In 2002–2003, their teacher union—the Springfield Ball Charter School Education Association, separate from the district union but affiliated with the Illinois Education Association (IEA) and NEA—created its first contract with the board (Nicole Gales, personal communication, April 19, 2013). For the first time, teachers had a set system to determine salaries, bargaining power in determining the number of days and hours worked, and greater transparency around how all of these decisions were made.

This first agreement was an improvement over the salary secrecy that teachers faced before, but teachers still felt that they were behind the district in terms of pay (Rupcich, personal communication, June 11, 2013). Having a union opened up the possibility for negotiating, but the actual changes to the work schedule and teacher pay in the 2002 contract had been slight. At the same time, the board continued to push for an innovative pay system that would set the school apart (Delich, personal communication, September 22, 2013, and May 10, 2013).

In 2009, the union and the board agreed to a new portfolio-based pay system as a compromise. Under the new system, teachers get regular raises based on years of experience at the school but have the option to earn additional raises by presenting a portfolio documenting their growth as educators. The portfolio contains a number of different elements: "artifacts, rich descriptions, surveys, audits, standardized test data, assessments, units, lesson plans, student work samples, documents, evaluations, projects, team logs, reports, articles, professional development, and other examples of information" (Gales, personal communication, April 19, 2013). Hope Kennell, president of the teacher union, stressed that the portfolio is designed to give a well-balanced look at teachers' work: "You can show your contribution to the school and your contribution to the students in your classroom" (personal communication, May 21, 2013). Evidence from teachers' portfolios is combined with feedback from their evaluations to determine promotions.

Not all teachers were initially happy with the portfolio system and the time it required. But, according to Kennell, most teachers have grown to like the new system and voted to maintain it in the next contract. "They like having the voice and having the chance to have an input into what they're doing in the classroom and what they're doing for the school" (personal communication, May 21, 2013).

Flexible Responses to Changing Workplace Demands. Founded in 2000, Amber Charter School, a K–5 school in East Harlem with a strong character program and Spanish instruction, was one of the first charter schools in the city and also the state of New York. The school's founding board and administrators were supportive of unions. Jon Moscow, one of the school's creators and an original codirector of Amber, had himself been a rank-and-file union organizer in computer typesetting shops in New York City some decades previous, and he and other leaders at the school had never been fully comfortable with a nonunion school model. So when the UFT approached Amber leaders during the school's first year about unionizing their teachers, the board and administrators welcomed them and helped facilitate the discussion with the school's teachers, who were also by and large supportive of the union (Jon Moscow, personal communication, September 20, 2013). At the end of the school's first year, teachers at Amber joined the UFT—the district union for New York City Public Schools, which is affiliated with the New York State United Teachers (NYSUT), AFT, and NEA—and began working with the union to develop a collective bargaining agreement that would be unique to Amber.

Amber's contract is short—originally just 6 pages and now about 20 pages long, compared to the 200-page New York City district contract (Amber Charter School & United Federation of Teachers, 2010; Lake, 2004). Over the years, a number of union leaders have supported "thin" contracts like Amber's as a flexible option for school districts and charter schools alike. Having a thin master contract, which is supplemented by a Personnel Policy and Procedures Manual, gives Amber teachers and administrators a clear understanding of essential compensation, benefits, and employment issues while leaving plenty of room to respond to changing workplace demands without constantly going through formal negotiations.

In our interviews, teachers at Amber were enthusiastic about their contract. Kathleen McCann, a 4th-grade teacher who was finishing her 5th year at Amber, said that the contract "gives everyone a common framework to work in, so that when something comes up we all know . . . this is how we're expected to do X, Y, and Z." She described the thin contract as a "good balance" between the extremes of extensive, highly specific contracts and "flimsy" contracts that provide few protections: "It's that nice middle ground where you still have flexibility to address stuff as it comes up" (personal communication, April 18, 2013). Francina Yaw, a 2nd-grade teacher, added that having the support of a union representative has helped Amber staff members to negotiate effectively, "to extend the conversation with the school" and "take it a step further" when teachers are unhappy about a policy (personal communication, April 19, 2013).

Principal Vasthi Acosta likewise thinks that the teachers' contract does a good job of setting up a framework of clear expectations while leaving her enough freedom to be an effective leader. In describing the multistep process for firing a teacher at the school, which is outlined in the contract, Acosta said that the sometimes lengthy process of identifying and addressing concerns is worthwhile. "I think that's only fair. I think people need to know why they're being fired and they need to know that they've been given every chance to correct what's been identified as a weakness. . . . I mean, it is a burden, but that's part of the job, isn't it?" (personal communication, April 11, 2013).

Because of the flexibility of Amber's contract, teachers and administrators have been able to work out quick solutions to problems that might have otherwise escalated. Jennifer Antolino, a 3rd-grade teacher and union chapter leader at the school, described a time when teachers were concerned about a new state rule requiring every grade-level team to prepare and submit all lessons for a module in math and humanities. Teachers were worried about how they would complete this time-consuming task, and they brought their concerns to Antolino who asked the principal if the teachers could leave early or have more prep time during the day to complete the work. The school countered with an offer of a $1,000 stipend to compensate teachers for the work, which teachers happily decided to accept (personal communication, May 17, 2013).

High teacher retention also points toward staff satisfaction at Amber: 89% of teachers returned to the school in 2010–2011 (New York State Education Department, 2013). "I have to say, I think the union helped

Amber because teachers stay," Antolino explained. "[At] other charter schools, the turnover is incredible. And it's not like that here" (personal communication, May 10, 2013).

Sometimes issues still arise that require contract negotiations. Although Amber has a thin contract, the daily schedule is part of this agreement. A few years ago, Acosta found that the daily student dismissal process was taking longer than expected, requiring a permanent schedule change for teachers to make sure that students were supervised. This adjustment required negotiating a change to the contract, "and that was a pain in the neck, I have to admit," Acosta explained. "It was frustrating that I had to go and negotiate [to extend the teacher workday by] an additional 5 minutes, where in a nonunionized school that would not have happened" (personal communication, April 11, 2013). But this example is the exception, underscoring the fact that Acosta is able to work out most issues with her staff quickly and amicably by working directly with teachers.

Outside union leaders agree that Amber provides a model for how union contracts can be negotiated to account for the differences between charter schools and traditional public schools. In 2003 then-UFT leader Randi Weingarten drew on Amber as an example when advocating for "thin" contracts to preempt New York Schools Chancellor Joel Klein's union reforms. "What if you had trust, fairness, and collaboration substitute for lock-step rules?" Weingarten asked. "Except for things like salaries, pensions, medical, safety, due process and things covered by law, maybe virtually everything else should be negotiable" (quoted in Herszenhorn, 2003). UFT Vice President of Academic High Schools Leo Casey echoed Weingarten's position in his 2009 statement before the New York City Council Education Committee. Arguing for the vision of charters first articulated by Albert Shanker, Casey (2009) highlighted Amber as an example of how "collective bargaining can take place in a way that respects both the uniqueness of a charter school and the professionalism of the educators who perform all of the essential work within it."

Springfield Ball Charter School and Amber Charter School came to be unionized in very different ways—at Ball, as the result of teacher vote after a heated conflict with management, and at Amber, through an amicable invitation from administrators. However, both schools made a decision to unionize, rather than being bound by state law to the collective bargaining agreements in their districts, and both have contracts written specifically for their school. This puts them in the minority of unionized charter schools and gives them an advantage in finding the right balance between protection and flexibility in their union negotiations. Striking such a balance can be more difficult for a charter school that is legally bound to a districtwide contract (see discussion of City Neighbors Charter School later in this chapter). Teacher voice in charter schools can perhaps be best facilitated through site-specific contracts or agreements that take into consideration the unique needs of the school.

A Tool for Improving Teacher–Administrator Communication

At both Ball and Amber, having a union has also helped facilitate a better relationship between teachers and administrators, making it easier to resolve issues that arise outside of contract negotiations. The most recent principals of Ball and Amber have made concerted efforts to encourage teachers to approach them with concerns and to listen to their feedback, but having a union has made establishing trust easier. The school union leaders serve as safe outlets for teachers to voice questions or concerns rather than approaching the principal directly. Likewise, administrators can test ideas with union leaders, gauging reactions before talking to the full staff.

The relationship between the union and administration at Ball has evolved over the years to become more amicable as the school found a principal who saw the positive side of teacher input. Nicole Gales, principal at Ball from 2006 to 2013, worked hard to create good communication with the union, holding biweekly meetings with union leaders. "We try to be proactive in our approach," she said, explaining that both administrators and the union have made a commitment "to get out in the front of a lot of issues" (personal communication, April 19, 2013). Hope Kennell agrees that the relationship between the union and administrators is "very close," with both sides paying attention to teachers' hopes and concerns "to keep things flowing smoothly" (personal communication, May 21, 2013). When an issue about scheduling or the calendar comes up, for example, Gales raises the question with the union during their biweekly meeting before making any proposals to the staff or the board. And when teachers have concerns or questions—for example, wondering what to expect on an upcoming professional development day—the union brings them to Gales's attention and encourages her to communicate with the whole staff.

The union serves as a helpful link between teachers and the principal. Gales adds that the union has also become a useful tool for her as a leader. "The union can also be supportive of the administration on things that I want to happen." She can pitch an idea to the union leaders, explaining her reasoning, and get the union's help in building wider teacher support. "It's not just all about restrictions and rules and that kind of thing.

It's really helping to join a partnership to support the teachers" (personal communication, April 19, 2013).

At Amber Charter School, Vasthi Acosta is well-known for being a principal who supports her teachers, from maintaining an open door policy to providing teachers with paid time for new extracurricular initiatives at the school. Having union representation has helped make sure that Acosta has honest communication with her staff. Acosta holds a monthly meeting with the school union chapter leader and the union chapter delegate, who are both teachers at the school, and she credits this regular meeting for helping to keep lines of communication open (personal communication, April 11, 2013).

Jennifer Antolino explains that as the union representative, she works hard to make sure that teachers know they can come to her with any issue and be confident that she will keep it confidential. In return, Antolino is able to give Acosta a frank assessment of what her staff is thinking, while protecting individual teachers. "Vasthi has mentioned to me several times that she's very happy that we have a union," Antolino told us. "Vasthi does not want her teachers to be unhappy. . . . [She] gets a lot more out of us when we're happy." Because Amber teachers have this union protection, "in the end, [Vasthi] always gets the truth about where the teachers are coming from," Antolino explained (personal communication, May 10, 2013).

As part of Amber's bylaws, the school also has a designated teacher representative on the Board of Trustees, adding another channel, in addition to the union, for teachers to voice feedback (Amber Charter School, 2012, p. 6). Francina Yaw has been the school's elected teacher representative for several years in a row. Teachers can come to Yaw confidentially with concerns, and she will raise those issues with the board and often the administration as well. Yaw added that teachers from Amber sometimes get together with other charter school teachers in the city through UFT ACTS, the New York City branch of the national AFT ACTS (Alliance of Charter Teachers and Staff). If teachers at another charter school are considering unionization, Amber teachers readily share "how having this foundation" has been an asset for the school (personal communication, April 19, 2013).

Maintaining Voice as a Network Grows

Springfield Ball Charter School and Amber Charter School are stand-alone schools, which, when it comes to promoting teacher voice, appears to be an advantage. Their contracts each address the needs of a single board, administration, and teaching staff. As a single school grows into a network of charter schools, new levels of oversight form. It can become more difficult to ensure that teachers' voices are heard and to design policies that work well for all campuses. As discussed in Chapter 2, teachers at the Chavez Schools in Washington, D.C., discovered this when their network expanded and added a Home Office, which seemed disconnected from teachers in schools. Former teacher Sarah Fine explained, "It just felt like there would be decisions that would come down the pipe from the Home Office that . . . were surprising" (personal communication, April 18, 2013). High Tech High, a network of charter schools in California that is discussed later in this chapter, experienced some of the same growing pains.

Green Dot Public Schools is a charter network of middle and high schools in Los Angeles that is unionized by design, with growth in mind. The network's founder, Steve Barr, is a former Democratic Party organizer and cofounder of the youth engagement organization Rock the Vote. Barr, who has now moved on to other education projects in New York and New Orleans, formulated his vision for the Green Dot schools by talking to teachers. "I spent a lot of time listening," he told *The Hechinger Report*. "What seemed to be very consistent with teachers was their inability to have a say in how decisions are made, how money is allocated, and their working conditions." Barr wanted to create a network of charter schools that would attract high-quality teachers and provide "R&D [research and development] for what school districts could become" (Carr & Barr, 2012). Cristina de Jesus, president and chief academic officer of Green Dot, explains that having a union was important "to be able to make apples to apples comparisons" between Green Dot and unionized school districts (personal communication, July 10, 2013). If charters are to provide lessons for traditional public schools, those insights are less likely to transfer if labor–management relations are radically different in the two sectors.

As the Green Dot network of middle and high schools has grown, from 140 students upon opening in 2000 to more than 10,000 students today, their union has evolved. Green Dot's teacher union, Asociación de Maestros Unidos (AMU), an affiliate of the California Teacher Association (CTA) and the NEA, was founded at the same time as the school, which has helped to build a spirit of collaboration between the two. "Our union is really trying to look at where we have common interests between our members and our management, and see how we can both meet as a team," explained Salina Joiner, president and former vice president of AMU (personal communication, July 8, 2013).

Together, AMU and Green Dot have developed innovative ways to maintain clear avenues for individual teachers to participate in organizational decisions while also introducing the efficiencies needed to run multiple campuses. Arielle Zurzolo, former AMU president, explained how growth has necessitated change: "I've heard stories of our first union meetings. You would have 8 teachers in a room, and they would all vote on every policy that the union adopted, and that's impossible when you have 550 teachers" (personal communication, July 26, 2013). De Jesus said that growth has forced Green Dot "to get a lot more transparent and explicit about our communication. We've had to build very formal and very structured ways to seek input from teachers on a regular basis" (personal communication, July 10, 2013).

The teacher union is a much larger organization at Green Dot than at Springfield Ball Charter School, where a stand-alone union represents just one charter school. AMU is run by a small executive board of five elected officers, and each of Green Dot's 19 schools has one or two site representatives for the union. Board members and site representatives are all paid stipends to compensate them for their time. When a teacher is elected president of AMU, she continues earning a salary but takes a leave of absence from her normal teaching duties so that she can devote 100% of her work time to union business (Green Dot Public Schools & Asociación de Maestros Unidos, 2013). (Unions in traditional public school districts often use similar arrangements.)

It would be easy for individual teachers to get lost in such a big organization, so AMU has taken steps to make sure that there are many opportunities for teachers to get involved at every level of the decision-making process. Zurzolo estimates that 95–100% of Green Dot teachers have direct interaction with the union. The AMU–Green Dot contract allots 45 minutes of professional development time per month to be used by AMU at each school, so union site representatives have an easy way to stay up-to-date with other teachers. When a big decision is being contemplated, like the recent process to create a new system for evaluating teachers, AMU and Green Dot seek input from teachers across the network through a tiered process, inviting them to participate in focus groups, learning sessions, and committees, and paying teachers for their time. And the network has done well meeting its goals for teacher retention; roughly 85% of teachers return each year (Joiner, personal communication, July 8, 2013; Zurzolo, personal communication, July 26, 2013; de Jesus, personal communication, July 10, 2013).

Another way that Green Dot and AMU have managed growth in their network is to have a single network contract but leave a number of issues to be decided at the school level. The small size and "community feel" are part of what attracted Salina Joiner to teach at a Green Dot school 7 years ago (personal communication, July 8, 2013). Although the network has grown considerably since then, allowing schools to make many of their own leadership decisions has helped to preserve this small feel. The contract stipulates, "Each school site and the Asociación agree to establish a teacher led school environment, where teacher talents will be utilized to their fullest potential, offering perspectives in administrative, curricular and extra-curricular decision making" (Green Dot Public Schools & Asociación de Maestros Unidos, 2013, p. 45). Many of the details of this leadership structure—who is on the school committees, what authority the committees have, when they meet—are left up to each school. If there is disagreement at a school—teachers at one campus, for example, complained that administrators were unfairly hand-picking teachers for leadership positions—then AMU leaders will step in to help find a solution (Joiner, personal communication, July 8, 2013).

Green Dot and AMU are still in the process of figuring out which decisions to leave to the school site and which to manage centrally. "We have had to adopt systems and create organizational structure as we go along," Zurzolo explained. This kind of evolution is possible in a union like AMU that has the "creativity and flexibility" afforded by starting with a clean slate, without a long history of "the way it's always done" (personal communication, July 26, 2013).

ALTERNATIVE STRUCTURES FOR TEACHER VOICE

Unions offer a number of benefits for charter school teachers. They tend to be able to negotiate formal and guaranteed protections for compensation and workplace issues, and they provide an outlet for teacher feedback and input into school decisions that can weather changes in the school administration. But unions also carry risks: In some cases, unions take a more adversarial stance than other methods of teacher participation; they introduce another form of bureaucracy; and, often by constraint of state laws, they sometimes focus more on bread-and-butter issues than on decisions surrounding curriculum and instruction.

We interviewed teachers at schools that employ other methods of securing voice, each with their own pros and cons. A small number of charter schools (and some noncharter schools) use a co-op model of leadership, where teachers are responsible for all of the duties of running a school that would normally fall to administrators. In cooperatives, where teachers make all the decisions, a union isn't necessary, as Ted Kolderie notes, because there is no separate management to bargain with (personal communication, June 4, 2013). These schools offer teachers unparalleled leadership and control, but in exchange, teachers assume a large workload. Other schools have a traditional divide between teachers and management but create a deliberate culture of collaboration by having relatively flat management structures and carving out time for working together. These arrangements have the potential to be more collaborative than a system based on union negotiations, but they also leave teachers with fewer protections on salary and workplace issues.

Teacher Co-ops

Soon after Minnesota passed the nation's first charter school law in 1991, a handful of residents from Henderson and Le Sueur, two neighboring farm towns, began developing plans to open one of the nation's first charter schools. Dee Thomas and a small crew of other educators, parents, and community members knew that they wanted to form something that would look totally different from a typical school but that, in Thomas's words, "would meet the needs of students much better than we've been meeting them in the past" (personal communication, June 13, 2013). They tossed around highly unorthodox ideas like having no classes or grades—an idea which made it to the final plan. And in a conversation with Ted Kolderie, one of the chief architects of the new charter school law, they came up with the idea of running the school as a teacher cooperative: "What if you didn't have employees? What if you owned the enterprise as a professional practice, much like a law firm or medical practice?" (Kolderie, quoted in Doug Thomas, 2007). The Le Sueur-Henderson region seemed an appropriate place for a co-op school to take root. As Dee Thomas explained, "Since we're in a rural Minnesota area, we have farmers' co-ops all over the place. So most of us had some experience working with a cooperative at some point in time" (personal communication, June 13, 2013).

Minnesota New Country School, a secondary school, opened its doors in 1994 and quickly attracted attention due to its unorthodox pedagogy and governance. In 1998 the *American Prospect* ran a profile of New Country, describing it as "a progressive open school with a high-tech spin" and highlighting a number of the unusual secondary school's distinguishing features: projects instead of classes and textbooks, no traditional grades, a year-round schedule, advisors instead of teachers, and personal learning plans for each student (Corson, 1998). Newspapers from the *St. Louis Post-Dispatch* to the *New York Times* ran stories on the school (Sievers, 1996; Traub, 1999). Most important for the future of co-op schools, New Country also attracted the attention of the Bill and Melinda Gates Foundation, which in 1998 pledged $4.5 million to start 15 new schools with a similar pedagogy and governance structure (Torres, 2000).

As a result of the Gates Foundation funding and other charter school initiatives, a number of other co-op schools opened modeled after New Country, including Avalon School, a secondary school in St. Paul, Minnesota, and IDEAL School, a K–8 school in Milwaukee, Wisconsin, both of which opened in 2001. There are a few dozen schools across the country today that use a co-op model or another teacher-run governance system (Education Evolving, n.d.). And New Country has stayed true to its individualized, small-school model. In the decade between 2002 and 2012, the school's enrollment barely grew, and the school has continued to earn accolades (Dyslin, 2012). The *Ladies Home Journal* selected New Country as one of its ten "Most Amazing Schools" in 2010, highlighting its "almost fanatical following among Minnesota families, with some students traveling as far as 100 miles a day, round-trip, to attend" (Guernsey & Harmon, 2013).

The co-op model asks much of teachers—making them responsible for all the decisions and duties normally assumed by administrators, from making a budget to coordinating school lunches—but offers unparalleled control in return. "As far as enabling voice, we're probably off the charts," boasted Carrie Bakken, a founding teacher at Avalon, noting that teachers "control all aspects" of the school (personal communication, June 18, 2013). Dee Thomas explains that a co-op school like New Country requires entrepreneurial teachers. "You will have more responsibility," she explains, "but along with that, you have more ability to make decisions and do different things" (personal communication, June 13, 2013).

New Country, Avalon, and IDEAL (which stands for Individualized Developmental Educational Approaches to Learning) all emphasize democracy and collaboration through their co-op structures. Gretchen Sage-Martinson, one of Avalon's founding teachers, finds that being forced to make management decisions collaboratively produces better results for the school. "Twenty-four brains *are* undoubtedly more powerful and smarter than one, and when we harness that power well we make really smart decisions." She also explained that having teachers make decisions together models civic engagement for the students, showing them that "if you want to fix something, you are the key to fixing it" (personal communication, July 2, 2013).

In curriculum and instruction this co-op model manifests itself through a balance of individual freedom and intense collaboration for teachers. Carrie Bakken described how teachers at Avalon can design their own seminar classes, which are offered to supplement students' individualized projects (personal communication, June 18, 2013). But co-op teachers are also constantly collaborating, in part because most of the work at New Country, Avalon, and IDEAL is done in an open floor plan, with groups of students and teachers working on different projects side by side. "When I was in a traditional school, I'd go in, shut my door, and do my thing for 42 minutes, and nobody really saw what I did except for the two scheduled visits from the superintendent each year," Dee Thomas remembers. At New Country, "everyone is in the open 24/7. Everyone sees everyone else. And you interact with all the kids in all the different groups" (personal communication, June 13, 2013).

The control that teachers in these co-op schools have over curriculum and instruction is similar to what you might find at other small, progressive, or nontraditional schools. What really sets co-op schools apart is the control that teachers have over other issues that are frequently completely in the hands of administrators, such as budgetary and salary issues. Different administrative duties are distributed to teachers, on a rotating basis. Gretchen Sage-Martinson took one of the lead teacher roles, assuming a number of administrative duties, for several years at Avalon. When setting salaries and looking at the budget, a lead teacher will start the process, but the entire staff must come to consensus on any decision. "If I am taking a look at the budget, and there's no way we can do cost-of-living raises this year," Sage-Martinson explains, "and I bring that to the staff, and 16 of us think that's a good idea, and 8 of us say absolutely not, we have to talk, until we get everybody to a place where we all agree" (personal communication, July 2, 2013).

Avalon and New Country use a "fist-to-five" voting system to make decisions by consensus. Staff members vote on proposals by holding up zero fingers (a fist, totally opposed) to five fingers (totally in favor). Any member of the staff can veto any decision, but teachers use the option judiciously since the voting system allows them to express dissent in more nuanced ways and encourages increased conversation to address concerns about an idea. For example, if an initial vote on an idea yields fists and/ or votes of one or two fingers, the staff spends time addressing concerns before moving forward.

Sometimes reaching consensus around financial issues means finding creative solutions. During a budget crisis brought about by state funding cuts, New Country needed to adapt to an operating budget that was 30% less than the year before. The school faced a choice between taking out a loan and cutting staff member salaries, but found a third way by asking staff members if anyone was interested in switching to part-time work; several people stepped up, and the crisis was avoided (Dee Thomas, personal communication, June 13, 2013). At IDEAL, teachers decided to accept shorter lunch hours and help out with playground and lunch supervision to save money on paying for other staff members to cover those duties. "When the budgets are really tight and it comes down to

making some of those decisions versus losing a teacher," said Kristin Leguizamon, "those are the ways we can work together to make things
work" (personal communication, May 10, 2013).

Making hiring and firing decisions collaboratively can also be a
challenge. Gretchen Sage-Martinson admits that there are times when
teachers at Avalon find themselves wondering, "Why don't we have a
principal?" particularly when difficult personnel decisions come up. But
while it might be easier to have an appointed principal in charge of deliv-
ering difficult decisions like the firing of a staff member, Sage-Martinson
says she thinks making tough decisions about personnel collaboratively
"makes us stronger" (personal communication, July 2, 2013). Avalon
surveys teachers, other staff members, parents, and students about each
teacher's work in order to get a full picture of staff members' performance. Experienced teachers serve as coaches and provide peer evaluations several times a year. If there are issues with a teacher's performance,
the school's personnel team gets involved early, to make sure the teacher
has as much support as possible. "It's way more effective to address any
issues and keep somebody than to get new employees," Carrie Bakken
explained. If a teacher continues to struggle and the personnel team rec-
ommends terminating the contract, the team will present the case to the
staff, explaining the problems and the interventions that were tried. Consensus of the full staff (minus the teacher in question) is needed to fire a
teacher (personal communication, June 18, 2013).

Even with some outside administrative help, teaching at a co-op
school places huge demands on teachers, ultimately limiting the appeal
of the model. Cris Parr, one of the teachers who founded IDEAL, as
well as two other Milwaukee teacher co-ops, described working at a co-
op school as a "phenomenal amount of extra work": "If you're dividing
up all of the administrative duties [among teachers], you have no life"
(personal communication, June 19, 2013). At Avalon, each summer
begins with staff divvying up duties that need to be taken care of before
the next school year. Teachers volunteer for different items, knowing
that they are collectively responsible for making sure that everything is
taken care of (Bakken, personal communication, June 18, 2013). Still,
national survey results show that many teachers are interested in this
opportunity. Farkas, Johnson, and Duffett (2003) found that 65% of
new teachers and 50% of veteran teachers were interested in working
at a teacher-run charter school. Likewise, in a 2014 national survey by
Education Evolving and Widmeyer Communications, 51% of all teachers rated their interest in entering a teacher partnership arrangement,
where teachers as a group make important school decisions, 8 or higher
on a 10-point scale.

The co-op model also works best in small schools; making decisions collaboratively with a staff of 100 teachers would be difficult. In 2012–2013, New Country served 111 students, Avalon enrolled 183, and IDEAL had 228 (NAPCS, 2013c). However, IDEAL began the school year in 2013 in its own building for the first time, and it is expanding to 300 students in the new facility. Kristin Leguizamon explains that, for now, they think 300 students is a rough size limit for having their co-op governance model run effectively (personal communication, May 10, 2013). After years of maintaining roughly the same size, New Country also began to expand in 2013, adding an elementary program. Both schools will still remain small, in the scheme of things, but their expansion will be an interesting test of the ability for co-op schools to grow.

Co-op schools face the financial and political hurdles associated with small schools, and they require teachers to manage a heavy work load; however, if these schools can manage the finances, navigate district politics, and find committed teachers, the co-op model has the advantage of building a strong school culture that does not rely on any one person to sustain it. In a traditional school, a charismatic principal can recruit a terrific group of teachers and achieve considerable success only to see the enterprise disintegrate once this principal moves on. Frustration with new leadership and a change in the direction of their old school was what led Kristin Leguizamon, Cris Parr, and a few other colleagues to start IDEAL. After teaching for 2 years at a Milwaukee public school known for its innovative pedagogical model, Leguizamon and Parr watched as a new principal made swift changes that undermined years of teachers' work to build a successful school. "[What was] considered [a] very successful program basically had been dismantled essentially by one person in a position of leadership," Leguizamon explained. She and the other founders of IDEAL had a vision to start a school where "everyone has ownership, and the fidelity of programming is based on the charter and on the investment of everyone. It's not just dependent on . . . one person's leadership" (personal communication, May 10, 2013).

Teachers at Avalon and New Country have also made an effort to keep power dispersed by making sure to have teachers' administrative roles rotate on a frequent basis. At Avalon, leadership of staff meetings even rotates each week, ever since teachers realized that running the staff meeting inevitably entails some power over how issues are discussed. The goal is to make sure that leadership remains collaborative. As Gretchen Sage-Martinson puts it, "It's never an us–them situation." Teachers work together constantly. "You always know how everybody's doing, and there's always somebody burned out, because it's hard. But we all can rally around and help that person out" (personal communication, July

2, 2013). Although the workload is heavy, Avalon has extremely high teacher retention: roughly 95% of teachers return to the school each year (Bakken, personal communication, June 18, 2013).

After cofounding IDEAL and then leaving to help start other co-op schools in Milwaukee, Cris Parr is now teaching in a traditional class-room. The most recent co-op school Parr helped start recently decided, based on the financial and administrative burden now facing small schools in Milwaukee, not to try to renew its charter. Parr is teaching 5th grade in a traditional district school in Milwaukee, "recuperating" from the work at co-op schools. She is quick to say that there is much she does not miss about working in a co-op school, particularly "the exhaustion" that came from constant battles with the district over school autonomy. She shared with a tone of joy—and some disbelief—"I'm no longer on ulcer medica-tion and migraine meds!" But Parr misses "the sense of ownership" that came from working at a co-op school. "I miss the problem solving that we did on a constant basis to do what was best for our kids" (personal communication, June 19, 2013).

Collaborative Cultures

A third model of teacher voice—"collaborative cultures"—is more amorphous than those of unionized and co-op schools. We included in this category any school-based governance structures or policies that facilitate collaboration and teacher input in school decisions, such as minimized management hierarchy, scheduled time for collaboration, and hiring by committee.

We looked at two schools with strong collaborative cultures that had different degrees of success in facilitating teacher voice across our full list of parameters. The High Tech High network in San Diego, California, has promising models for flat leadership and guaranteed collaboration time, but salaries, contracts, and working conditions still raise some con-cerns among teachers. City Neighbors Charter School, a K–8 school in Baltimore, Maryland, has a collaborative culture as well as union protec-tions around salaries and benefits; however, City Neighbors is part of a districtwide union contract that leaves them little site flexibility, which causes its own concerns.

Strengths and Limitations of a Collaborative Culture. Since its founding in 2000, High Tech High has attracted attention from government lead-ers, the media, and philanthropists for its innovative pedagogical model and student success. Now a network of 12 elementary, middle, and high schools in San Diego, California, High Tech High began as a single high

school that was the vision of veteran educators Larry Rosenstock and Rob Riordan. After working together in a large northeastern school district, Rosenstock and Riordan decided to start a school where they could build from scratch the educational innovations they had already spent years developing in the margins at traditional public schools (Riordan, personal communication, May 2, 2013). Rosenstock envisioned a school where the hands-on, project-based methods of vocational education were integrated with a demanding academic curriculum (personal communication, December 5, 2011). In a 1999 report *Seeing the Future: A Planning Guide for High Schools,* Riordan and several coauthors described their key principles for high school design, including personalizing education for each student, immersing students into the adult world, creating a common intellectual mission by eliminating academic tracking, and giving teachers ownership over their work (Riordan, Roche, Goldhammer, & Stephen, 1999). When Bush Administration Secretary of Education Margaret Spellings visited Gary and Jerri-Ann Jacobs High Tech High school—the original High Tech High—in 2008, she called the school "customized learning at its best," urging an expansion of the model (U.S. Department of Education, 2008).

In addition to its use of project-based learning and a focus on science and technology, High Tech High prides itself on student diversity (discussed in Chapter 6) and on the culture of collaboration among teachers, administrators, and graduate students at the network's own graduate school of education. "We knew from the beginning when we started High Tech High that if we were going to have a rigorous, engaged student learning environment, we also needed to create the conditions for a rich adult learning community," Rob Riordan explained. "We know if we want to model and convey 21st-century skills for kids, that our teachers need to be working in a 21st-century work environment, i.e., an environment where they have ample opportunities to try out ideas, collaborate with colleagues, and do problem solving and troubleshooting as they go along" (personal communication, May 2, 2013).

Teachers at High Tech High generally agree that the school has lived up to this goal. Bobby Shaddox, a teacher at High Tech Middle, describes the network as "set up to honor teachers and the practice of teaching" (personal communication, May 10, 2013). Stacey Lopaz, who has held a number of teaching positions in the network and was also director of one of the middle schools, explained that teachers at High Tech High schools are given "trust and freedom and responsibility," in issues ranging from curriculum and school design to schedules. In cases where, "traditionally, directors make decisions in isolation," at High Tech High "teachers are given a voice" (personal communication, May 10, 2013). Jeff Robin, an art teacher at High Tech High since its opening, summarized the difference in the amount of voice he has at High Tech High compared to his early positions in district schools: "This is heaven and those were hell" (personal communication, May 9, 2013).

One of the most basic ways that High Tech High fosters teacher voice and collaboration is by employing a relatively flat organizational structure. High Tech High purposely has few management and administrative roles and many teaching roles, in an effort to reduce bureaucratic oversight. Each High Tech High school has a relatively small administrative staff—"lean and mean," Rob Riordan calls it. Furthermore, all of the directors of High Tech High schools have previous experience as successful teachers in the network, so they bring the knowledge and perspective of a classroom educator to their leadership (personal communication, May 2, 2013). Bobby Shaddox describes his school's director as fulfilling multiple positions that you might see in other schools—"principal and vice-principal, and probably school counselor." As a result, Shaddox feels that it is easy for teachers to engage with the school's administrators: "The flat structure breaks down that hierarchy that exists in a lot of traditional schools. The director is really accessible if you're a teacher" (personal communication, May 10, 2013).

At the network level, Larry Rosenstock, the CEO and cofounder, and Ben Daley, chief academic officer, each have an "open door policy" for meeting with teachers and administrators from High Tech High schools. They actively work to make sure that staff members feel comfortable coming to them with ideas or concerns. Daley encourages people to "barge in" to his office, but he also makes it easy for teachers to schedule a time to meet with him or take advantage of set office hours. He reserves blocks of time for "meeting with anybody about anything" at the main campus and at the network's two outposts farther away in the county, to make sure he is accessible to staff from across the network. Still, Daley acknowledges that as the organization grows, it is a challenge to maintain open lines of communication (personal communication, May 29, 2013).

Within this minimally stratified management structure, High Tech High's central mechanism for facilitating teacher collaboration is a daily meeting block. During the first hour of the day, before students have arrived, teachers have 45 minutes devoted to collaboration, whether with a teaching partner, within a discipline, or with the whole school staff. Having protected time for meeting with colleagues each day ensures that teachers are constantly giving and seeking feedback on issues related to their classroom and broader schoolwide questions. Full-staff meetings are run democratically and provide an opportunity for teachers to raise issues that they think deserve whole-school attention. Issues raised during morning meetings might be directed to one of the school's standing "study groups" (committees), such as the professional development study group, or may lead to the creation of an ad hoc study group of teachers to look at a specific issue, such as dress code (Daley, personal communication, May 29, 2013). Sarah Strong, another High Tech Middle teacher, added that having a regular meeting time facilitates strong relationships among the staff (personal communication, May 9, 2013).

Another area of intense teacher involvement at High Tech High is hiring. Daley reflected that, with the exception of co-op schools, High Tech High has "as much teacher involvement in hiring as any school that I'm aware of" (personal communication, May 29, 2013). Teachers are involved in each step of the hiring process, from reviewing applications, to interviewing candidates and observing them teach sample lessons, to making final deliberations.

Finally, High Tech High has also worked over the years to increase the opportunities that teachers have to advance their careers and engage with colleagues on broader educational issues. The organization opened a teacher credentialing program in 2004, offering pathways to California state teaching credentials, and in 2007 the High Tech High Graduate School of Education (GSE), offering a master's degree program for experienced educators. Both programs are open to educators from the network and beyond. Both have highly collaborative structures, with teachers providing feedback on each other's work and engaging in broader conversations about education issues (Rob Riordan, personal communication, May 2, 2013). The GSE runs a peer-reviewed academic journal, *Unboxed: A Journal of Adult Learning in Schools*, which provides another outlet for High Tech High teachers, as well as other educators and professors from across the country, to share insights with a broader community of educators (Scherer et al., 2008).

Ben Daley has also worked on developing other ways for teachers to pursue leadership roles in the organization without permanently leaving the classroom. High Tech High is committed to helping some of their best teachers become school directors, but because of the network's lean administration, there are not that many noninstructional positions to fill. Furthermore, there is a tension between creating leadership opportunities for teachers and keeping effective teachers in the classroom. Daley stresses that it is important, alongside helping some teachers grow into administrative positions, to find ways for effective and experienced teachers to take on new roles while staying grounded in classroom teaching. Daley is working on building a teacher "sabbatical" program at High Tech High whereby teachers can decide for themselves what issues or areas of practice or policy they are interested in exploring or refining.

With funding from the semiconductor company Qualcomm, High Tech High launched the Qualcomm Digital Learning Fellowship, which allows teachers to apply to spend a year working on a project of interest to them, then return to the classroom afterwards. A physics teacher spent a year making movies for online courses, for example, and a multimedia teacher took the year to learn computer coding, which she will now incorporate into the art projects that her students pursue (Daley, personal communication, May 29, 2013).

While High Tech High offers many avenues for teacher voice, the school does not have a teacher union, and school leaders and teachers alike expressed skepticism toward the value of teacher unions. Both Riordan and Rosenstock had negative experiences in the past with union bureaucracy, finding that the district and union were both obstacles to innovation (Riordan, personal communication, May 2, 2013). Teacher Jeff Robin came to High Tech High after many frustrations dealing with the San Diego school district and teacher union, where he felt the union supported bad teachers and wielded too much power in determining teacher placement (personal communication, May 9, 2013).

However, the system of teacher voice at High Tech High, based on school culture rather than a more structured union relationship or co-op governance model, has proved vulnerable in several key areas. As High Tech High has expanded—the network now contains 12 schools—leaders have struggled to maintain teacher voice. High Tech High has faced some of the same growing pains that the Green Dot schools experienced, for example, in making the transition from school-based calendar decisions to having a central network calendar. But whereas Green Dot has created a specific structure to get individual teacher input on calendar decisions through a survey which is then reviewed by a calendar committee that includes teachers, High Tech High is still figuring out a logistically feasible way to include teachers in the process. Daley notes that although the calendar is a mundane example, the same struggle between efficient decision making and diffuse power "plays out across a whole range of issues. How do you get that tension right?" (personal communication, May 29, 2013).

Concerns about salaries were also widespread among the High Tech High teachers we interviewed. When High Tech High first opened in 2000, teachers' salaries ranged from $40,000 to $60,000 a year—higher than the $34,000 a year average salary for educators in the San Diego Unified School District at the time (Hardy, 2001). By 2013, however, salaries for teachers at High Tech High lagged behind those of their public school peers. Faced with state funding cuts, the network did not raise salaries for 6 years. "Our conversation to teachers is along the lines of—

we're not letting teachers go, we're saving jobs, but we can't increase salaries," Riordan explained. He felt that teachers understood the rationale for the lack of raises: "They understand that they're not getting a raise, but nobody is being let go" (personal communication, May 2, 2013). However, the teachers we talked to did not feel that decision-making around salaries was transparent. Stacey Lopaz noted that the salary freeze is a "source of teacher frustration" and that concerns about salaries are "the kind of thing that people complain about to each other" but might not feel comfortable sharing with their school director (personal communication, May 10, 2013).

The process of dismissing or renewing teachers was another area in which High Tech High teachers noted a breakdown of communication. Sarah Strong recalled the feeling of uncertainty as a beginning teacher at High Tech High about whether or not her contract would be renewed, since all teachers are on one-year contracts. "I think every teacher in their 1st or 2nd year [thinks] . . . I really want to be asked back, and I hope I'm doing well enough!" (personal communication, May 9, 2013). Stacey Lopaz agreed that teachers at High Tech High, particularly those who are new to the organization, sometimes have a nagging worry that they will be let go. Although most teachers who have been at the school a few years "feel very confident in their positions," Lopaz said, some newer teachers "would probably prefer if there was better communication about contract renewal" (personal communication, May 10, 2013). Lopaz supports High Tech High's one-year-contract model as a method for keeping a high bar for teacher quality, though she still sees room for improvement around communicating with teachers about their performance. Teachers who are dismissed have had conversations with their director prior to that decision, but other teachers may have received less feedback on their performance, leaving some feeling anxious about contract renewals even when their performance is strong.

High Tech High teachers' concerns and confusions about salaries and contracts illustrate one of the chief limitations of relying on a collaborative culture to facilitate teacher input in school decisions. Minimal management hierarchy, open door policies, and guaranteed time for collaboration do not change the fundamental power imbalance between teachers and administrators, when the latter group retains final decision-making power over all employment and compensation decisions. Despite valuing the openness of his bosses to provide office hours and meeting times, Bobby Shaddox noted that not every issue can be comfortably addressed in this setting. "You may not feel confident about going in to the person who negotiates your contract and saying, I want to talk to you about the way that you're running the meetings," he said. "Although I always felt safe with these types of conversations, I think that all teachers feel varying levels of comfort with addressing issues directly with the director" (personal communication, May 10, 2013).

Still, while there are holes in High Tech High's model for promoting teacher voice, teachers emphasized the positive ways in which the network empowers them, particularly as compared to other schools. "At High Tech High teachers feel safe to speak up, have a role in decision making at schools, and are happier and more productive than at any other school I've ever worked at or supported," Lopaz said (personal communication, October 21, 2013).

Combining a Collaborative Culture with Unionization. Monica O'Gara, one of the founding teachers at City Neighbors Charter School in Baltimore, Maryland, leads her 1st-grade class of 22 students more as a guide than as a boss. Preparing her students for work time on a Thursday in late May, 2013, O'Gara explained one by one where each student would work and what that student would be doing. Despite the rapid approach of summer vacation, students listened with rapt attention as O'Gara gave many different instructions, each based on how best to support a student or group of students. O'Gara checked in with students to see how far along they were into various projects—have you finished the drawing? —and find out in which ways they would prefer to work—at an easel or on the floor? Once she finished with all of the instructions, students moved to their various stations efficiently and began their independent or group work.

The relationship between the principal and teachers at City Neighbors has some things in common with the way that O'Gara manages her classroom. At City Neighbors, the principal of the school serves as the keystone of the school's governance, imagined as a stone arch in which each block is a member of the school's governing board. The principal is a key player, holding together the arch of board members that include a teacher representative and a student from the school, both full voting members of the board. But the primary role of the principal and the full arch is to support teachers, rather than supervise them, and teachers in turn support students.

Teachers at City Neighbors Charter School, a K–8 school that is now part of a family of three City Neighbors schools in Baltimore, rave about the collaborative culture at their school. Biz Manning, a special education teacher, "felt fettered" at her previous school but feels empowered at City Neighbors: "I matter here. I can teach how I want to teach, and I have a really supportive administration" (personal communication, May 30, 2013). Teachers at City Neighbors are drawn into school decisions at every level; as 4th-grade teacher Joan Jones explained, the school looks to hire teachers "that want to be involved in more than just the classroom and teaching" (personal communication, May 30, 2013).

Part of this success is due to the leadership style of principal Mike Chalupa, whom teachers described as respecting teachers' knowledge and communicating well. All the teachers we talked to mentioned Chalupa's effective encouragement of collaboration. But established collaborative governance structures at City Neighbors help ensure teacher voice in more permanent ways that should withstand a change in administration. "We have a culture and a process and protocol about how decisions are made," Bobbi Macdonald, the school's founder and executive director, explained. "They're made collaboratively, and it's a distributed leadership model" (personal communication, August 16, 2012).

The Governance Arch is a central way that City Neighbors facilitates voice for not only teachers but also parents and students. Macdonald started City Neighbors based on tenets of student, parent, and educator collaboration; student diversity; and constructivist education, the theory that students create their own understanding through experience and re-flection. "From the very beginning," Macdonald told us, "the design of our school was created to make it so there is a pathway . . . allowing people to create together." Teachers, parents, and administrators can all participate in different board committees, from the Diversity and Inclu-sion Committee to the Accountability Committee, each of which is led by a board member (personal communication, August 16, 2012). Most major school decisions are made by these collaborative committees, either through one of the standing committees or by assembling an ad hoc com-mittee. The standing committees deal with issues ranging from finance to community engagement, while ad hoc committees have dealt with topics such as playgrounds, greening, or expansion.

At the school level, City Neighbors also encourages collaboration among teachers and administrators through weekly professional develop-ment time. Every Wednesday, students have a half-day of school while teachers have time to collaborate with one another and the principal. For instance, Tracy Pendred, a 3rd-grade teacher, described how the teach-ers wanted to know more about their students' experiences in previous grades, in order to serve them better. To this end, the faculty agreed to create K–3 intervention meetings to discuss students across grades so teachers can get to know students and their individual needs before they start teaching them. Macdonald stressed that "it's inherent in the design of our school that the teachers should have a way of being around the table passionately arguing about the curriculum and looking at student work together" (personal communication, August 16, 2012). Wednesday afternoon meetings help give teachers the forum for these discussions.

Under Maryland law, City Neighbors is part of Baltimore City Public Schools and is bound to the district's collective bargaining agreement. In some respects, teachers at City Neighbors were grateful for the protections that a union contract provides. Peter French, who teaches middle school social studies, stated firmly that he "wouldn't work anywhere that doesn't have [a union contract]." For fellow teacher Peter Redgrave, the union's legal protections are important, providing teachers with a safety net in case of a liability suit, for example. Monica O'Gara, a veteran teacher, and Biz Manning, a more recent addition to the City Neighbors team, agreed that younger teachers in particular benefit from the protections of a union-negotiated contract in terms of salary, benefits, and job security (French, Redgrave, O'Gara, & Manning, personal communication, May 30, 2013).

But the Baltimore Teachers Union (BTU) has also been a source of frustration for City Neighbors teachers, who find themselves bound to a districtwide contract that does not always meet the needs of their specific school. "I am fed up with this union," O'Gara pronounced. She thinks the BTU has at times failed to put children's needs first. For example, the union previously asked teachers to "work to rule"—performing only contractual duties—in opposition to principals in the district asking to devote some teacher planning time to faculty meetings (personal communication, May 30, 2013).

Many teachers at City Neighbors complained that the union did not do enough to resist the district's new contract, which was driven by the Race to the Top initiative and contains a teacher performance pay system tied to student test scores. City Neighbors' involvement with the new contract started out to be supportive. In September 2010, Baltimore City Schools and the Baltimore Teachers Union held a press conference at City Neighbors Charter School to announce a new contract that both sides hailed as an important step forward. Macdonald was excited when they had asked to host the conference at one of their campuses. "I love being known, and I love getting our name out there" (personal communication, August 16, 2012).

Within a month, however, opposition to the contract was brewing, and a teacher from City Neighbors was leading the charge. Peter French, who had been with the district for 19 years, argued that the contract promoted "increased principal control, teacher competition, and teaching to the test" (quoted in E. L. Green, 2010). The school's union representative and social studies teacher, French is well-known at City Neighbors and beyond for teaching his students about civic engagement, which fits well with the spirit of the school. "We're a grassroots group," Macdonald told us; "we're all about activism" (personal communication, August 16,

2012). Several of French's class projects—from mock trial reenactments of Vietnam-era war crime tribunals to picket-line protests of community efforts to close Read's Drug Store, the historic site of a 1955 civil rights–era sit-in—have even gotten newspaper coverage (Associated Press, 2011; Fanning, 2009).

French's opposition to the contract tested the bounds of teacher voice at City Neighbors. Bobbi Macdonald was put in an awkward position when Andrés Alonso, CEO of Baltimore City Public Schools, called to check in on the teacher who was rabble-rousing around a contract that both the district and the union had lauded. But Macdonald stood up for French. "He is awesome," she told Alonso. "He is a fabulous organizer, and he feels passionately about this, and I'm proud he's on my staff" (personal communication, August 16, 2012).

The new contract ultimately passed on the second vote, after the union sent representatives into schools to garner teacher support, but City Neighbors teachers overwhelmingly continued to oppose the new performance pay system. Most saw the test-based accountability system as counter to the spirit of collaboration in their school and decided as a staff to send principal Chalupa to negotiate the right of teachers in a school to submit a modified system to the district for approval. As a result of these negotiations, all schools in Baltimore now have the option of applying for a waiver from a variety of contractual elements including the performance pay system by submitting their own plans.

Meanwhile, perhaps the biggest testament to teacher empowerment at City Neighbors is the consistently positive feedback that teachers give about working at the school. The glowing endorsements we heard from teachers were echoed by data from the annual TELL (Teaching, Empowering, Leading, and Learning) Maryland survey for 2013. City Neighbors teachers provided dramatically higher ratings of their school's climate, leadership, and structures than their counterparts in the district: 100% of City Neighbors teachers agreed that their school has "an atmosphere of trust and mutual respect," compared to 69.9% of teachers across the district.

STUDENT OUTCOMES

The academic results from the schools highlighted in this chapter offer a look at the success that is possible in charter schools with strong teacher voice, reinforcing research evidence of the positive effects of teacher input, collaboration, and unions discussed in Chapter 2. Guided by the original vision of charter schools as models of good practices for district schools, we specifically chose successful schools with teacher voice. We did not investigate a link between teacher voice and academic success or compare the schools' performance to that of schools with less teacher voice, charter or otherwise. And we acknowledge that performance could be attributable in some measure to student self-selection, as discussed in Chapter 4. Instead, the schools in this chapter serve as important examples that charter schools can have strong teacher voice and show impressive results at the same time.

As a rough overview of student achievement, we looked at performance on state standardized tests in reading and mathematics for all students, and specifically low-income students, in each school. (See data in the Appendix.) We compared the percentage of students scoring proficient or above at each school with the proficiency averages for the district and state in which each school is located. These are intended as rough points of comparison only, as they do not control for demographic differences between schools, districts, and states.

Using this yardstick, the charter schools highlighted in this chapter have strong reading achievement. At seven of the eight featured schools (or flagship campuses, in the case of charter networks), the percentage of students passing state standardized tests in reading exceeds the district averages. And at five of the eight schools, students beat state proficiency averages in reading. Low-income students at these schools are also beating the odds, compared to other low-income students in their state and district. At all eight schools, low-income students beat the average proficiency rates in reading for low-income students in their district, and at seven of the schools, low-income students beat state averages for low-income students as well.

Results in mathematics are more mixed, but still promising. At six of the eight schools, low-income students beat district averages for proficiency on state standardized tests in math, and at five of these six schools, the average for all students beats the district average as well. The other two schools, City Neighbors Charter School and Minnesota New Country School, have below-average math achievement, as compared to their districts and states; however, these two schools also serve an above-average proportion of special education students.

The schools highlighted in this chapter have also shown success in a variety of different ways. While we will not provide an exhaustive list of their accomplishments, the following gives a sense of the breadth and quality of distinctions:

- Amber Charter School (2011) won competitive federal government grants for Enhancing Education Through Technology and Teaching American History.

- Avalon School (2013) has been recognized by the Washington, D.C.–based Character Education Partnership for its programs fostering good citizenship and conflict resolution.
- City Neighbors (n.d.) has won several awards for its arts and environmental curricula, and the Maryland State Department of Education recognized City Neighbors in 2009 for growth in student test scores.
- Green Dot Public Schools (n.d.) graduates 74% of its seniors across the network—far surpassing the graduation rate of 53% across Los Angeles Unified School District (LAUSD) and 42% among neighboring schools. Furthermore, almost half of all Green Dot students graduate having completed the University of California and California State University's college-going course requirements (specifying number of years of study needed in each of seven subjects), compared to just one in five students across LAUSD and only one in eight students in neighboring schools.
- High Tech High (n.d.) sends 98% of its graduates across the network to college, about 35% of whom are first-generation college students. Furthermore, National Student Clearinghouse data shows High Tech High grads persist through college at high rates: 86% of all 2007 High Tech High graduates and 64% of the network's low-income grads had graduated college or were still enrolled 5 years out (Larry Rosenstock, personal communication, November 22, 2013).
- IDEAL School (2013) has been identified by the Wisconsin Department of Public Instruction 7 years in a row as a School of Recognition for "beating the odds" by showing strong academic achievement among low-income students.
- Minnesota New Country School was highlighted in a U.S. Department of Education report for its work closing the achievement gap for special education students (WestEd, 2006).
- Springfield Ball Charter School is a top-performing school in the Springfield, Illinois, district (Beck, 2013), and in 2012 one of the school's 8th-graders was honored for academic excellence by the Illinois Network of Charter Schools (n.d.).

CONCLUSION

The strong performance of the schools that are the focus of this chapter adds to the evidence that teacher voice can improve school cultures and student outcomes. The workplace protections of a union can create a sustainable working environment, even as a charter network grows, and establish channels of communication between teachers and administrators. Furthermore, co-op schools like Avalon and other collaboratively structured schools, such as City Neighbors, demonstrate that innovation and flexibility, key advantages of the charter model, might be best achieved when teachers are central players in the development of a school.

Unionization, co-op governance, and creating a collaborative culture each empower teachers in different ways. The path for teacher voice in charter schools moving forward might well call for experimenting with the advantages of each route. What if a school had a strong collaborative culture and its own union, with a site-based contract? Could parts of a co-op governance model be adapted to a larger school by separating grades or departments into different decision-making teams? The flexibility of a charter school is the ideal vehicle for testing these innovations.

What is not in doubt is that charter schools are capable of embodying Al Shanker's original vision of schools that empower teachers—and that there are some exciting examples out there on which to build.

6

Charter Schools
That Integrate Students

IN THE 60 YEARS SINCE *Brown v. Board of Education* (1954), the school integration movement has seen a number of shifts, from fighting de jure segregation to addressing de facto segregation; from focusing solely on race to considering socioeconomics, disability, and language; and from building solutions with fixed student assignment to incorporating more parent choice. In recent years, integration has taken a back seat to discussions about testing and accountability in national education policy debates, but a small army of educators and policymakers has continued to fight for more integrated schools. Over the past decade, for example, the number of school districts that pursue socioeconomic integration has grown from just a handful to more than 80 districts spanning the country, from Cambridge, Massachusetts, to Bloomington, Minnesota, to Salina, Kansas (Kahlenberg, 2012). And now, a small but growing number of charter schools are joining the charge for school integration.

Although charter schools today tend to be more racially and economically segregated than traditional public schools, there is great potential for charters to reverse this trend. Charter schools, like public magnet schools, are uniquely suited to create integrated student bodies. As schools of choice, they are not as constrained by residential segregation as are most public schools. And as schools created from scratch, with particular visions, they have the potential to draw interest from diverse income, racial, and ethnic groups.

The innovative charter schools we highlight in this chapter have consciously integrated students from different racial and economic backgrounds. And in developing practices to overcome some of the challenges of enrolling and serving a diverse student body, they have identified strategies that could help other schools—charter or not—create successful integration programs (see also Kahlenberg & Potter, 2012; Potter, 2013; these are the sources for some portions of this chapter).

We chose schools to highlight in this chapter, as in Chapter 5, with the goal of telling powerful stories, showcasing charter schools that integrate students and sharing some of their best practices. We focus on eight high-achieving charter schools or networks that are actively committed to seeking a diverse student body:

- Blackstone Valley Prep Mayoral Academy (network), Cumberland and Lincoln, RI
- Capital City Public Charter School (pre-K–12 school), Washington, DC
- City Neighbors (network), Baltimore, MD
- Community Roots Charter School (K–8 school), Brooklyn, NY
- DSST Public Schools (network), Denver, CO
- E. L. Haynes Public Charter School (pre-K–12 school), Washington, DC
- High Tech High (network), San Diego, CA
- Larchmont Charter School (K–12 school), Los Angeles, CA

Profiles of the schools are provided in the Appendix. Two of the schools listed above, City Neighbors Charter School and High Tech High, were discussed in Chapter 5 because they are also on our list of schools with teacher voice, and they will be discussed again in Chapter 7 because they are examples of both teacher voice and student diversity. Another school with both teacher voice and intentional student diversity, Morris Jeff Community School in New Orleans, is discussed only in Chapter 7 because it is still in the early stages of developing its model.

In looking at diverse charter schools, we used an absolute measure as a baseline for selecting schools that offer students the academic and social benefits of a racially and socioeconomically integrated classroom. The schools (or flagship campuses, in the case of charter networks) that we highlight in this chapter fall within 20 percentage points of a 50% low-income, 50% middle-class mix, based on free and reduced-price lunch eligibility as a measure of low income. (The exception is Community Roots Charter School, which comes close to this demographic mix and has recently adopted steps to diversify further.) In terms of racial and ethnic diversity, we looked for schools where there was enough racial diversity to avoid having a clear dominant group at the school. No single racial or ethnic group makes up more than 60% of the student body at any of the schools we highlight. (See Sidebar 6.1 for discussion of how we chose these demographic targets.)

In this chapter, we examine the promising strategies for enrolling and serving a diverse student body employed by the high-achieving charter schools we investigated. First, we look at strategies for diverse enrollment. In order to create an integrated student body, schools have developed

---

SIDEBAR 6.1. THE IDEAL SOCIOECONOMIC
AND RACIAL MIX IN CHARTER SCHOOLS

Socioeconomic Diversity Goals

Research dating back a number of years suggests the strongest benefits of integration are found in schools that are no more than 50% low-income, defined as eligible for free or reduced-price lunch (Kahlenberg, 2001). This goal also dovetails with national demographics, in which 48.1% of students are eligible for subsidized lunch (U.S. Department of Education, NCES, 2012d).

In the case of charter schools, there is good reason to believe there is some flexibility in the 50% rule of thumb, so we suggest that charter schools aim to have populations in which between 30% and 70% of students are low income. As discussed in Chapter 3, low-income charter school parents—who have taken the time to apply to a charter school—may be more motivated and have greater social capital than low-income parents in traditional public schools. Furthermore, research on racial/ethnic diversity in K–12 schools shows that 70% is a threshold at which a group is at risk of becoming a dominant culture (McConahay, 1981); applied to the economic balance in a school, this may suggest that a middle-class population of more than 30% is needed to create a school with a mixed-income culture.

In addition, it is important to note that the 50% guideline, using free and reduced-price lunch data from more than 2 decades ago, is likely to be affected by substantial differences in the free and reduced-price lunch program 20 years later. Free and reduced-price lunch eligibility has risen rapidly in recent years, and not all of the rise can be explained by changes in the real economic conditions of students. From 1988 to 2009, the percentage of public school students eligible for free or reduced-price lunch (available to families earning up to 185% of the federal poverty line) rose from 35.1% to 44.6%, a 27% increase. Over the same period of time, the percentage of school-age children in families earning below 200% of the poverty level grew from 38.1% to 40.0%, an increase of just 5% (U.S. Census Bureau, 1991, 2010).

The discrepancy between free and reduced-price lunch and census data could be the result of undercounting in the 1980s and 1990s, or overcounting 2 decades later. The accuracy of free and reduced-price lunch data is complicated by a number of factors including self-reported income, families not returning forms, and financial pressure on schools to report high free and reduced-price lunch numbers. According to a 2009 study by analysts at Mathematica Policy Research, 15% of school lunch applicants erroneously received a benefit greater than their eligibility, while 7.5%

SIDEBAR 6.1. *Continued*

---

received a benefit less than what they actually qualified for, due to household reporting errors or administrative mistakes (Ponza, Gleason, Hulsey, & Moore, 2009). Either way, the fact that the underlying meaning of free and reduced-price lunch data has changed suggests the old 50% guideline (using a relative undercount of eligible students) should be updated in today's context to a somewhat higher level.

In suggesting an ideal mix of 30–70% low-income students in charter schools, we recognize that in high poverty districts, the result could be a marginal increase in the proportion of low-income students in the traditional public schools. For example, creating a 50% middle-class charter school in an 80% low-income district might mean the other schools rise on average to 81% or 82% low-income. We nevertheless support the creation of these new socioeconomically integrated charter schools, just as we support integrated magnet schools that marginally increase poverty concentrations in traditional public schools.

We take this position for two reasons. First, we believe there are strong benefits to creating a net plus in the number of socioeconomically integrated options available to students. We do not believe it is justified, educationally or morally, to hold low-income students hostage in an 80% low-income district, preventing them from attended an economically integrated school just because others will go from 80% to 81% or 82% low-income.

Second, there is reason to believe that the creation of a subset of strong, economically integrated charter or magnet schools can have the effect, over time, of creating additional middle-class interest in the public schools in higher-poverty districts. The demographic makeup of the public school population in a district is not fixed. If successful integrated schools are created in mixed-income areas, it is possible that the success of these schools will change the calculations of some middle-class parents, making them more willing to use the public schools than to exit to the private school system or move to more affluent areas. In the DSST lottery for 2006, for example, only 36% of student applications came from district schools in Denver, while 40% came from private or out-of-district public schools (Kurtz & Gottlieb, 2006).

By facilitating this virtuous cycle, it is possible that the 80% low-income school district, with the presence of strong, economically mixed charter and magnet schools, could, in the long haul, create more and more opportunities to attend good, socioeconomically integrated schools for larger and larger numbers of low-income students.

SIDEBOX **6.1.** *Continued*

Racial and Ethnic Diversity Goals

With respect to racial and ethnic diversity, we believe the goal should be for schools to facilitate the maximum amount of integration. One marker of that integration is a school in which no racial or ethnic group represents a majority. In this situation, schools would have the best chance of developing a multicultural environment in which no one group dominates. This goal would also track with national statistics among school children. Enrollment projections from the U.S. Department of Education's National Center for Education Statistics (NCES) (2012c) forecast that White enrollment in public schools will fall below 50% by 2016.

Another marker of success is a school in which a critical mass of students exists for various racial and ethnic groups. This concept of *critical mass* has been widely recognized in the higher education arena, where research suggests the healthiest and most robust discussions take place when members of minority groups do not feel isolated and do not feel they have to "represent" their racial or ethnic group in conversations (CollegeBoard Advocacy & EducationCounsel, 2009). In higher education, critical mass has been estimated as having been met when a school has at least 30% minority representation (M. F. Green, 1989). At the K–12 level—and particularly in the lower grades—critical mass is important also for encouraging tolerance, reducing stereotypes, and facilitating cross-racial friendships (Welner, 2006). Research on K–12 settings suggests that a school's culture is at risk of being dominated by one group if that group constitutes more than 70% of the school's population (Ma & Kurlaender, 2005; McConahay, 1981). Furthermore, the federal district court in *Comfort v. Lynn School Committee* (2003) noted that the benefits of a diverse classroom continue to increase along a continuum past critical mass thresholds as the school population becomes more racially balanced (Welner, 2006).

Landing somewhere in the middle of these various recommendations, the diverse charter schools we profile in this chapter have no one racial/ethnic group constituting more than 60% of the population.

---

educational programs that appeal to a wide range of families, and some have chosen their location strategically. Schools also target recruitment to create a socioeconomically and racially/ethnically mixed applicant pool, and some use weighted lotteries to ensure that diversity is maintained once families apply.

We next outline the ways schools are mindful of diversity in their daily operations. Many of these charter schools have developed strategies to differentiate instruction for the wide range of experiences and abilities represented at their school while preserving the benefits of an integrated classroom. Some place special emphasis on recruiting and serving students with special needs, English language learners, and students in need of social or psychological services. And some schools have specific programs to encourage social interaction among students of different backgrounds. These practices form a toolbox that other educators, parents, and community members can use to start diverse charter schools or diversify enrollment at existing schools. Furthermore, many of the lessons— particularly those on strategies for serving diverse learners and promoting social integration—are also applicable to district schools.

Finally, we examine evidence suggesting that, in these schools, the creation of diverse student bodies and thoughtful attention to diversity in the classroom coincides with high levels of academic achievement and positive outcomes for all students.

ENROLLING A DIVERSE STUDENT BODY

During Teach for America's 20th anniversary summit in 2011, some 1,300 people chose to attend a panel discussion on "Segregation in American Schools and Its Impact on the Achievement Gap." Alongside some of the other session choices, with upbeat and self-confident titles like "Creating a Culture of Greatness" or "Changing Education Through Social Entrepreneurship," the panel on segregation stood out for suggesting a blind spot for energetic reformers.

Bill Kurtz, CEO of DSST Public Schools, addressed the crowd of present and former teachers and school leaders. DSST is a network of socioeconomically integrated charter schools in Denver, Colorado, named for its founding school, the Denver School of Science and Technology. Kurtz challenged what has been a central paradigm for much of the education reform movement, the idea that "90–90 schools"—where 90% of students are racial/ethnic minorities and 90% are low-income—should be the primary arenas for reform. "Don't get me wrong," he explained. "It's very important to bring great schools to communities that don't have them. . . . But I also believe that we can accomplish similar goals by creating schools that transcend those communities and bring kids from all different backgrounds together" (Teach for America, 2011).

Sharply challenging the work of fellow reformers, Kurtz declared, "Right now our movement is very skewed to one paradigm, and we need multiple paradigms. . . . I have no faith that we as a society will be able to solve our problems together if we don't have the most formative institutions in our society committed from the beginning to create a diverse community with the youngest of our society" (Teach for America, 2011).

Kurtz is one of a small group of charter school leaders—growing in number—who have chosen to prioritize student diversity in their school missions, not only because they see integration's civic value but also because they view it as an educational asset. As Kurtz (2011) wrote after the Teach for America summit, "All students—minority, White, high-income and low-income—are far better prepared to succeed in college when they have been given the opportunity to learn and work with diverse peers." However, in a landscape in which many equate the term *charter school* with *90–90 school*, enrolling a diverse student body requires thoughtful planning and outreach.

Appealing to a Wide Range of Families

Since charters are schools of choice, creating a diverse student body begins with attracting a wide range of families. Supporters of racially homogeneous charter schools are quick to point out that they exist because parents choose them, that they represent self-selection rather than forced segregation. Integrated charter schools also rely on parent choice. In order to achieve diverse enrollment, they must offer a program that will attract families from across the socioeconomic spectrum and from many racial/ethnic groups.

Some policymakers and education reformers are skeptical about the possibility of creating schools that cater to the needs and desires of families from many different backgrounds. In his book *The Diverse Schools Dilemma*, Michael Petrilli (2012), a supporter of diverse schools and president of the Thomas B. Fordham Institute, the conservative-leaning education think tank, worries that low-income and middle-class families want fundamentally different things in a school. "Students either call their teachers by their first names or they don't. Either they wear uniforms or they don't. It's hard for schools to meet the needs of poor kids while also meeting the expectations of affluent parents," he explains (p. 56). "No excuses" pedagogy has been a popular approach in charter schools and has shown promising results for low-income students in some cases, but would middle-class parents want to send their kids to a school with rigid discipline and an extended day (see Sidebar 6.2)? And would low-income parents want to send their students to a school with a more progressive pedagogy and less clear-cut disciplinary model?

Some of these concerns may be overblown. Data on parents' school priorities from a 2013 study conducted by Petrilli's own Fordham Institute showed that parents' preferences are remarkably consistent across different income groups. The survey asked parents to rank a list of student goals and school characteristics. Parents of all incomes were likely to value a strong reading and math curriculum: This was the top-ranked school characteristic, on average, in each of four different income brackets. Learning good study habits and self-discipline was also the first or second ranked student goal within each income group. Wearing uniforms or studying a foreign language, however, were low priorities across all income groups. Some variation in preferences did exist; however, the overall ranking of preferences was fairly consistent across income brackets (Zeehandelaar & Winkler, 2013).

The charter school leaders we interviewed found that it was relatively easy to attract families from many different backgrounds as long as they had a high-quality program. Bill Kurtz explained that the academic success of DSST Public Schools attracts families from across the Denver area. DSST opened in 2004 as a single school—the Denver School of Science and Technology (now called DSST: Stapleton High School)—that was started with funding from the Bill and Melinda Gates Foundation and a number of smaller donors. Early buzz about the school focused on the state-of-the-art facilities, newly built on land donated by a real estate company with residential developments planned for the same area, and extensive use of technology—every student received a laptop (Beauprez, 2002). By its 3rd year, the school was drawing applications from students in more than 65 schools across the Denver area—including many private and out-of-district public schools (Kurtz & Gottlieb, 2006). Some higher-income families were skittish about the school in its early years, but enthusiasm grew once DSST graduated its first class of high school seniors, sending students to prestigious colleges such as Stanford and MIT. "We're really proud of the fact that we have kids from all over the city in our schools who feel comfortable in our schools [and] who see us as not a school serving this population or that population," Kurtz explained. "We have parents literally pulling kids from the most elite private schools in Denver to come to our schools, and we have homeless kids who are coming to our schools. It's really phenomenal" (personal communication, December 13, 2011).

Karen Dresden, founding principal and head of school at Capital City Public Charter School in Washington, D.C., said that different parents choose the preschool–12 school for different reasons, which is possible because Capital City offers a rich academic program. Capital City is an Expeditionary Learning school, which is a whole-school model (including recommendations for curriculum, pedagogy, and professional development) that focuses on project-based learning. First-graders, for example, spend the spring semester studying honeybees, investigating everything

---

SIDEBAR 6.2. "No Excuses" Model in Integrated Schools

The label "no excuses" describes a popular style of charter school that focuses on raising the achievement of low-income kids through a clearly defined pedagogy and culture. These schools frequently feature strict discipline codes, school uniforms, and an extended day with more time on academic subjects. They usually hold out college as the ultimate prize for students and emphasize success on standardized tests and an attitude of respect as important tools for reaching that goal. Prominent examples of schools that are frequently described as using a "no excuses" model include the KIPP charter schools across the country; Uncommon Schools network in Massachusetts, New York, and New Jersey; and YES Prep charter schools in Houston, Texas.

Proponents of "no excuses" pedagogy frequently argue that low-income children need a different type of school environment than middle-class children, since they typically have less support and enrichment at home (see Chapter 1). This rationale would seem to make a "no excuses" school incompatible with socioeconomic integration. However, some integrated charter schools have borrowed elements from the "no excuses" model while successfully attracting parents from a wide socioeconomic spectrum.

Blackstone Valley Prep Mayoral Academy, a regional charter school network in Rhode Island, fits many of the characteristics that come to mind with a "no excuses" model. It has a strict discipline system. Students wear uniforms and have a longer school day and school year. Programming during the summer and on some Saturdays offers targeted support for students. Jeremy Chiappetta, the Executive Director of Blackstone Valley Prep, prefers the term "high expectations" or "no excuses lite" to describe their approach. "Honestly, the entire branding needs to be reframed in a positive way," he explained. "Hence we have adopted 'high expectations, high support.'" Chiappetta summarized their approach by explaining, "We'll do whatever it takes to make sure that children are successful" (personal communication, November 26 & 30, 2011).

Blackstone Valley Prep, however, is a socioeconomically integrated school, started by the Rhode Island Mayoral Academies, a nonprofit that supports regional charter schools in the state. The student body at each of the network's three schools is about 65% low-income, 35% middle-class (NAPCS, 2013c). The school has been able to attract both higher- and lower-income families.

Chiappetta said that middle-class families' reactions to the school model vary. The extended school day, for example, can be viewed as a downside or an advantage by middle-class families. According to Chiappetta, one family with a stay-at-home mother pulled their child out of the school after

SIDEBAR 6.2. *Continued*

deciding that the extended day was too long. Another family in which both parents are doctors was attracted to Blackstone Valley Prep for the extended day because it allows them to have their child in a stimulating environment all day without coordinating other after-school opportunities (personal communication, November 30, 2011). Journalist Dana Goldstein (2011) visited Blackstone Valley Prep and likewise found that some middle-class families objected to the strict discipline and long school day, while others embraced it. The school reports that attrition of low-income and middle-class families is about equal, and they have been able to maintain steady middle-class enrollment. (Other schools, such as E. L. Haynes Public Charter School, a pre-K–12 school in Washington, DC, mix progressive ideology with "no excuses" practices in a way that attracts a socioeconomic cross-section of students.)

It is important to break the assumption that all charter schools are "no excuses" schools; in fact, most of the integrated charter schools that we studied were built on progressive educational philosophies. Furthermore, there is a separate debate over which educational philosophies are best for which students. Some "no excuses" schools have produced impressive results for low-income students, but many others have not (see, e.g., Pondiscio, 2013; Thompson, 2013). Still, it is enlightening to see that a "no excuses" model can be compatible with integration. It is possible to combine enthusiasm for charter schools that provide high expectations and clear-cut methods with a desire to provide all students with a diverse learning environment.

from bees' life cycle to colony collapse disorder, and learning the skills of observation, critique, and revision by creating multiple drafts of scientific drawings. Their learning culminates in a presentation that includes a musical and video presentation as well as a guided tour of classroom exhibits in which family members and teachers ask students questions about their work.

For some parents, Expeditionary Learning is the biggest draw at Capital City, and, according to Dresden, these parents are more likely to be middle-class and White. But other parents are drawn to the school's social curriculum, arts and fitness programs, or after-school activities. "People like that it feels like a well-resourced school," she explained. For other families, in particular many of the school's Latino families, a nurturing environment is the priority. "There's a sense of safety that's really important," Dresden noted. "We're a small school. We really care about kids" (personal communication, November 16, 2011).

City Neighbors Charter School, a K–8 school that is part of a family of three charter schools in Baltimore, similarly attracts parents through a variety of channels. Like Dresden, Bobbi Macdonald, the school's founder, noted that middle-class families were more likely to be attracted to the school's instructional model, which follows a progressive philosophy that emphasizes project learning, the arts, and student empowerment. Other parents find the school because they're looking for a safe environment, they live nearby, or they hear from others that City Neighbors is a good school. City Neighbors works hard to involve parents and explain the school's philosophy. "Those people who might not have understood [our instructional model] at the beginning become the most passionate ambassadors for City Neighbors because they see the difference," Macdonald explained (personal communication, August 16, 2012).

Intentional Location

The northeast corner of Rhode Island is home to four communities with contrasting demographics. Cumberland and Lincoln are higher-income suburban towns, while Pawtucket and Central Falls are lower-income cities. Median household income across the four communities ranges from $32,759 in Central Falls to $75,445 in Lincoln (U.S. Census Bureau, 2013, n.d.). In the two suburbs, 13 out of 14 schools perform near or above the state average. In the cities, on the other hand, only 10 out of 20 schools meet or exceed state average performance (Rhode Island Department of Education, 2013b).

At Blackstone Valley Prep Mayoral Academy, a charter network founded in 2009, students come from all four of these communities. The yellow and navy uniforms worn by all Blackstone Valley Prep "scholars"— as even the youngest students at the network's elementary and middle schools are called—are designed to emphasize similarity, but the student body is nevertheless a diverse bunch (see the Appendix profile). In 2013 Blackstone Valley Prep exceeded state performance averages, a distinction that just four of the 34 district schools spread across Cumberland, Lincoln, Central Falls, and Pawtucket shared (Rhode Island Department of Education, 2013b).

By locating in an area accessible to parents of different incomes and ethnicities—and by making sure that all families have transportation to the school—charter schools can increase their chances of attracting a diverse student population. Blackstone Valley Prep is one of several charter networks we studied that began by identifying a geographic opportunity for integration that traditional public schools were neglecting. Blackstone Valley Prep's two elementary schools and one middle school (a high school is being planned) are "Mayoral Academies," a particular type of Rhode Island charter school that was written into law in 2008. The idea, as proposed in a report commissioned by the Democratic mayor of Cumberland, Daniel McKee, was to start "diverse, regional public schools designed from the beginning to achieve great results for students at a reasonable cost to taxpayers" (Public Impact, 2008, p. 2). Mayoral Academies have several features distinguishing them from other charter schools in the state: exemption from district collective bargaining agreements and state pension plans, for one, but also intentional regional diversity. (Rhode Island's district charter schools, by contrast, may be bound to collective bargaining agreements and constrained by district enrollment boundaries.) Mayoral Academies are formed through partnerships between mayors of neighboring communities and are instructed to "enroll a diverse student body, including students who reside in both distressed urban and other districts" (Public Impact, 2008, p. 16). By locating at the nexus of urban and suburban communities, Blackstone Valley Prep is able to enroll a socioeconomically and racially diverse student body.

While Blackstone Valley Prep is designed to integrate students across a demographically stratified region, other charter schools strategically chose to locate in diverse neighborhoods. Larchmont Charter School in Los Angeles, California, was started by a group of middle- and higher-income parents from Hollywood who were frustrated that the demographics of their community, one of the most diverse neighborhoods in Los Angeles, were not reflected in the area's schools. Starting with a meeting in a parent's backyard in 2004, the group planned a school that would reflect the diversity of Hollywood and the surrounding area, both by recruiting low-income students who were attending low-performing and overcrowded district schools and by getting wealthier parents, many of whom were turning to private schools, to opt back into the public system. Brian Johnson, former Executive Director of Larchmont Charter School, explained that he believes education reform requires getting involvement from all segments of society: "We need families and leaders from all backgrounds to get in the game about public education. And part of that is bringing back communities that have left for private schools and independent schools" (personal communication, November 23, 2011).

Capital City Public Charter School in Washington, D.C., was also intentionally planned for a mixed-income area, providing an initial base of diversity that has helped the school retain an integrated student body even after moving to a new location. When Capital City opened its doors in 2000, it was housed in a space above a CVS Pharmacy on a street corner in Columbia Heights, one of the more racially and socioeconomically diverse neighborhoods in the city. The three other corners of that intersection all contained empty lots, and some of the founding parents—who migrated from a public elementary school in one of D.C.'s wealthiest neighborhoods—backed out after that location was chosen, feeling that it was not safe (Karen Dresden, personal communication, November 16, 2011). Even after committing to the school, some parents were wary of the neighborhood during the school's first few years; one parent was startled when her 7-year-old daughter walked right past police officers pulling their guns to stop a street fight at the neighboring CVS Pharmacy on the way out of the building (Lord, 2003). But Columbia Heights bordered Adams Morgan and Mount Pleasant, two neighborhoods also known for their diversity, and proved an excellent location for recruiting families of all backgrounds to apply to the school.

As Capital City grew, however, moving into two other locations nearby to accommodate its transition from an elementary school to a K–12 model, the school wanted more space to house all grades together. Columbia Heights also changed rapidly; the empty lots cornering the school's old space gave rise to a new mall with a Target, an upscale beer and wine store, and a number of restaurants. Housing prices in the neighborhood skyrocketed, and middle-income housing options were increasingly scarce, while public housing and million-dollar homes remained.

In order to serve all grades in one campus, Capital City moved in fall 2012 to a new location three miles away near the neighborhoods of Brightwood and Takoma. The new area is also racially and economically diverse, and, according to Dresden, has more middle-income housing (personal communication, November 16, 2011). Capital City has taken over an abandoned district public school building and now has outdoor space for P.E. and Expeditionary Learning projects. And the school easily maintained an integrated student body in its new location in part because it had already developed a reputation for diversity. The parents we talked to had heard about Capital City through a variety of means, but most heard about it through family or friends. Building a diverse initial group of families at the school helps perpetuate diverse enrollment.

Targeted Recruitment

When Barack Obama was elected president in 2008, Capital City Public Charter School's name was thrown around as one of the options for a school where his daughters might attend (Yglesias, 2008). While Sasha and Malia Obama ended up at a private school instead, President Obama and the First Lady visited Capital City in February 2009, Obama's first visit to a public school as president. After talking to 5th-graders and reading to 2nd-graders, President Obama (2009) called Capital City "an example of how all our schools should be." "We are very proud of this school," the president said, "and are interested in duplicating its success across the country" (quoted in Expeditionary Learning Schools, 2009).

This national attention is a testament to the strong reputation that Capital City has developed. By its 3rd year, the school received 375 applications for 37 spaces (Mathews & Blum, 2003). But when the school first started, leaders had to put considerable effort into recruiting applications to make sure that their applicant pool was diverse. Dresden described Capital City's successful efforts to increase the number of Latino families, a demographic that was underrepresented during the school's first few years. Capital City partnered with community organizations that provide other services, such as health care or after-school programs, and capitalized on the trust that these organizations had already built with members of the Latino community in order to boost applications (personal communication, November 16, 2011).

E. L. Haynes Public Charter School, another Washington, D.C., preschool–12 charter, also uses recruitment strategically, targeting underrepresented populations. At the beginning, E. L. Haynes marketed aggressively to families of different economic and cultural backgrounds by conducting extensive recruitment drives at a variety of neighborhood locations. "When we first got started, we recruited from in front of grocery stores, to coffee shops, to preschools," said Jennifer Niles, the school's founder and head of school. "If there was a community organization that I could find, I would go to it" (personal communication, December 19, 2011). Now that E. L. Haynes is a top-ranked charter school in the city and receives many applications from families who hear about the school through its reputation, E. L. Haynes focuses all of its recruitment efforts on low-income and non-English-speaking families, who may have less access to information about local schools.

At Larchmont Charter School, school leaders adjust their recruitment strategies on a monthly basis. The school's administrative team looks at census and Nielsen data for the surrounding neighborhood and sets the goal of having their student body mirror that diversity. Students are not chosen based on their individual race or ethnicity. Rather, the school designs a recruitment plan at the beginning of the year outlining its strategies and the community groups with which it plans to partner. Every month, school leaders look at the racial, ethnic, and socioeconomic breakdown of the lottery pool to measure their progress and adjust strategies if needed. Brian Johnson, the school's former executive director, explained that recruitment is a job involving many people. In addition to partnering with community groups, churches, Head Start programs, other schools, and places of employment, school leaders rely heavily on parents. "We're leveraging our community of parents internally," Johnson said. "Can you knock on doors for us? Can you come with us to do presentations? Can you introduce us to community leaders we should be talking to?" (personal communication, November 23, 2011). By being conscious of diversity in marketing and outreach, the school can recruit a diverse lottery pool.

Weighted Lotteries

In addition to targeted recruitment, most of the charter schools we studied use weighted lotteries to ensure diverse enrollment. By building a preference based on income or geography into the school's otherwise random selection, schools can guarantee that their diverse lottery pools translate into diverse admissions.

Although the charter schools we studied are interested in racial and ethnic diversity as well as socioeconomic diversity, their weighted lotteries avoid the specific use of race. In the 2007 Supreme Court ruling in *Parents Involved in Community Schools v. Seattle School District No. 1*, the court struck down school assignment plans in Seattle, Washington, and Louisville, Kentucky, which treated individual students differently by race. And in the 2013 Supreme Court decision in *Fisher v. University of Texas* involving higher education, the Supreme Court endorsed the goal of racial diversity but ruled that universities have "the ultimate burden of demonstrating, before turning to racial classifications, that available, workable, race-neutral alternatives do not suffice." As a result, lotteries that rely on an individual student's race or ethnicity may not be an option for charter schools. (See further discussion in Chapter 8.)

Furthermore, some states (and the District of Columbia, where Capital City and E. L. Haynes are located) prohibit charter schools from using weighted lotteries to promote diversity or have unclear policies on the practice. Even in states where they are permitted, charter schools face additional restrictions on the use of weighted lotteries if they want to remain eligible for federal start-up funds, an important funding source for many charter schools during their first three years of operation (U.S. Department of Education, 2014). Still, lotteries that are not based on individual race, but weight students based on family income, geography, parents' educational status, or the racial makeup of a neighborhood, for example, can be a powerful tool for creating a diverse student body.

Several of the charter schools we studied have lottery preferences based on family income. Blackstone Valley Prep simply reserves the first 50% of seats in their lottery for low-income students. The remaining seats are awarded regardless of income, so the actual percentage of low-income students at the school exceeds 50%. At Larchmont Charter School, the lottery mechanism is more complicated and more closely controls outcomes. School leaders estimate the percentage of families in the local area that would qualify for free or reduced-price lunch based on census data—42% in 2011, for example—and set that as their target. They then use a carefully designed algorithm that is updated each year, depending on what percentage of that year's lottery pool qualifies for free or reduced-price lunch. The algorithm adjusts the weight given to qualifying students in order to help reach the school's target percentage of low-income students.

Other charter schools use geographic markers in their lottery to ensure diversity. High Tech High, a network of elementary, middle, and high schools in San Diego, California, uses a lottery that weights only by zip code, seeking an even distribution of students from across the area. Because of the residential segregation in the area, the result of the zip code lottery is a socioeconomically and racially diverse student body. "Zip codes predict socioeconomic status exquisitely well and ethnicity almost as well," explained Larry Rosenstock, the school's CEO and founding principal. Furthermore, zip codes have the advantage of being a fairly impersonal marker. "90216 [or any other zip code] is a number, so you're not objectifying anybody," Rosenstock added. "That's what we like about it" (personal communication, December 5, 2011).

Community Roots Charter School, an elementary and middle school in Brooklyn, New York, also recently added an address-based preference in the school's lottery. The school's K–5 campus occupies the third floor in a New York City public school building that is nestled between three expansive public housing complexes in Fort Greene, an economically and racially mixed neighborhood. Diverse enrollment in a diverse neighborhood is central to the mission of the school, which opened in 2006 with a 47% low-income enrollment. As the popularity of the school grew, however, Community Roots began to see a decrease in the percentage of low-income students at the school. In particular, students living in the neighboring public housing developments saw their chances of being admitted plummet as more middle-class families found out about the school and applied. In 2012–2013, Community Roots began reserving 40% of the spaces in their incoming kindergarten class for students living in public housing. Like many charter schools, Community Roots has a sibling preference, and half of incoming kindergarten seats are usually filled by siblings (of all economic backgrounds). The school chose 40% as the set-aside for students living in public housing so that a small slice of seats—about 10%—would still be open enrollment. School leaders expect the percentage of low-income students schoolwide to increase gradually year to year as student cohorts admitted through the new lottery move through higher grades (Allison Keil, personal communication, May 15, 2013).

DSST Public Schools uses a hybrid of income- and geography-based preferences. DSST works with the school district to determine the enrollment preference at each campus based on the communities in which the schools are located and with the goal of having diverse student bodies at each school. Some DSST schools then hold a separate lottery for students who are eligible for free or reduced-price lunch or who reside in a particular geographic region.

One unfortunate result of diversity strategies that rely on a lottery is that many families who apply to diverse charter schools do not get admitted. The documentary films *Waiting for Superman* and *The Lottery* told heart-wrenching stories of low-income families who pinned their hopes on a high-achieving, high-poverty charter school but in many cases were not admitted (Guggenheim, 2010; Sackler, 2010). There is plenty of heartbreak in the lotteries for diverse charter schools as well. High Tech High, for example, receives more than 7,000 applications to fill just a few hundred spots (Larry Rosenstock, personal communication, December 5, 2011). Community Roots Charter School was ranked the fifth hardest charter school to get into in New York City in 2010, with spaces for just 6.6% of those who entered the lottery (Otterman, 2010a).

This clear demand from parents is one of the reasons why we need more diverse charter schools, but the lottery system is also a reminder of why charter schools alone cannot solve the problem of segregation in public schools. The families that are not chosen in the lottery deserve integrated schools as well. We need more magnet schools that consciously integrated students, and we need to tackle de facto segregation in district schools. Furthermore, we should facilitate connections between charter schools and traditional public schools, seeing charters once again as a laboratory setting where innovative models can be created, tested, and refined, then shared with other schools. Indeed, the programs and strategies that integrated charter schools have developed to serve a diverse student body, which are discussed in the following section, could be useful tools for other diverse schools, charters or not.

SERVING A DIVERSE STUDENT BODY

Socioeconomic and racial school integration is a strong tool for improving student outcomes. Low-income students' performance rises in mixed-income settings, and all students receive the cognitive benefits of a diverse learning environment (see Chapter 3). However, serving a diverse group of students also presents challenges. Students arrive with a wide range of previous experiences, and teachers must differentiate instruction to meet their varied needs.

Furthermore, while socioeconomically and racially integrated schools can offer some benefits even if academic and social environments still show a degree of socioeconomic and racial stratification (see, e.g., Schwartz, 2010), integration is a more powerful tool when it reaches not just schools but also classrooms, cafeterias, and playgrounds. Students of all backgrounds gain a competitive edge by learning to understand differences and build relationships with people from other racial/ethnic or socioeconomic groups.

Mindful of these challenges and goals, the charter schools we highlight in this chapter are developing ways to make the most of a diverse learning environment by actively promoting integration in academic and social settings, for students of all backgrounds and needs. Some schools use innovative strategies for blending the benefits of leveled instruction and heterogeneous classrooms. Furthermore, while the charter sector as a whole has a mixed record on serving special student populations, some successful diverse charter schools prioritize supporting English language learners, serving students with special needs, and providing social and psychological services. And a few integrated charter schools are also tackling the more elusive problem of how to encourage students of different backgrounds to interact socially while building tolerance and respect.

Tools for Differentiating within an Integrated Classroom

First thing on a May morning, a group of about a dozen 6th-, 7th-, and 8th-graders at City Neighbors Charter School in Baltimore watched as one of their classmates dunked his arm in ice water, squirmed until he could stand the cold no longer, and yanked it back out again. Kate Seidl, the school's reading specialist and librarian, and Peter Redgrave, a middle school science teacher, led the class in recording data and observations from the experiment, part of an investigation of how body mass index affects people's perceptions of cold. With curly hair and wearing a patterned skirt with dragons on it, Seidl looked a bit like Ms. Frizzle, the energetic schoolteacher from *The Magic School Bus* children's book series. Like the students in *The Magic School Bus*, the City Neighbors kids were wary of the crazy-sounding experiment at first, but ended up enthralled. In the middle of class, the power went out—one of the hazards of being located in an older building—but students barely noticed.

This short science class was one of the daily tutoring sessions that City

Neighbors calls "intensive learning periods." For half an hour each morning, middle school students attend highly specialized small-group lessons. Intensive learning periods are one of the tools that City Neighbors uses to differentiate instruction without dividing students into leveled tracks.

Mixed-income schools can draw criticism from both directions with respect to how well the school community and individual classrooms are integrated. On the one hand, students in diverse schools are sometimes separated into tracked classes along lines that mirror socioeconomic status, and students may further self-segregate during free time. In that situation, middle-income and low-income students are cheated out of some of the peer interactions and access to broader social networks that diversity can offer. On the other hand, schools that intentionally maintain heterogeneous classes must consider the research suggesting that these classes can negatively affect the academic progress of higher achievers (Brewer, Rees, & Argys, 1995).

Research suggests that it is possible, by offering all students a single challenging curriculum, to reduce the achievement gap without harming the highest performers (Burris, Wiley, Welner, & Murphy, 2008; Rui, 2009). However, ability grouping remains a hotly debated topic that is particularly relevant at socioeconomically diverse schools, where students enter school with a wide range of knowledge and skills (see Petrilli, 2012). How can mixed-income schools best support lower-achieving students without hurting the higher-achievers?

Intensive learning periods are one of City Neighbors' answers to this dilemma. This half-hour block provides an opportunity for extra support or enrichment in different subjects, allowing teachers to meet different students' needs while still teaching most of the academic time in mixed-ability classrooms. For example, some students may spend their intensive period receiving extra writing support while others attend an enrichment intensive period building robots.

Intensive learning periods have several features designed to create effective support and enrichment without losing the benefits of heterogeneous classrooms. First, groupings are flexible. Over the course of a year, students take up to three different intensive classes with three different groups of peers, giving teachers multiple opportunities to adjust placements based on individual needs. Seidl said that City Neighbors designed this unique schedule "because we know we have to be as responsive as possible." She said they see middle school as a pivotal time for intervening to support and challenge students: "This is the place to catch kids" (personal communication, December 14, 2012). Second, topics are often highly specialized blends of different skills and subjects, grouping students by strengths or affinities and areas for growth at the same time. The science class investigating body mass index and perceptions of cold was part of an intensive period on science writing that grouped students who struggle with nonfiction writing but who have shown an interest in science. It is not the case that all intensive classes are strictly enrichment or strictly support, nor do all the high-achieving students end up in one set of intensive periods and the low-achieving students in another. Third, the intensive period is focused but short. This is an all-hands-on-deck operation; all middle school staff members pitch in during intensive time to ensure low student-teacher ratios. As a result, a lot of targeted instruction is fit into 30 minutes, leaving most of the day available for students to attend mixed-ability classes.

As at City Neighbors, educators at High Tech High are committed to grouping students by mixed ability as much as possible. "It's not just diversity in admissions," said CEO and founding principal Larry Rosenstock. "It's also integration in practice once they've arrived" (personal communication, December 5, 2011). Rosenstock started High Tech High after running a large public high school in New England where overall enrollment was racially and socioeconomically diverse, but instruction was carried out in leveled tracks that produced highly segregated classrooms. Rosenstock is committed to making sure that High Tech High's diverse enrollment translates into diverse classrooms and rich interactions between students of different backgrounds.

High Tech High's project-based learning is a prime tool for differentiating instruction in an integrated classroom. Sarah Strong, a teacher at High Tech Middle, explained that projects "naturally differentiate" by setting up open-ended problems with multiple pathways for exploration (personal communication, May 9, 2013). Students who are more advanced in a subject can approach a project from a higher level, exploring information in greater depth and creating a more complicated final product, while others will work with a narrower interpretation of the task. At the same time, projects are also "vehicles for integration," as Bobby Shaddox, another High Tech Middle teacher, described. "In projects you have people collaborating, solving problems together, and doing work together" (personal communication, May 10, 2013). High Tech High art teacher Jeff Robin added that this collaboration ripples into students' social interactions, encouraging students to become friends with classmates from a wide range of backgrounds. "[Students] have a reason to be friends because they might be somebody's partner in the next couple weeks, and you want to get to know each other," Robin explained (personal communication, May 9, 2013).

The system for honors classes at High Tech High is another way that the school offers differentiated but integrated instruction. As High Tech High grew, leaders at the school realized they needed to offer honors classes so that students could have the weighted grade point averages that selective colleges look for in admissions. Separating the highest-achieving students from their peers, however, would have gone against the school's policy of integrated classrooms. Instead, High Tech High decided to offer some classes with an honors option, allowing interested students to take the class at the honors level by completing extra assignments. Under this model, all students still get the benefits of a heterogeneous classroom. Furthermore, making the honors option visible and accessible to all students encourages participation. More than 70% of students at High Tech High ultimately take an honors course, according to Rosenstock (personal communication, December 5, 2011).

Serving Special Populations

Successfully serving a diverse group of students requires not only differentiating instruction to address different ability levels and experiences but also serving the needs of specific populations. We have focused our discussion of diversity on social class and race/ethnicity because of the large body of research on the harms of socioeconomic and racial segregation, as well as the benefits of integration along these lines. However, there is crucial work to be done to make sure that charter schools are adequately enrolling and serving students with special needs and English language learners. Existing research suggests that many charter schools have very poor records on this front, raising legal as well as ethical concerns (see Chapter 3). Some of the integrated charter schools that we studied, however, are strong counterexamples. These schools actively recruit and enroll special education students and English language learners and provide robust support programs that focus on integrating students with mainstream classes as much as possible.

Community Roots Charter School serves a large special education population and focuses on providing a full spectrum of services in an inclusive environment. Allison Keil and Sara Stone, cofounders of Community Roots Charter School, met in graduate school at Bank Street College of Education in New York City, a school known for its progressive educational philosophy. They decided to start a school together that would combine their passions—Keil's vision for socioeconomic and racial diversity and Stone's mission for a school that is fully inclusive of students with special needs (Keil, personal communication, May 15, 2013).

During the school's early years, Keil and Stone went to every Head Start in the neighborhood and also visited preschool programs for students with special needs to recruit students (Keil, personal communication, December 15, 2011). About 20% of students at Community Roots have special needs (see the Appendix). Each class at Community Roots is cotaught by two teachers, one with general education certification and one with special education certification. Teachers work together to plan and differentiate lessons. They may lead writing lessons on the same topic targeting different skill levels simultaneously in two halves of the room, for example, or they might both pull small groups during a work time. There is a room devoted to occupational therapy and physical therapy at Community Roots, but you will also see students using some therapeutic tools—such as bands, balls, and mats—in the hallway right outside their classroom, taking a quick break before rejoining the class.

E. L. Haynes Public Charter School in Washington, D.C., is another strong example of a school that serves all students. Founder and Head of School Jennifer Niles started planning E. L. Haynes back when she was a fellow with New Leaders for New Schools, a competitive program for training leaders of urban schools, interning as a resident principal at Capital City Public Charter School. The vision for the school, which Niles and a group of 40 friends, colleagues, and community members developed at a meeting on a rainy Saturday afternoon in 2003, was to help all students achieve at high levels side by side.

Roughly a quarter of all students at E. L. Haynes are English language learners, and the school of about 1,100 students has more than a dozen teachers on its English Language Learning team. The school translates all information sent home into Spanish and is considering adding Amharic translation as well, as the number of Ethiopian immigrant families at the school increases (Niles, personal communication, June 9, 2013).

Furthermore, E. L. Haynes devotes considerable resources to providing seven full-time social workers and one full-time psychologist at the school. Niles explains that many students living in extreme poverty suffer from posttraumatic stress disorder or face other obstacles at home that can be significant barriers to academic success. Middle-class families at the school may not be aware of these additional supports for their neediest students. "We run almost a whole other school that most people never see," Niles explained (personal communication, June 9, 2013). But by addressing the needs of English language learners and students with psychological, emotional, or social issues within an integrated learning environment, E. L. Haynes helps ensure that all students succeed.

Cultures That Encourage Integration

The kindergarten classrooms at Community Roots Charter School in New York have a map on the wall filled with pins marking where each student lives. A cluster of pins surrounds the school's location in Fort Greene, others are scattered throughout Brooklyn, and a few lie far out in other boroughs. The map is a tradition at the school, and it makes an impression on students; when we talked to 5th-graders about their neighborhoods, they started by explaining, "In kindergarten, we had a map of where everyone lives." The map is part of kindergartners' semester-long exploration of families, which lays the groundwork for a diverse community at the school. Kindergartners discuss how families are similar and different. Over the course of the semester, each student's family comes in to be interviewed by the whole kindergarten class. The projects send a strong message to students and families that all are welcome and that Community Roots is a place where they will be encouraged to share, learn about one another's perspectives, and ask questions about differences.

Community Roots is one of several charter schools we studied that have developed creative strategies to make sure that diverse enrollment translates into diverse participation and interaction. These schools take a proactive approach to difficult conversations about diversity, provide students with opportunities to interact and connect across demographic groups, and reach out to parents of all backgrounds.

Addressing Diversity Proactively. Diversity was integral to the vision for Community Roots from the start and is a selling point for many of the school's teachers and families, but the school's strategies for getting the most out of a diverse community have evolved over the years. Codirector Allison Keil explained that simply filling a room with students from a range of socioeconomic, racial, and ethnic backgrounds does not ensure that students will all feel welcomed or make connections with each other. "I think we can bring people together, and it can look like a really nice picture, and then when you don't push on it, certain parts of the population feel like they have more access or less access," Keil explained. "We have lots of programming here specific to pushing on that" (personal communication, December 15, 2011).

Keil is particularly mindful of the message about diversity that Community Roots sends given the greater context of segregation in many of New York City's public schools. Community Roots' K–5 campus is located on the third floor of the P.S. 67 building, sandwiched between P.S. 67 below and a district special education school above. Colocation is a common, and controversial, practice for New York City public schools (see Ravitch, 2013; Sahm, 2013). The relationship between Community Roots and the two other schools sharing the building has at times been tense, particularly during a debate about the school's expansion to add middle school grades. P.S. 67, now known as the Charles Alexander Dorsey school, was the first African American School in Brooklyn, started in 1815 as an independent school and taken over by the city of Brooklyn in 1841, at which point it was renamed "Colored School Number One" (P.S. 67 Charles A. Dorsey, 2012). When Community Roots first opened in 2006, the student body of 100 kindergartners and 1st-graders was 59% Black, 22% White, 7% Hispanic, and 12% other races or ethnicities (NAPCS, 2013c). As students entered the school's space on the third floor of P.S. 67, Community Roots' White students were among the first such students ever to enter that building. Keil works hard to support the school's vision for diversity while being sensitive to the history of the school building and neighborhood.

Community Roots Charter School created a full-time staff position specifically charged with making sure that the school is serving all parts of the school community. Sahba Rohani started at Community Roots as a kindergarten teacher and is now the Director of Community Development, a position that she and Keil invented as they saw the need to increase programming to bring the diverse community together. Rohani's warm personality and the trust that she has established with families are important ingredients in the success of her work. During the week that we visited the school, Rohani had an evening outing with students who had won "dinner with Sahba"—staff and teachers go by their first names—at the school's silent auction fundraiser. Walking down the hall in the morning, she was stopped by a parent with a newspaper clipping to share—an article that the parent herself had written. "I'm so proud to read this," Sahba responded. "I'll text you." But Rohani has also helped develop a number of programs fostering interaction at Community Roots that could be replicable models.

Rohani and Keil, together with a small self-selected group of dedicated staff members, have come together to form a "Diversity Working Group," whose mission is both to support staff and to create a developmentally aligned antibias approach that can be infused into the curriculum already in place from kindergarten to grade 8 at Community Roots. This group strives to create a sequence of concepts, language, and ideas around (but not limited to) race, class, gender, and sexuality to be taught throughout the years at Community Roots. The work is steeped in research, a deep understanding of the developmental stages of children, and knowledge and insight into the school's community and culture. They hope that this work could serve as a guide for their school and others (Rohani, personal communication, May 15, 2013).

Community Roots is also striving to make sure that leadership at the school, in addition to enrollment, is diverse. Rohani has created a leadership program for 5th-graders designed in part to change students' concept of what a leader looks like. At the beginning of the year, 5th-graders of all backgrounds apply to be Community Builders, volunteering to spend their lunch and recess time helping in younger grades. Community Builders make sure that students are included in activities and become role models for younger children. "If a person is lonely, I can go to them and ask what happened," a 5th-grade boy explained. Rohani said the school is also committed to making sure that it is recruiting staff that represents the diversity of the students so that students are interacting with and learning from a diverse group of adults as well as a diverse student body.

E. L. Haynes Public Charter School and DSST Public Schools also take active approaches to facilitating conversations about diversity at their schools. All staff members at E. L. Haynes participate in an intensive Race and Equity Education Seminar series during the summer, when they first join the school and for multiple cycles afterwards. These trainings have grown into a hallmark of the E. L. Haynes model. "It really is why many people choose to work here and stay here," said founder Jennifer Niles. The training series seeks to enable participants to develop the skill, will, and courage to fight institutional racism. The goal is for educators to leave with a better ability, as Niles phrases it, "to talk about race across difference." She explained that most people in our society lack the tools to talk about racial and socioeconomic differences with people who do not share their background, but these conversations are crucial in a diverse school. "As a school, we can't let a social taboo limit the thinking we do about what's best for kids" (personal communication, June 9, 2013).

At DSST Public Schools, embracing diversity means engaging the full school community in difficult dialogues. Bill Kurtz, the network's CEO, described a time when a DSST school held a schoolwide discussion in response to an incident where one student called another student a racial slur. Addressing diversity is about "real situations, not about a curriculum," Kurtz said. "I think we work hard to embrace those challenges and create authentic situations where race—and income, in some ways—are talked about" (personal communication, December 13, 2011).

Mixing Up Students. Sahba Rohani talks about the importance of creating "small, intimate spaces where diverse communities can come together" (personal communication, May 15, 2013). Every Wednesday afternoon at Community Roots, for example, classrooms are converted into woodworking shops, yoga studios, yearbook offices, and bakeries as part of Community Open Work—COW, for short. Parents, grandparents, and community members volunteer to lead or assist workshops on a variety of extracurricular topics of their choosing. Students rank their preferences for COW sessions, and the school staff assigns groups strategically, looking to create diverse groups where students can interact with other children and adults with whom they might not normally spend time.

In some diverse schools students disperse to different neighborhoods after classes and rarely see one another on evenings, but Community Roots facilitates opportunities for interaction outside of the school day as well. Through the school's Play and Learning Squads (PALS), for example, small groups of Community Roots students and their parents go on weekend or afternoon outings or do craft or cooking projects at one family's home. As with COW groupings, teachers assign the squads strategically, with an eye toward matching students who would not otherwise spend time together outside of school hours. "PALS is sort of like a mix-up," one 5th-grade girl explained. "These aren't the kids I normally talk to. It's to make friends."

Inviting Parents. Parent involvement can be a contentious issue for charter schools, but it is another area in which diverse schools can encourage integration. Getting families from all backgrounds engaged in school activities is valuable for multiple reasons. Students benefit academically and socially when their own parents are engaged. The school community becomes stronger when families of all backgrounds feel like active participants in their children's education and are valued by the school for their contributions. Reaching out to parents also creates opportunities to build more diverse social connections among students and their families (Wohlstetter et al., 2013). Involving parents across different socioeconomic and racial/ethnic groups can be a challenge, however, because of economic or cultural barriers to participation in school activities and volunteer opportunities (see Chapter 3).

Charter schools generally have a leg up in parent involvement. As opposed to district schools that enroll all students within their boundaries, charter schools have only families where someone—a parent, grandparent, aunt, social worker, or friend—was involved enough in a child's education to apply for the school. This is an inherent advantage at schools of choice, including public magnet schools, and is one of the reasons why we need to strengthen partnerships between charter schools and traditional public schools so that the benefits of community involvement can be shared across schools. Furthermore, many charter schools—including City Neighbors Charter School, Capital City Charter School, and Larchmont Charter School—have parent volunteer requirements, expectations, or requests. In general, we favor encouraging parent involvement but oppose volunteer requirements, as they could discourage low-income families from applying to charter schools.

Nevertheless, some charter schools, with and without parent volunteer policies, have developed important strategies for engaging parents of many different backgrounds that could be applied in traditional public schools. At Blackstone Valley Prep, for example, the Family Leadership

Council (similar to a parent–teacher organization) is co-led by one urban and one suburban parent, to help ensure that voices from across the community are heard and to encourage parents of different backgrounds to interact. In addition to providing support for the school and teachers, the Family Leadership Council provides support to families within the school community. Tracey Dann (2012), a past suburban cochair of the council, explained in a blog for RI-CAN, a state advocacy group pushing for education reform: "When someone in your family is sick, we bring them food. When someone is between apartments, we help with their scholar's laundry. . . . We do anything we can to help one another because a stable home means a stable scholar. In the end, everyone rallies to keep our children on a path to college." Building on shared interests makes family activities accessible to all. "Our best programming was centered around the things we have in common, instead of our differences," Dann explained. These activities include "canned food drives or potluck dinners, used uniform sales, concerts showcasing the scholars' art and music skills, dances, as well as math and science nights" (personal communication, November 14, 2013). Ana León, who served as urban cochair alongside Dann, explained that the Family Leadership Council is particularly intentional about including families who do not speak English, who are often afraid to come to school meetings. Parent volunteers reach out to these families in person, over the phone, and by email, letting them know there will be translators at events and helping them feel welcome (personal communication, November 15, 2013).

Blackstone Valley Prep's parent committee's structure emphasizes diverse participation and community cooperation. As a result, the school has been relatively successful in encouraging participation across demographics and building social connections between families from the four different communities served by the school, without a parent volunteer policy. "I believe that a lot of our cross-cultural family conversations and connections that happen are the beginning of what could be a really great positive social influence," said Jeremy Chiappetta, the network's executive director (personal communication, November 30, 2011).

City Neighbors Charter School does have a policy asking parents to volunteer but works hard to structure volunteer opportunities that are accessible to people with different schedules and skills. The school asks parents to volunteer 40 hours a year, but coming to any school event or meeting, such as a class play or parent conference, counts toward these hours. Other volunteer opportunities fall at different times of the week and involve different types of work. A stapling or mailing job can be sent home with a child, completed by a parent during the evenings, and sent back. Maintenance help fixing a cubby or building a playground often happens on weekends. Kate Seidl, the school's librarian and literacy specialist, described one parent volunteer, an Ethiopian immigrant, who comes to the school whenever he has free time—without advance notice—and helps shelve library books (personal communication, December 14, 2012). There is no punitive action for families that do not fulfill their hours, but a parent from the school's board will call families to check in and see if there are volunteer opportunities that will work for them. Without a parent volunteer policy, the practice of providing many different ways and times for involvement would still be a valuable way of encouraging diverse participation.

STUDENT OUTCOMES

The academic results from these diverse charter schools are promising, if anecdotal, affirming the evidence of the benefits of integration in traditional public schools. As in the case of the charter schools with teacher voice highlighted in Chapter 5, we chose these diverse charter schools specifically because they were successful, keeping in mind the notion that charter schools were originally intended to incubate best practices that could be used in other schools. An investigation of the link between diversity and academic success was outside the scope of our research, and as discussed in Chapter 4, self-selection may be a factor in the schools' performance. Rather, we use these examples to demonstrate that diverse charter schools can show impressive results.

As in Chapter 5, we looked at each school's student achievement on state standardized tests in reading and math, for all students and low-income students. And, without controlling for demographics, we compared the percentage of students scoring proficient or above with the proficiency rates in the district and state in which each charter school is located. (See data in the Appendix.)

Based on this rough comparison, reading achievement is particularly strong at the charter schools highlighted in this chapter. At all eight schools (or flagship campuses, in the case of charter networks), the percentage of students passing state standardized tests in reading exceeds the state average. More tellingly, low-income students at all eight of these schools beat the average proficiency rates for all low-income students in both their state and district.

Math results are more uneven but still strong overall. At six of the eight schools, low-income students beat district averages for proficiency on state standardized tests in math, and at five of the eight schools, low-income students also beat proficiency averages in math for their low-income peers statewide. Parallel to results seen in Chapter 5, the two schools with below-average math achievement, City Neighbors and Community Roots, both serve above-average proportions of special education students.

Some of these schools are making impressive progress in reducing the income achievement gap. At Blackstone Valley Prep, for example, both low-income students and all other students beat the average proficiency rates for their peers statewide by sizable margins. Furthermore, the gap in proficiency rates for low-income students versus other students is smaller at Blackstone Valley than it is statewide. In 3rd-grade reading, Blackstone Valley's income achievement gap is roughly half the size of the statewide gap, and in math the school's gap is about a third smaller than the statewide gap (New England Common Assessment Program, 2012a; see also the Appendix). In addition, early results from DSST's work opening a new campus in the building of a failing middle school suggests that changing the mix of students in a school may even be a valuable method of helping to turn around struggling schools (see Sidebar 6.3).

A variety of awards and distinctions also speak to positive results at socioeconomically integrated charter schools. The list of accolades is long, but here are a few highlights:

- DSST: Stapleton High School, flagship campus of the DSST Public Schools (n.d.), was one of three finalists out of more than 1,000 schools that entered the 2010 Race to the Top Commencement Challenge, a national competition judging schools' commitment to college- and career-readiness.
- In 2013 the Rhode Island Department of Education (2013a) classified Blackstone Valley Prep's founding elementary school as a "commended" school, the highest level in the state's school quality rankings, earned by just 9% of schools across the state.
- In 2011 the California Department of Education ranked Larchmont Charter School (n.d.) in the top 10% of all schools with similar demographics across the state, based on standardized test results.
- Capital City Public Charter School (n.d.) and E. L. Haynes Public Charter School (n.d.) have each won the Fight for Children Quality Schools Initiative award, granted each year to outstanding schools in Washington, DC.
- Capital City has also been named an Expeditionary Learning "Mentor School," an honor that recognizes the school as one of the highest performing Expeditionary Learning schools and gives it the chance to showcase best practices to other schools.
- E. L. Haynes has also won three EPIC awards, granted by the

New Leaders' Effective Practice Incentive Community (EPIC) to urban schools showing the greatest student achievement gains.

- Community Roots' cofounders, Allison Keil and Sara Stone, received a 2013 Alumni Award from Bank Street College of Education (n.d.) in recognition of their work and the school's success.

- As previously mentioned in the list of distinctions in Chapter 5, City Neighbors Charter School (n.d.) has been honored for its arts and environmental curricula and for growth in student test scores, and High Tech High (n.d.) has an impressive college-going rate of 98% for a student body that includes 35% first-generation college students.

CONCLUSION

Many factors are at work in the success of the diverse charter schools we highlight in this chapter. These schools stress a number of design principles in addition to socioeconomic integration, from project-based learning to longer class time. Furthermore, students who won the lottery to attend these schools may have the advantage of having parents who are more engaged in their education than students who did not enter the lottery. Still, when combined with the wide body of research showing the academic advantages of giving low-income students the chance to attend economically integrated schools, these stories give hope that more schools, charter and otherwise, can produce positive results for students through consciously integrated enrollment and instruction.

These schools are cutting against the grain. Integration is not one of the buzz words in education reform circles, and when "diversity" comes up, it is often code for "underrepresented minority." Jeff Robin, an art teacher at High Tech High, recalled a group of visitors from Washington, D.C., who remarked that the school was "not very diverse" because its population—which is roughly 33% White, 11% Black, 41% Hispanic, and 13% Asian (see the Appendix)—didn't fit their definition of *diverse*, which was "95% African American" (personal communication, May 9, 2013). Prioritizing truly diverse learning environments requires a shift in thinking.

Jeremy Chiappetta (2012) was initially reluctant to work at a diverse school. An alumnus of Teach for America who taught in New York City and Providence, Chiappetta is passionate about helping low-income students succeed and was unsure when the opportunity arose to run a regional charter serving urban *and* suburban students. "What tipped the

---

**SIDEBAR 6.3. INTEGRATED CHARTER SCHOOLS
AS A TURNAROUND STRATEGY?**

One of the persistent challenges in public education is how to improve the nation's lowest-performing schools. Data across decades shows that chronic underperformance is incredibly hard to fix (Smarick, 2010). In recent years the federal government and local districts have turned to charter management as a new hope for improving failing schools. Federal School Improvement Grants, designed to support school turnaround efforts, allow for "restarting" the school under charter management as one of four allowed strategies. However, the results of these efforts have been lukewarm so far, and school turnaround remains a significant challenge, even for charter operators with many successful schools under their belts (U.S. Department of Education, 2012b).

School turnaround efforts usually involve changing the principal, teachers, or management at a school. But because the nation's lowest-performing schools are overwhelmingly high-poverty, it might be possible in some cases to take a different approach (Balfanz & Legters, 2004). What if we changed the mix of students in a struggling school, rebalancing enrollment so that the school did not serve a concentration of the most disadvantaged students?

The story of Cole Middle School in Denver, Colorado, highlights some of the difficulties of school turnaround but also shows the potential for socioeconomic integration as a new strategy to pursue. In 2004 Colorado state officials announced that they would shut down Cole Middle School, located in Denver, because of the school's low performance on state tests. The State Board of Education began searching for a charter organizer to take over the school and awarded the contract to KIPP. In August of the following year KIPP reopened the school as Cole College Prep—the network's one and only venture into school turnaround (A. B. Anderson & DeCesare, 2006).

Cole College Prep struggled during its 1st year and closed after its 2nd. From the start, the school faced a number of difficulties, including high staff turnover, insufficient funding, and lack of community support. Rich Barrett, the principal at Denver's other KIPP school, supported Cole College Prep through its 1st year. At the start of the 2nd year, he told the *Denver Post,* "Would I do it again? Absolutely not. . . . I would not transform a school again" (quoted in Sherry, 2006a). Van Schoales, a program officer for the Piton Foundation, which funds education initiatives in Denver, said that KIPP "made some serious mistakes in their leadership decisions" (quoted in Sherry, 2006b). KIPP announced midway through the school's 2nd year that they would not enroll new students in the fall. According to the *Denver Post,* KIPP decided to abandon the project because they failed to find an

---

SIDEBAR 6.3. *Continued*

---

effective principal. Richard Barth, CEO of KIPP, said, "We had a challenging start at Cole. . . . We killed ourselves to give [the students] a much better education." But without the right school leader, Barth said, "we're not going to go out and promise a great school" (quoted in Sherry, 2007). *Washington Post* columnist and KIPP supporter Jay Mathews (2009a) called the effort "a failure."

From 2007–2011 the Cole campus underwent a number of transitions, including the creation of Cole Arts and Science Academy (CASA), a preschool through 8th-grade program. In fall 2012, after being invited by a group of parents and CASA administrators, DSST Public Schools took over the middle school grades at Cole.

DSST Public Schools is known in Denver and nationally for its successful socioeconomically integrated charter schools, but taking over a struggling school was new territory for DSST, as it had been for KIPP. DSST benefited from increased stability at the Cole campus since the opening of CASA but still faced a significant challenge. In 2011, less than 30% of 5th-graders at CASA passed the state standardized tests in reading and math, compared to more than 60% of 5th-graders statewide (Colorado Department of Education, 2013b).

In keeping with the network's integrated model, DSST: Cole Middle School enrolls students from the low-income, high-crime neighborhood surrounding the school as well as additional students from across Denver. DSST: Cole provides guaranteed slots to all rising 6th-graders from CASA (about 60 seats) and fills an additional 80 sixth-grade seats through a lottery of applications from students throughout the district. In 2012–2013 the school still had relatively high levels of poverty compared to other DSST campuses: 77% of students at DSST: Cole were eligible for free or reduced-price lunch, compared to 47% of middle school students at DSST: Stapleton, the founding campus. But DSST: Cole had lower poverty levels than its feeder school, CASA, which enrolled 94% of students eligible for free or reduced-price lunch (Colorado Department of Education, 2013b).

Initial results from DSST: Cole are promising. In 2011–2012 the school exceeded state targets for academic growth and reducing gaps in achievement, and it was the top-ranked middle school in the city that year, according to the School Performance Framework released by Denver Public Schools (Colorado Department of Education, 2012). Bill Kurtz, CEO of DSST Public Schools, said in December 2011 that he was optimistic about the school's future. He sees the school's success thus far as a testament to the strength of DSST's model. "It's one thing to open a school in a middle-upper-income neighborhood that low-income kids come to. It's another to

---

SIDEBAR **6.3.** *Continued*

---

open it in a really challenging neighborhood that then middle- and upper-income families come to," he explained. "I think it demonstrates the brand that we've been able to establish and that people want what we have to offer and are willing to do things they may not otherwise have done because of the promise of great education and the promise of a really vibrant learning community" (personal communication, December 13, 2011). Indeed, in 2012–2013, DSST: Cole continued to be one of the district's highest-rated middle schools (Colorado Department of Education, 2013a). The school's initial success also suggests that socioeconomic integration could be an important tool in the persistent challenge of school turnaround.

---

scales for me to join the diverse schools work was a conversation with a mentor—a Rhode Island urban superintendent," Chiappetta wrote in *BVP Musings,* the blog he runs for Blackstone Valley Prep. "She suggested that if my goal was to serve urban poor kids well, then the *best* way to do so was to lead a truly diverse school." Now Chiappetta is an advocate for integrated schools, and Blackstone Valley Prep has a strong record of success with students of varied backgrounds.

Diverse schools provide the opportunity, as E. L. Haynes' Jennifer Niles phrased it, "to demonstrate that all students can achieve at high levels all together" (personal communication, December 19, 2011). As American society becomes increasingly diverse and globally connected, the experience of learning in a diverse school setting is more important than ever. In the words of Brian Johnson, former executive director of Larchmont Charter School, "In order to prepare our kids to participate and lead in the 21st-century diverse society, we've got to be giving them opportunities to learn from and with children who have different experiences than they do, from the very beginning" (personal communication, November 23, 2011).

The schools in this chapter are exciting examples of a different model for charter school success that deserves more attention but has thus far been overshadowed by the quest to make high-poverty charter schools work. These successful integrated charter schools demonstrate that diverse learning environments can foster the success of all students, and they provide a set of tools and strategies that other charter schools—and traditional public schools with diverse enrollment—can adopt.

7 Charter Schools That Combine Teacher Voice and Student Diversity

THE HIGH-POVERTY, NONUNIONIZED MODEL for charter schools has grabbed the attention of the media, philanthropists, and policymakers in part because it stems from an appealing broader strategy for education reform: "whatever it takes." The key to fixing high-poverty, racially isolated schools, the theory goes, is for teachers to do whatever it takes to help students succeed: working long hours, visiting students' homes, giving rides to school, or even making morning wake-up calls. Students learn that they, too, are responsible for doing whatever it takes to make it to college—finishing homework, coming to school on Saturdays and in the summer, and following a strict code of behavior. According to the "whatever it takes" mantra, students in high-poverty schools can succeed given enough extra support, and freedom from unions allows these schools room to push teachers to go the extra mile. Geoffrey Canada—whose work founding the Harlem Children's Zone is profiled in a book titled *Whatever It Takes* (Tough, 2008)—argued that his charter schools are not unionized because a union contract would be too inflexible. As we noted in Chapter 4, Canada claimed: "It kills innovation; it stops anything from changing" (quoted in Vasagar & Stratton, 2010). This seductive theory, that poverty and segregation are just excuses for teachers, provides a simple and dramatic narrative in which unions are the villains and vanquishing them makes great things possible.

On the other end of the spectrum of educational strategies, the original vision of charter schools articulated by Albert Shanker—which we are seeking to revive and update in this book—is driven by the fundamental ideal of democracy. In this framework, the school is a model of workplace democracy in which teachers are not simply workers who implement the directives of principals but are active participants in decision making. Students see workplace democracy in action, underlining the lessons found in civics books. Furthermore, students in economically and racially integrated schools learn on a daily basis the animating vision of American democracy—that we are all social equals, all deserving of a seat at democracy's table. In a 21st-century context, this model of education also prepares students for success in an economy that requires critical thinking and collaboration. If "whatever it takes" is the mantra behind nonunionized charter schools with concentrated poverty, then "education for a 21st-century democracy" should be the rallying cry at charter schools that intentionally integrate students and empower teachers in school decisions.

Although teacher voice and integration are deeply connected, we do not mean to suggest that the two always go hand in hand in charter schools today. To the contrary, as we talked to experts and educators, we found that the overlap between the two spheres of interest was relatively small. Indeed, some supporters in one camp specifically rejected the other. The legislation for Mayoral Academies in Rhode Island, which gave rise to Blackstone Valley Prep Mayoral Academy, proposed a new type of charter school that would integrate students across a region but that would also be exempt from the state's normal collective bargaining agreements and rules about pay, benefits, and tenure. Mayoral Academies were designed to be integrated and nonunion. Likewise, StudentsFirst, the education advocacy organization founded by former chancellor of District of Columbia Public Schools Michelle Rhee, opposes teacher unions on most policies but has recently begun to highlight socioeconomic integration as a successful school reform strategy (Bayer, 2013). On the other end of the spectrum, some of the unionized charter schools that we studied, such as Amber Charter School in New York City and the Green Dot network in Los Angeles, embraced some elements of a "whatever it takes" strategy to serve a high-poverty student body, at the same time that they stressed teacher voice.

However, we did find a handful of American schools open today that employ both prongs of Shanker's plan to consciously integrate students while also empowering teachers. At City Neighbors Charter School in Baltimore, teacher voice and student diversity come together to create a democratic school environment. Meanwhile, at the High Tech High network in San Diego, teacher leadership and an integrated student body are tools for teaching 21st-century skills. (Both schools were also discussed in Chapters 5 and 6.) In addition, in this chapter we discuss a third charter school, Morris Jeff Community School in New Orleans, which is in the early stages of building a model that empowers teachers and integrates students.

MODELING DEMOCRACY: CITY NEIGHBORS CHARTER SCHOOL

When Albert Shanker proposed the creation of charter schools in 1988, the concept represented the culmination of decades of his thinking about how schools could strengthen our democracy. If charter schools were structured correctly, Shanker believed, they could serve as the ultimate embodiment of democratic values, even more so than traditional public schools (Kahlenberg, 2007b; also source for remainder of this section).

Democracy was central to Shanker's overall vision of education. As a graduate student in philosophy at Columbia University in the late 1940s and early 1950s, Shanker was taught by the disciples of John Dewey, the great American philosopher and educator, who spent 3 decades at Columbia until retiring in 1939. Dewey famously argued that education and democracy were inseparable, because genuine education required freedom of thought and true democracy required an educated populace of critical thinkers who could fairly evaluate candidates for public office.

Dewey also believed that free trade unionism was central to democratic societies. Dewey was the holder of card no. 1 in New York City's local of the American Federation of Teachers, which was founded in 1916 as an alternative to the older and larger National Education Association. Whereas the NEA leadership was dominated by administrators and principals, the AFT was part of the labor movement and held a charter from the American Federation of Labor (AFL). The AFT's founding motto was "Education for Democracy, and Democracy in Education." Giving teachers democratic voice in the workplace would strengthen schools and also model for children democratic values.

When Shanker became president of the AFT in 1974, he came back time and again to the importance of democratic values and rarely gave a speech or wrote an article that did not invoke democracy. Shanker was a Social Democrat, a group for whom the philosopher Sidney Hook said that "democracy is not merely a political concept, but a moral one" (quoted in Kahlenberg, 2007b, p. 266). Democracy was Shanker's touchstone, just as the marketplace is for conservatives. Shanker thrived on being president of a teacher union because in so doing, he stood at the intersection of America's two grand institutions furthering democratic values: public schools and trade unions.

So it is no surprise that democratic ideals were center stage when Shanker envisioned a new kind of school, built from scratch. These new "charter schools" would essentially be a more purely democratic version of traditional public schools. If public schools did not in practice always live up to 19th-century educator Horace Mann's ideal as institutions that educated the children of the rich and poor and different races and religions side by side, integrated charter schools could go beyond neighborhood segregation to realize the concept more fully. Likewise, if unionized schools did not always tap into the knowledge, ideas, and expertise of teachers, charter schools might do so by allowing small groups of teachers to try new things. Shanker's fight for teacher voice in charter schools was connected to the idea that in democratic institutions, individuals' opinions and expertise should be valued. As institutions that empowered teachers and integrated students, charters could do in practice what even the regular public schools often failed to accomplish: create genuinely democratic environments.

City Neighbors Charter School in Baltimore is one place where Shanker's democratic vision is alive and thriving. At City Neighbors, teacher voice and student diversity are driven by a common appreciation for diverse voices. Bobbi Macdonald, the school's founder, explained that "democracy and public education" were at the heart of the founding philosophy at City Neighbors, which was heavily influenced by Dewey, Vygotsky, Piaget, and constructivist educational theory (personal communication, August 16, 2012). This pluralist approach unites City Neighbors' focus on empowering teachers and integrating students: The school community values having different strengths, talents, and voices represented among both teachers and students. Furthermore, giving teachers voice in school decisions empowers them as advocates for the needs of diverse learners. "There is a very strong teacher voice for the best interest of the kids," special education teacher Biz Manning explained (personal communication, May 30, 2013). City Neighbors operates as a vibrant democracy, where teachers are important voices in school leadership and students represent the full racial and socioeconomic diversity of their community.

TEACHING 21ST-CENTURY SKILLS: HIGH TECH HIGH

More than 2 decades after Shanker proposed charter schools, voice and diversity are also important principles in preparing students for success in a rapidly changing economy. According to the Partnership for 21st Century Skills (n.d.), a coalition of business leaders, educators, and policymakers founded in 2002, success in our evolving economy requires a combination of the "3Rs"—which they interpret broadly to include many core subjects such as reading, mathematics, science, civics, history, and foreign language—and the "4Cs": "critical thinking and problem solving; communication; collaboration; and creativity and innovation."

Socioeconomically and racially diverse schools are ideal environments for teaching the 4Cs. Different cultural and family experiences may lead to different learning styles and ideas. When students interact, they have to learn how to share their perspective, consider other points of view, work through differences, and find common ground.

Furthermore, teaching the 4Cs successfully requires teachers to build and practice these skills themselves. When teachers participate in making school decisions, they engage in collaboration, problem solving, critical thinking, and innovation. Teachers who understand these skills firsthand and use them regularly are better positioned to help students build their own toolkits of 21st-century skills.

At High Tech High, teacher voice and student diversity are both important ingredients in the school's focus on preparing students for success in college and beyond. Rob Riordan, cofounder of High Tech High, sees a strong connection between these two pillars of the school's model. "If we're asking teachers to model and foster 21st-century skills, they need to be working in a 21st-century environment," he said. Furthermore, "it's really important for teachers to be designers in addressing the diversity that is before them in their classrooms . . . to create in a classroom a community of learners." Likewise, Riordan explained, students need opportunities to interact with peers from different backgrounds in order to learn collaboration and flexibility, and to prepare them for work in diverse workplaces (personal communication, October 17, 2013).

The intersection of teacher voice and student diversity is evident in High Tech High's project-based curriculum. Art teacher Jeff Robin explained that project-based learning relies on having strong teacher voice from faculty with expertise in a variety of different fields. At the same time, this method of instruction is also built to accommodate students with diverse backgrounds, interests, and approaches to learning. "We are not making widgets," Robin said. "We are trying to expose the students to educational endeavors that appeal to them." Robin cites this intersection of "personalization, student voice and choice, and teacher ownership" as the crux of project-based learning (personal communication, October 14, 2013). Sarah Strong, a teacher at High Tech Middle, explained the connection this way: Having strong teacher voice encourages a culture of "confidence, creativity, and risk-taking" among teachers. These values are passed on to students, "who come to embrace all types of diversity—ethnic, socioeconomic, academic" (personal communication, October 14, 2013).

MOVING FORWARD: MORRIS JEFF COMMUNITY SCHOOL

Founded in 2000 and 2003, respectively, High Tech High and City Neighbors are middle-aged, as far as charter schools go. Between 1999 and 2013, the number of charter schools nationwide nearly quadrupled (NAPCS, 2013c). Now we see interest in combining teacher voice and student diversity also cropping up in newer charter schools, such as Morris Jeff Community School, a charter elementary school in New Orleans that opened in 2010. Tiana Nobile first became involved with Morris Jeff in the middle of Mardi Gras earlier that year. Nobile, a teacher at another school in New Orleans at the time, had heard about a neighborhood group opening a charter school that fall, and she volunteered to join their procession, beating a drum and handing out flyers to the crowds of parade watchers. "That was my first exposure to Morris Jeff," Nobile explained. "That's what's really exciting, because it came straight from the community" (personal communication, June 28, 2013).

Morris Jeff Community School, a charter elementary school in New Orleans' diverse Mid-City neighborhood, was the result of a multiyear grassroots campaign by neighborhood residents to create a new community school. Mid-City families were frustrated that their local elementary school, Morris F. X. Jeff Elementary School, had been shuttered after Hurricane Katrina. They hoped to start a new community-supported elementary school that would provide a diverse student body with a rigorous curriculum. Nobile signed on as one of the founding teachers and is now also copresident of the school's recently created teacher union.

In a city where schools are sharply divided racially and the teacher union was all but dissolved after Hurricane Katrina, Morris Jeff is a rare specimen: a unionized charter school that intentionally seeks a diverse student body. The school is particularly interesting for our research because student diversity and teacher voice have been important principles at the school from the beginning and are integrally related in the school's model.

As a relatively new school, Morris Jeff is still developing core features of its program. After spending 3 years building its academic program, the school was authorized as an International Baccalaureate World School in September 2013, the first elementary school in Louisiana to earn that distinction (Lingenfelter, 2013). And the school's union, Morris Jeff Association of Educators (an affiliate of the NEA), is also just getting off the ground after being formally recognized by the charter school board in May 2013. "This is new for everyone," said Patricia Perkins, the school's principal, who has worked as a teacher and administrator for almost 40 years. New Orleans school officials and residents are watching to see how this experiment turns out. "We're in a glass bubble right here," Perkins explained. "We've had a lot of eyes on our school" (personal communication, July 1, 2013).

Diversity has been part of the vision for the school since the beginning, but enrolling a diverse student body is a constant balancing act. Before opening, Morris Jeff conducted extensive student recruitment campaigns that involved volunteers "from all walks of life," according to Perkins (personal communication, July 1, 2013). The work paid off. Morris Jeff opened with a student body that was 58% low-income, 55% Black, 36% White, and 9% Hispanic, Asian, or other races/ethnicities—roughly mirroring demographics in the city (NAPCS, 2013c). Morris Jeff now enrolls most new students in preschool, which has its own mechanism for economic diversity. As part of a statewide preschool program, Morris Jeff receives state funding to enroll 40 four-year-olds who are eligible for free or reduced-price lunch in its preschool class, while a remaining 20 seats are offered to nonqualified families on a paid basis (Perkins, personal communication, July 1, 2013).

The ongoing nature of building a diverse school leads directly to Morris Jeff's emphasis on teacher voice. "[A diverse school] requires teachers who are engaged in crafting and molding that diversity because it has to be constantly tended. . . . We have to be working together," Perkins explained (personal communication, July 1, 2013). Teacher voice was a topic of discussion early in the school's planning. Some of the founding community members were originally wary of charter schools because of their national reputation as antiunion. When the steering committee decided that starting a charter school would be their best option, they were mindful about building time for collaboration into the school schedule and making sure that teachers would feel free to organize. Teacher collaboration and participation were outgrowths of the school's focus on student diversity. Rowan Shafer, a founding 4th-grade teacher and co-president of the teacher union, explained: "I don't think diversity just means different cultures but diversity of opinions and diversity of voice. And I think what made our school work from the beginning is diversity of voice" (personal communication, June 27, 2013).

The decision by teachers to form a union in 2013 was driven by a desire to make sure that the collaborative relationships established during the school's first few years will continue as the school grows. Aaron Forbes, the school's founding Spanish teacher, said that the idea of starting a teacher union grew out of teachers' conversations about collaboration. "As any organization builds up, you need more structure set in place. . . . As we were adding more and more students, more and more teachers, we were finding that we needed more opportunities to be able to get together, talk together, collaborate, share ideas" (personal communication, July 1, 2013). Teachers wanted to formalize some of the school's informal mechanisms for collaboration and communication among teachers, administrators, the board, families, and the community (Nobile, personal communication, June 28, 2013). And, as Rowan Shafer said, they believed that "teachers unions make schools better." She and other teachers observed that "when we have the time to get together as a group of professionals and share ideas, we come up with great things that help our school" (personal communication, June 27, 2013).

Teachers at Morris Jeff are also mindful of the impact that their example could have on other schools in the city. Before Hurricane Katrina, New Orleans had a thriving teacher union, the largest in the state. However, after Katrina the Orleans Parish School Board laid off all teachers in New Orleans schools and declined to bargain with the teacher union. Since then, the United Teachers of New Orleans has not formally represented any teachers, and the union is a frequent scapegoat for explaining educational woes that plagued the district for years before Katrina hit. "So there is certainly a rich history of teachers unions in the city," Shafer said. "Being the first teachers union in the city post-Katrina certainly brings a lot of that up. We stand on powerful teachers union shoulders" (personal communication, June 27, 2013).

Morris Jeff Association of Educators hopes to show that teacher unions can encourage collaboration and help fight for children. At the board meeting in which the union was officially recognized, Forbes told the board, "We are driven by two, unwavering goals: providing the highest quality education to ensure all children achieve their maximum potential and transforming the landscape for teacher organization and development in New Orleans" (quoted in "The Lens," 2013). Forbes hopes that Morris Jeff Association of Educators will serve as a model of a teacher union that "represent[s] the needs of our students. Unions are supposed to act as mechanisms that allow for collaboration between teachers, the staff, the administration, the students, the parents, the larger community. We want to get back to that" (personal communication, July 1, 2013).

Although it is too soon to weigh in on the school's overall success, Morris Jeff seems to be heading in the right direction. The student body is socioeconomically and racially diverse, teachers are actively engaged in conversations about how to improve the school, and students have shown impressive test score growth in the school's first years. Proficiency rates on state standardized tests in mathematics rose from 54% for 3rd-graders in 2011–2012 to 83% for 4th-graders the following year, with English proficiency rising from 61% to 95%, beating state and district averages (Louisiana Department of Education, 2012, 2013b). As school leaders and community members from New Orleans and beyond look at this model of voice and diversity in action, they may well see much to emulate.

CONCLUSION

For the moment, City Neighbors, High Tech High, and Morris Jeff are part of a rare breed among charter schools. To be sure, there are other charter schools that integrate students and empower teachers to different degrees. For example, Springfield Ball Charter School in Springfield, Illinois, where teachers at the school formed a union to promote voice, also has a racially and economically diverse student body, which formed quite naturally. Conversely, Community Roots Charter School in Brooklyn, New York, which is dedicated to enrolling and serving a diverse student body, promotes collaboration within grade-level teams. But it is particularly rare to find schools that are passionate and intentional about infusing both missions throughout their work.

"Whatever it takes" is a catchy philosophy of school improvement, while the blend of teacher voice and student diversity that we have dubbed "education for a 21st-century democracy" may be somewhat harder to grasp immediately. Indeed, our interviews suggest that many of the teachers and administrators at diverse schools with teacher voice had not thought much about the connections between these two elements before our discussions.

But while the first slogan, which encourages managerial freedom and sidesteps demographic concerns, has the virtue of simplicity, teacher voice and student diversity are backed by years of research. Furthermore, the democratic vision that animates these principles goes to the fundamental purpose of American public education. Like Shanker, the late Manning Marable, a historian, social critic, and fighter for racial and economic justice, saw public education as the key to creating a successful democracy:

> I believe that real academic excellence can only exist in a democracy within the framework of multicultural diversity. Indeed, our public school systems, despite their serious problems, represent one of the most important institutional safeguards for defending the principles of democracy and equality under the law. . . . Public education alone has the potential capacity for building pluralistic communities and creating a lively civic culture that promotes the fullest possible engagement and participation of all members of society. In this sense, the public school is a true laboratory for democracy. (Marable, 2002, pp. 133–134).

Students educated in diverse groups, led by teachers and administrators who themselves model democracy, have the best chance of succeeding in an evolving 21st-century society and economy.

8

Expanding the Charter School Models

We can encourage more charter schools like City Neighbors, High Tech High, and Morris Jeff, which embody the original vision of empowering teachers and desegregating students, by changing public policy and philanthropic priorities. In this final chapter, we discuss lessons gleaned from the experiences of the charter schools highlighted throughout the book as well as recommend policies and practices to encourage expansion of these models. We begin with public policies to promote schools that empower teachers, then consider those that facilitate student diversity. We also discuss how foundations might encourage these schools, and we conclude with suggestions for sharing the lessons learned at charter schools with other schools.

ENCOURAGING TEACHER VOICE IN CHARTER SCHOOLS

In an ideal world, charter school teachers would be able to choose from a variety of avenues for voice—forming their own union, joining a district union, creating a teacher co-op, or participating in collaborative governance in cooperation with administrators. However, a number of obstacles have to be overcome in order to open all of these pathways. The charter school sector can be hostile to teacher unions, and teacher unions can sometimes be unresponsive to the concerns of charter school teachers. Forming a union from scratch is labor intensive, but participating in the district union can in some cases lead to conflicting agendas. Alternative models for promoting teacher voice can be difficult to sustain and replicate.

There are a number of ways that states, districts, teacher unions, authorizers, and charter schools could help clear pathways to teacher voice in charter schools, emphasizing flexibility and multiple options.

How Can We Ensure That Charter Schools Are Open to Teacher Voice?

Charter schools have a mixed record of openness to teacher unions, which in part explains why 88% of charter schools are nonunion (NAPCS,

2011). Furthermore, forming a union at a charter school can be a complicated process, and laws differ from state to state. States, charter schools,
teacher unions, and authorizers should take the following steps to make
sure charter school teachers have the option to unionize and share their
views through other channels:

- *State charter school laws should give teachers at charter schools the
  option to bargain collectively, including joining the district teacher
  union.* Five states (Illinois, Maine, New Hampshire, Pennsylvania, and Washington State) currently bar teachers at charter
  schools from joining the district collective bargaining unit
  (NAPCS, 2013b). Forming a separate collective bargaining unit
  may afford teachers more flexibility, but it also requires more
  work to form a union from scratch. Teachers at charter schools
  should have the option to join with other teachers in their district to bargain collectively if they want.
- *State charter school laws should give charter teachers the option of
  forming their own union.* Because charter schools thrive on flexibility, being automatically involved in the district collective bargaining agreement may not always be appropriate. At the same
  time, because charter schools are usually small and therefore
  cumbersome to organize, charter school laws should provide
  teachers an automatic opportunity to vote on the creation of a
  union during the charter school's first year of operation. Instead
  of making a nonunion environment the charter school default
  option, as is usually true today, teachers would be given an affirmative choice to decide whether or not to form a union and
  could also vote again on the matter at any time.
- *Federal and state law should clarify that charter schools are covered by state public unionization laws.* Although charter schools
  usually hold themselves out as public institutions, some charters have fought union organizing drives by seeking to declare
  themselves private institutions for the purpose of labor law. Federal and state law should clarify that charter schools are public
  schools and public institutions in the eyes of the law, including
  labor law.
- *Unions should reach out to charter school teachers.* Teachers at
  charter schools may not know about the option to form a union
  or may not know how to start the process. The AFT formed the
  Alliance of Charter Teachers and Staff (AFT ACTS) to support
  union chapters in charter schools and spread information to
  other charter school teachers about unionization options. How-

ever, the AFT represents only a small fraction of all unionized charter schools (24%), while the NEA represents the majority (89%—13% are represented by both unions) (NAPCS, 2011). The NEA is reaching out to charter schools in some areas (see Walker, 2013), but there is still much ground to cover.

- *Authorizers should penalize charter school operators that engage in union busting or unfair labor practices.* Operators should be held accountable for good management, which includes using fair labor practices. For example, authorizers should intervene when charter school operators block organizing efforts or refuse to recognize a teacher union. In such cases, authorizers could put schools on probation with requirements to end unfair practices or send an arbitrator to impose a first contract. And in the most egregious cases, charter schools with records of unfair labor practices should not have their charters renewed without new provisions to ensure a fair and legal workplace. When reviewing labor practices, authorizers should consider, among other factors, school resources spent on legal fees associated with blocking a union.

- *Charter schools could appoint teacher representatives to their governing boards.* Unions are not the only way to facilitate teacher voice. When Minnesota's charter school law was first passed, it required a majority of each charter school's board to be composed of teachers employed at the school. (The law has since been relaxed to require at least one teacher on the board.) Currently, six states (Connecticut, Delaware, Hawaii, Minnesota, Nevada, and Virginia) require charter school boards to include a teacher representative, while two states (Louisiana and Missouri) forbid charter teachers from sitting on governing boards (Wohlstetter et al., 2013). Where unions do not represent charter teachers, we favor the model of reserving seats for teachers on charter school boards.

How Can We Balance Specificity with Collective Action in Charter Teacher Unions?

The chief advantage of charter schools is that they are small-scale operations where decisions are localized, but this strength can be diluted if union policies are not tailored to a specific school. Thus being a part of a district collective bargaining agreement can be a constraint on innovation in charter schools. At the same time, a central reason why unions are useful tools is that they provide strength in numbers. If charter schools organize individually, they are missing out on the benefits of joining a network of teachers that can shape education decisions both locally and nationally. Here are our recommendations for balancing these demands:

- *In cases where charter schools are bound by state law to be part of the district union, state laws should also provide that school districts and teacher unions give charter school teachers the option to negotiate a site-specific contract or memorandum of understanding (MOU).* For example, charter school teachers could vote on an agreement for a modified daily and yearly schedule or a different teacher evaluation system. Long-term agreements between charter school operators and district unions—such as the 10-year agreement on teacher salaries struck between the Baltimore Teachers Union and KIPP Baltimore (see Chapter 4)—could also add additional flexibility by eliminating the burden of yearly renegotiating.
- *Unions created to serve teachers at specific charter schools can affiliate with national and state teacher unions.* Under that arrangement, unions receive the benefits of being part of a larger advocacy group without sacrificing flexibility to operate in ways that suit their school best. All of the teacher unions at the unionized charter schools we highlighted have national affiliations with the NEA or AFT.
- *Charter school unions could strive to create "thin" contracts.* Shorter contracts can offer teachers basic protections while leaving flexibility for administrators and teachers to work together on other issues as they arise. Traditional district contracts usually specify work hours, establish a pay structure based on experience and degrees, and contain lengthy due process procedures for dismissing teachers. A thin contract, however, might refer to a "professional work day" instead of set hours, use alternative qualifications for determining salaries, and have a shortened process for dismissing teachers based on "just cause" (Russo, 2010a). A thin contract is used at some of the charter schools we highlight in this book.

How Can We Expand Alternative Models for Teacher Voice in Charter Schools?

By design, charter schools are an ideal venue for experimenting with alternative structures for promoting teacher voice other than teacher unions. There are some promising examples of charter schools run by teacher co-ops as well as schools that encourage teacher voice through school-specific structures such as a flat leadership model and designated time for collaboration. However, these models are more nuanced and fragile than a union-based approach to teacher voice. In order to expand teacher co-ops and collaborative cultures effectively, we suggest the following strategies:

- *Larger charter schools could incorporate elements of the teacher co-op model at the department level.* Since teacher co-op schools are run collaboratively, and usually by consensus, the model is naturally constrained to smaller schools where the staff is small enough to gather and make decision en masse. This model could be applied to larger schools, however, by giving grade-level teams or subject departments some of the same responsibilities and freedoms of a teacher co-op. Teachers in a department could work together to make all of the department's budget and hiring decisions, for example. A lean administrative team could help coordinate among different department co-ops.
- *Teachers at charter schools with collaborative cultures could work with a union to adopt a "thin" contract to address salaries, benefits, and due process.* While flat management structures, committee-based decision making , and reserved time for collaboration are effective ways of incorporating teacher voice into many elements of school governance, including instructional issues and hiring decisions, it is difficult to have meaningful teacher input on issues directly related to employment and compensation without a safety net. Teachers need to know that they can raise these issues without risking their job security, and even in a school with a high degree of trust and collaboration, that is difficult when teachers' only option is to approach administrators directly. However, by forming a union to address these core employment issues—leaving decisions about other school matters to the collaborative structures already in place—charter school teachers might have the best of both worlds: flexible, authentic collaboration and clear expectations around employment and compensation.

ENCOURAGING STUDENT DIVERSITY IN CHARTER SCHOOLS

In order for charter schools to be effective vehicles for integration, we need tools and incentives for promoting diverse enrollment as well as protections against choice-driven segregation. Federal, state, and local policies could do more to expand tools, incentives, and protections. Furthermore, as charter schools create strategic plans for socioeconomically and racially diverse enrollment, they need guidance about the legal options and limits placed on the consideration of race in student school assignment.

How Can We Structure School Choice to Promote Integration?

School choice has the potential to either increase or decrease socio-economic and racial integration in public schools. However, in practice, charter schools have often led to greater levels of segregation (see Chapter 3). This is consistent with the school-choice literature which finds that completely unregulated choice often exacerbates segregation (Fuller & Elmore, 1996; Wohlstetter et al., 2013). Gary Miron notes that to the extent that charter schools do not often provide an array of distinctive pedagogical approaches, parents end up choosing instead based on the socioeconomic and racial makeup of the student body (Burns, 2010). While the exceptions we discuss prove that charter schools can be used for integration, the general trend toward increased segregation with increased school choice calls for judicious policies to help avoid this outcome and encourage integration instead (see also Orfield & Frankenberg, 2013).

We think that charter schools are an important tool for integration, despite the risks posed, for several reasons. First, school choice is already a reality for most middle-class families, who often move to school districts in which high housing prices effectively exclude low-income families. According to a 2012 report from the Brookings Institution, a majority of all families already exercise some form of choice over their child's school, including 27% of families selecting their home based on access to good schools (Whitehurst, 2012). Choice is not going away for middle-class families; even if we limit public-choice options such as charter schools and magnet schools, many of these families will have the option of selecting private schools or choosing to live in attendance zones for higher-performing public schools. Our best hope of leveling the playing field is to expand public-choice options for low-income families.

Second, while we should continue to work to integrate schools across districts or regions, this is challenging work that takes time to implement. We should simultaneously pursue integration at the school level, slowly increasing the number of integrated options available to students and providing laboratories to develop best practices for diverse education that can be expanded to other schools. Creating a diverse charter school from scratch is often easier than integrating existing public schools and can be an important first step in increasing overall integration. Whereas existing high-poverty traditional public schools can be hard to integrate because they may have negative reputations that endure even as the school improves, charter schools have a chance for a fresh start. Furthermore, families, teachers, and community members that witness the success of these diverse schools can become advocates for school integration more broadly. As noted in Chapter 3, integrated charter schools in high-poverty areas could start a virtuous cycle of attracting middle-class families and encouraging greater integration in schools across a metropolitan area.

Third, the politics of choice and segregation are changing; choice and integration can be complementary goals. Past trends have generally shown choice and integration to be opposing forces, with parents selecting more segregated schools when given the choice and integration carried out through forced reassignment. But many parents now have an appetite for diverse schools, as shown by the long waitlists at the integrated charter schools highlighted in Chapter 6. Michael Petrilli, author of a book advising middle-class parents who are interested in sending their children to diverse schools, explains that an influx of young professionals in American cities has opened up new opportunities for integrated urban schools: "In almost all of our great cities you see this happening, that many Gen X parents and Millennial parents want to live in the city. Many of us grew up in the bland suburbs, we don't want that same blandness for our own kids" (Nnamdi & Petrilli, 2012; see also Petrilli, 2012). Furthermore, researchers Allison Roda and Amy Stuart Wells (2013) from Columbia University found that White, advantaged parents in New York City were interested in sending their children to diverse schools and were troubled by segregation, but they needed more quality integrated school options from which to choose. A study from the Thomas B. Fordham Institute likewise found that there is a strong core of parents for whom an integrated school is a big draw: about a fifth of all parents place learning "how to work with people from diverse backgrounds" among their top educational preferences for their children (Zeehandelaar & Winkler, 2013, p. 6).

Thoughtful choice plans can create integrated schools without limiting parent choice. In Cambridge, Massachusetts, for example, student assignment is based on parent preference and socioeconomic balance at each school. Parents rank their choices for schools, and a computer algorithm assigns students based on these preferences and a control to make sure that each school is within a certain range of socioeconomic balance. In sharp contrast with the heartbreak seen at some charter school lotteries, roughly 90% of parents in Cambridge typically receive one of their top three choices. Under controlled choice, parents in some ways have *more* choice than they would in an "uncontrolled" choice system: They are free to choose schools based on pedagogy, curriculum, extracurricular options, or even location—rather than demographics. Low-income and middle-class parents alike know that their children will not be socioeconomically isolated, regardless of which school they attend (Kahlenberg, 2001). Opening a number of diverse charter schools across a region, with lotteries weighted for diversity, could create a similar dynamic.

Fourth, the charter school community could yield powerful allies for school integration. The enormous growth of charter schools over the past 2 decades has resulted in sheer numbers and energy that are a dynamic force in shaping the direction of public education in our country. If integration advocates convince more charter school operators, educators, and families that socioeconomically and racially integrated schools can be both in-demand and effective, there could be a powerful lobby for policies that support integration in charter schools and beyond.

Given these opportunities and risks, improved federal, state, and district policies, as well as increased authorizer oversight, can help shape charter schools as a tool to help, not hurt, school integration in the following ways:

- *States should allow charter schools to enroll students from across a region.* In states where charter schools are bound by district lines or other smaller zones, new provisions for interdistrict charter schools, akin to Rhode Island's Mayoral Academies (see Chapter 6), should be an option. Likewise, when charter schools are required to give preference to applications from the surrounding neighborhood, these preferences could be capped below 100% of seats, so that charter schools may balance serving the immediate neighborhood with increasing integrated options across the region.
- *States should require that funding be provided for transportation to charter schools, at least for all low-income students.* Many state charter school laws fail to provide charter schools with funding for student transportation that is equitable to that of other public schools (see NAPCS, 2013b). Charter schools that do not provide transportation may exclude families who are unable or unwilling to provide their own transportation, a group likely to be disproportionately low-income. Providing transportation funding will remove this potential barrier as well as make it easier to use charter schools to integrate students across a region.
- *States should require that all charter schools participate in the National School Lunch Program to provide free or reduced-price*

meals to eligible students. Based on a nationally representative
sample, the federal Schools and Staffing Survey found that
17.2% of charter schools did not participate in the federal free
or reduced-price lunch programs as of 2011–2012, compared to
just 3% of traditional public schools (Bitterman, Gray, Goldring,
& Broughman, 2013). Low-income families may be deterred
from enrolling at a charter school that fails to provide free or
reduced-price meals. States should require all charter schools to
provide this important resource for needy students.

- *States and the U.S. Department of Education Office for Civil
  Rights should enforce existing state laws and federal desegregation orders that regulate charter school enrollment.* A 2009 study
  found that while 16 states had laws that permit or require charter schools to take positive steps to manage socioeconomic and
  racial/ethnic diversity, these laws are rarely enforced (Frankenberg & Siegel-Hawley, 2009). Similarly, a 2007 study found
  that state statutory language on charter school enrollment had
  no discernable effect on the student body composition at charter schools (Eckes & Trotter, 2007). States should take active
  steps to educate charter schools about the laws on student diversity and monitor schools for compliance.

- *Authorizers should require charter schools to provide recruitment
  plans detailing outreach to special education students and English
  language learners.* Proposals for new charter schools should
  include plans for how the school will specifically reach and
  serve these students, and renewal of a school's charter should
  consider evidence that the school has enrolled special education
  students and ELLs as well as provided students with appropriate
  services and supports.

- *The federal Charter Schools Program (CSP) of the Elementary
  and Secondary Education Act of 1965 should adjust competitive
  preferences to encourage integrated charter schools.* The competitive preference priority in CSP for schools that promote diversity, currently up to 4 points out of 100, should be increased to
  at least equal the weight of the priority given to schools serving
  a low-income demographic, which is currently 9 points out of
  100 (U.S. Department of Education, 2012a). And determina-
  tion of which charter schools are "high-quality," a prerequisite
  for charter expansion and replication grants, should include
  consideration of whether the school promotes diversity. (For
  technical assistance, see Mead & Green, 2012; National Coalition on School Diversity, 2011.)

- *Federal grant programs and state laws should allow charter schools to use a variety of weighted lotteries to promote integration.* Until recently, federal start-up funds and replication grants through CSP were limited to charters that use a blind lottery, with exceptions made only in cases where a weighted lottery was otherwise required by federal or state law or was used to give preference to students seeking to transfer out of a failing school (U.S. Department of Education, 2011). In January 2014, the U.S. Department of Education released new guidance allowing charter schools to give increased weight to applications from low-income or educationally disadvantaged students in their lottery. This guidance creates important new opportunities for charter schools to encourage diverse enrollment while receiving CSP funds. However, the U.S. Department of Education can and should go further to allow other types of lotteries weighted for diversity, such as those that balance low-income and middle-class enrollment based on geography and those that reserve a set portion of seats for low-income students or ELLs. Furthermore, states should specifically allow weighted lotteries designed to promote integration. Currently states have varied and often unclear policies on the legality of weighted lotteries (see NAPCS, 2013b).
- *Charter school authorizers should hold all charter schools, including high-poverty schools, accountable for results.* Authorizers could work to close failing high-poverty charter schools and apply heightened scrutiny to applications for new charter schools from operators of high-poverty schools that struggle academically.

What Is the Legal Status of Using Race in Student Assignments?

In Chapter 6, we identified a set of promising strategies for promoting diversity in charter schools: programs that appeal to a wide range of families, intentional location, targeted recruitment, and weighted lotteries. While a weighted lottery is the surest tool for guaranteeing that a school reaches its integration goals, it also requires schools to make critical decisions about the use of demographic data in enrolling a socioeconomically and racially integrated student body (Kahlenberg, 2013; also source for much of the rest of this section).

We support leading with the use of socioeconomic status rather than race/ethnicity for two reasons. First, a long line of evidence suggests that the socioeconomic mix in a school drives achievement even more than the racial mix. Research has generally found that the academic benefits of racial desegregation came not from giving African American students a chance to sit next to Whites, but from giving poor students of all races a chance to attend predominantly middle-class institutions (Kahlenberg, 2006). The well-regarded Coleman Report, for example, found that the "beneficial effect of a student body with a high proportion of White students comes not from racial composition *per se* but from the better educational background and higher educational aspirations that are, on the average, found among Whites" (Coleman et al., 1966, p. 307). More recent research confirms this notion (Kahlenberg, 2001; see also Rumberger & Palardy, 2005). Indeed, UCLA professor Gary Orfield (1978), a strong proponent of racial desegregation, notes that "educational research suggests that the basic damage inflicted by segregated education comes not from racial concentration but the concentration of children from poor families" (p. 69). Of course, schools are about much more than raising test scores, and racial integration is important to create democratic citizens who appreicate diversity. However, socioeconomic integration is worth pursuing for its own sake, not merely as a proxy for racial integration.

Second, we support socioeconomic integration because it can indirectly produce racial and ethnic diversity in a manner that is legally unassailable. Racial integration is valuable in and of itself because it shapes the kind of society we want, but using race directly is fraught with legal limitations. In 2007 the Supreme Court severely limited that option by striking down voluntary (as opposed to remedial and court-supervised) race-conscious student assignment plans in the case of *Parents Involved in Community Schools v. Seattle School District*, decided jointly with *Meredith v. Jefferson County Board of Education*. However, unlike voluntary racial integration plans, socioeconomic integration programs are on very sound legal footing. Even opponents of using race in student assignment concede that using socioeconomic status in student assignment is perfectly legal (see, e.g., Brief of Amicus Curiae, United States, 2007; Brief of Amicus Curiae, Pacific Legal Foundation, 2007).

Furthermore, while employing race is, by definition, the most efficient method of promoting racial integration, the evidence suggests that socioeconomic integration in many cases can produce a substantial racial dividend. African American and other minority students are almost three times as likely to be low-income as White students. For example, among public school students nationally in 2009, only 29% of Whites compared to 74% of African Americans and 77% of Latinos were eligible for free or reduced-price lunch (Aud, Fox, & KewalRamani, 2010). And within the universe of low-income students, poor Blacks are more than five times as likely to attend high-poverty schools as poor Whites (U.S. Department of Education, NCES, 2012d).

Given this legal and educational background, we recommend the following strategies for using demographic data to increase integration in charter schools:

- *Charter schools should be permitted to use weighted lotteries based on socioeconomic factors or geography.* Some of the charter schools we highlighted in Chapter 6 used lotteries based on income (measured using eligibility for free or reduced-price lunch) to reserve seats for low-income students. Others based lotteries on geographic preferences designed to track socioeconomic status: reserving seats for residents of public housing or seeking an even distribution of students from across an area. Charter schools could use geographic preferences in other ways as well, for example, locating in a low-income area and reserving seats for students from the neighborhood while recruiting middle-class families from other neighborhoods. In addition, schools could weight a lottery based on other socioeconomic factors, such as parents' educational background.
- *Charter schools should be permitted to monitor aggregate socioeconomic and racial/ethnic composition of their lottery pool and adjust recruitment strategies.* By looking at overall demographics of applications, charter schools can identify underrepresented populations and target recruitment of these groups. Decisions should be based on aggregate data, not individual students' race/ethnicity.

BUILDING PHILANTHROPIC SUPPORT FOR CHARTER SCHOOLS WITH STUDENT DIVERSITY AND TEACHER VOICE

In recent years philanthropic support has been a powerful force in shaping and expanding charter schools. From its founding in 2005 through 2013, the Charter School Growth Fund (n.d.) has invested more than $185 million in philanthropic funds from a variety of contributing foundations to support the growth of 40 CMOs serving 160,000 charter school students across the country. The Walton Family Foundation (2013b) spent almost $160 million in 2012 alone on education reform initiatives, the bulk of which went to support charter schools or lobby for public policies to support school choice. By comparison, the FY 2013 budget for the federal Charter Schools Program was roughly $242 million (U.S. Department of Education, 2013). Private funding for charter schools, stunningly, is on a similar scale to federal funding.

There is debate over whether or not private funding for charter schools is a positive development. Significant private funding could undermine the public purpose of charter schools, particularly if money comes with strings attached. Furthermore, it could lead to the creation of unsustainable programs that will face a crisis if and when private funding dries up. However, increased private support for public education has the potential to accomplish many good things, particularly if it steers education in a promising direction that public funding can maintain. Furthermore, since studies show that charter schools generally receive less funding per student than traditional public schools, private funding streams may, by necessity, be a more permanent fixture in the charter sector (Huerta & d'Entremont, 2010).

It is difficult to know exactly how much private funding charter schools receive. Many charter schools do not report private sources of revenue on federal surveys, and studies suggest that levels of private funding vary widely among charter schools (Miron & Urschel, 2010). Some charter schools may receive little or no private funding, but there are also CMOs that receive millions of dollars in a single year.

Many of these top recipients of private funding are charter schools that focus on serving high-poverty student bodies. According to the Million Dollar List, a project of the Lilly Family School of Philanthropy (2013) at Indiana University that tracks publicly announced gifts of $1 million or more, KIPP received more than $90 million from foundations, corporations, and private donors in 2007. Harlem Children's Zone received almost $75 million in private funding in 2010. Alliance College-Ready Public Schools (n.d.), a charter network of 22 schools in Los Angeles that serves a population that is 95% eligible for free or reduced-price lunch, received almost $50 million in 2007. In 2003 private funders gave almost $9 million to Aspire Public Schools, a CMO with schools in California and Tennessee that describes itself as "one of the nation's top-performing large school systems serving predominantly low-income students" (Aspire Public Schools, 2013). And IDEA Public Schools, a network of high-poverty, "no excuses" charter schools in Texas, received over $8 million in 2009.

There are some exceptions to this pattern. A few economically integrated charter schools have seen large philanthropic support as well: A private donor pledged $7 million to DSST Public Schools in 2011, and High Tech High received more than $7 million in private support in 2006 (Robles, 2011; Lilly Family School of Philanthropy, 2013). And while the high-poverty charter school networks highlighted in the previous paragraph are largely nonunion, Green Dot Public Schools, the unionized charter network in Los Angeles, has also received significant private support from foundations such as the Bill and Melinda Gates Foundation, the Edna McConnell Clark Foundation, the Wasserman Foundation, and the Eli and Edythe Broad Foundation, to the tune of more than $16 million in 2007 (Lilly Family School of Philanthropy, 2013).

But integrated and unionized charter schools often face an uphill battle in attracting funding from foundations. Some philanthropists may associate teacher unions with the status quo or actively oppose unionization (Gyurko, 2008). And because private funders understandably want to get the biggest bang for their buck, they may be reluctant to invest in schools where a significant portion of students come from middle-class backgrounds—instead favoring schools that serve an almost exclusively low-income population.

One exciting new development on this front comes from New Schools for New Orleans (NSNO), a nonprofit organization created in 2006 to help turn around public education in New Orleans, where as of 2013–2014 about 90% of students attend charter schools (Jindal, 2013). As one of several endeavors, NSNO uses funding from a number of private foundations as well as federal grants to support the creation and replication of successful charter schools in the city. NSNO has had a hand in launching nearly 25% of New Orleans' open-enrollment public charter schools.

In 2013 NSNO made its first large investment in a racially and socioeconomically diverse charter school, Bricolage Academy, which opened in fall 2013. Neerav Kingsland, NSNO's CEO, said that evaluating the proposal for Bricolage prompted "a reflective moment for our own organization." According to Kingsland, some people in NSNO wondered, "Why are we putting money behind this school where half the kids don't really need our money?" Others, however, took the stance that "this is innovative. This could be the future of the city, and we need not be so myopic around closing the achievement gap with no excuses charters." Ultimately, many were convinced by the argument that there is an advantage to not overwhelming a school with high-need students. "Even if you reject the idea that diversity in itself is good, there's kind of a more pragmatic level," Kingsland explained. "If you think of the difference of having 100% of your students needing 5 hours of tutoring a night (or whatever) to catch them up . . . you could make an argument that it might actually be better [to have an economically integrated school] devote a significant amount of resources to 50% of students, the low-income students" (personal communication, July 29, 2013).

Kingsland sees the funding of Bricolage as the opening of new possibilities for NSNO, and he hopes national funders will follow suit:

I definitely think national funders would be wise to be investing in this, for two reasons. . . . I think it's worth expanding this sector because I think it has strong potential to increase achievement and to create more vibrant societies where people aren't growing up in bubbles. I also think, to be honest, it's sound politics. So long as the charter world and the "KIPP-TFA [Teach for America]" world is considered something that is for poor people of a certain color, I think that limits your ability to really change the country and change the way the country educates children. (personal communication, July 29, 2013)

There are compelling social, academic, pragmatic, and political arguments for making these investments in diverse schools.

Likewise, there is a strong case for supporting unionized charter schools, in part because there are more possibilities for transferring lessons from charter schools to traditional public schools when both sectors have similar labor structures. As noted in Chapter 5, Steve Barr, founder of Green Dot Public Schools, which has attracted large philanthropic investments, explained that he chose to create a charter network with a teacher union as a form of research and development for the broader public school system (Carr & Barr, 2012). Investments in unionized charter schools may have a greater chance of "multiplying" by influencing other schools and shaping the direction of large school districts.

Foundations should consider increasing support for charter schools that build 21st-century skills and reinforce democratic values. They could diversify their philanthropic portfolios by supporting more charter schools that educate students in integrated settings and make teachers active participants in school decisions. As a starting point, we suggest several models for exploration:

- Private funders could support new schools or fund the expansion of successful charter schools that focus on student integration or teacher voice.
- Foundations could fund rigorous research on outcomes for low-income students in integrated versus high-poverty charter schools.
- Foundations could offer grants to teacher unions to strengthen charter school outreach and develop strategies for more flexible union–management relationships.

SHARING LESSONS WITH OTHER SCHOOLS

Chapters 5 and 6 reveal promising practices at charter schools for promoting teacher voice as well as for enrolling and serving diverse student bodies. While some of these strategies are specific to charter schools, many are applicable to schools across sectors. For example, district schools with diverse populations could use some of the charter schools' strategies for differentiating students without tracking, encouraging social integration, and engaging families of different backgrounds. School districts and teacher unions could embrace tools that charter school unions use to balance teacher voice with flexibility, such as "thin" contracts and site-based agreements or MOUs.

As explained in Chapter 1, Albert Shanker originally envisioned charter schools as doing just this—testing and developing new methods that could be shared with other schools. Thus far, however, charter schools and district schools have more often been engaged in competition instead of collaboration. Sharing these lessons requires building new pathways for communication:

- *District, charter, and private schools could form neighborhood partnerships.* City Neighbors Charter School, for example, is part of the Northeast Schools Alliance, a partnership among three schools in northeast Baltimore: City Neighbors, a district public school, and a private parochial school. Funded by the Baltimore-based Goldseker Foundation, the partnership facilitated joint marketing and mutually beneficial neighborhood projects and sparked a "Progressive Ed Summit." Now an annual event hosted by City Neighbors, the summit convenes teachers from district, charter, and private schools to participate in professional development, share best practices, and form new connections.
- *Charter schools could help lead districtwide reform initiatives.* E. L. Haynes Public Charter School in Washington, DC, for example, is a pioneer in charter–district collaboration. The school is leading the DC Common Core Collaborative, an initiative funded by D.C.'s Race to the Top grant that is helping teachers citywide to become effective instructors using the Common Core State Standards.
- *Foundations could give charter schools funding to develop tools for sharing their successful practices.* Educators at Community Roots Charter School, for example, are creating a guide for an antibias

teaching approach that they hope to share with other diverse schools.

- *Charter schools and graduate schools of education could form partnerships for teacher training.* Blackstone Valley Prep Mayoral Academy in Rhode Island, for example, hosts student teachers from Rhode Island College in a yearlong fellowship program that pairs them with lead teachers. As mentioned in Chapter 5, High Tech High has taken teacher training further and established its own accredited graduate school of education, enrolling not only teachers and administrators from within the network but also those from other schools, charter and noncharter.

- *State laws should not allow the creation of for-profit charter schools.* For-profit charter operators are currently allowed in more than four-fifths of states with charter laws (NAPCS, 2013b). In 2010–2011, 12.3% of charter schools across the country were operated by for-profit Education Management Organizations (NAPCS, 2013c), including nearly 80% of all charter schools in Michigan (Kain, 2011). These for-profit charter schools, particularly online schools, generally have a poor record of promoting student achievement. K12 Inc., the nation's largest for-profit online charter school operator, collects millions of dollars each year in state, local, and federal funds; spends millions in advertising; and posts miserable outcomes for students. K12's online schools have below-average proficiency rates on state standardized tests and graduation rates below 50% (Miron & Urschel, 2012).

    The very purpose of for-profit charters is to maximize profits for shareholders, capturing as many markets as possible. The ultimate success of for-profit institutions would be the elimination of public schooling. By their very nature, for-profits do not seek to collaborate and share knowledge with traditional public schools. Instead, for-profits risk tainting the entire charter school enterprise.

THE FUTURE OF TEACHER VOICE AND STUDENT DIVERSITY IN CHARTER SCHOOLS

The current thrust of the charter school sector, toward nonunion workplaces and segregated schools, is troubling for at least two reasons. First and foremost, it is bad for kids. Having vibrant teacher voice can help build a strong school climate and increase student achievement. Likewise, students in socioeconomically and racially diverse schools have shown greater academic achievement and social awareness than peers in more homogeneous settings. When schools diminish teacher voice or enroll segregated student bodies, students miss out on these important benefits.

Second, it is unimaginative. If comparing all charter schools to all district schools is "like asking whether eating out is better than eating at home" (Ted Kolderie, quoted in Hawkins, 2011), then concentrating resources into the propagation of nonunionized, segregated charter schools is like going to a buffet and only eating the dinner rolls.

Charter schools should start with big dreams, creative ideas, and experimentation—not repetition of one mediocre model. City Neighbors Charter School in Baltimore, for example, was born out of monthly discussions that founder Bobbi Macdonald hosted in her living room, where Northeast Baltimore families gathered and asked, "If we could have the best school we can imagine, what would it be?" "This chance to design a school together was just incredible," Macdonald said (personal communication, August 16, 2012). Why waste that chance by capitulating to de facto segregation and assuming all or nothing when it comes to unionization? Why not try to increase socioeconomic and racial school integration through charter schools? Why not use charter schools to rethink traditional notions of teacher voice?

Changes to federal, state, and local policy, as well as increased private support, can help encourage innovation in charter schools around these two issues. But there is room to grow even before structural changes take place. We have blueprints to follow in the form of existing charter schools that empower teachers through unions, co-ops, or collaborative cultures, as well as those that integrate students from diverse socioeconomic, racial, and ethnic backgrounds.

Albert Shanker's ideas for charter schools, formulated more than 2 decades ago, turn out to be a powerful vision for educational innovation in a new century. Charter schools can address the educational demands of a 21st-century society by giving students the chance to work with a diverse group of peers and treating teachers as 21st-century professionals engaged in collaboration, critical thinking, and problem solving. Teacher voice and student diversity, largely forgotten goals from the earliest ideas about charter schools, may hold the best hope for improving charter schools—and thereby illuminate a path for strengthening our entire system of public education.

Appendix:
Profiles of Charter Schools Featured in Chapters 5–7

LIST OF FEATURED CHARTER SCHOOLS

Charter Schools with Teacher Voice
1. Amber Charter School
2. Avalon School
3. Green Dot Public Schools
4. IDEAL School
5. Minnesota New Country School
6. Springfield Ball Charter School

Charter Schools with Teacher Voice and Intentional Student Diversity
7. City Neighbors
8. High Tech High
9. Morris Jeff Community School

Charter Schools with Intentional Student Diversity
10. Blackstone Valley Prep Mayoral Academy
11. Capital City Public Charter School
12. Community Roots Charter School
13. DSST Public Schools
14. E. L. Haynes Public Charter School
15. Larchmont Charter School

METHODOLOGY USED IN THE PROFILES

- Unless otherwise noted, all data are for 2012–2013. *Denotes 2011–2012 data.
- Low-income is defined as eligible for free or reduced-price lunch.
- In the case of charter networks, demographic and student achievement data are provided for the original school/campus, with the rationale that these flagship campuses have been operating for the longest time and thus have the best data available.

- Notes on information in student achievement data tables:
  - » **Bold** text indicates the school beats the district average for that group of students in that subject, *italics* indicates it beats the state average, and ***bold italics*** indicates it beats both the district and the state averages.
  - » Composite test data for all grades were used when possible; otherwise, the highest grade available was used, with the rationale that usually students in upper grades have spent more time at that school than those in the lower grades.
  - » When it was not possible to compare to a similar grade bracket in the state or district, we compared to all grades in the state or district.
  - » We compared school averages to averages in the state and district in which they are located. This is intended as a rough point of comparison only. In many cases the charter schools are their own Local Education Agencies, are not part of the local district, and may enroll students from outside the district boundaries. Furthermore, these rudimentary comparisons between schools, districts, and states do not control for demographic differences.
  - » Most data tables are named "% Students Proficient or Above on State Standardized Tests," but the schools located in California (#3, 8, and 15) have tables named "Academic Performance Index (API)." The State of California assigns each school, Local Education Agency, and subgroup an Academic Performance Index (API) from 200 to 1,000 to reflect the overall academic performance and growth of that group. The API is calculated using student performance data from statewide assessments across different subjects.
- Notes on sources:
  - » Much of the information for these profiles was drawn from *The Public Charter Schools Dashboard* created by the National Alliance for Public Charter Schools (2013c).
  - » Additional sources are listed at the bottom of each profile.

PROFILES OF THE CHARTER SCHOOLS

Charter Schools with Teacher Voice

---

1. Amber Charter School, New York, NY
www.ambercharter.org/

Mechanism for teacher voice: Unionized by design; founders at Amber welcomed the union. Amber teachers are part of the United Federation of Teachers (UFT), the district union for New York City Public Schools, which is affiliated with the New York State United Teachers (NYSUT), AFT, and NEA. Amber teachers have a site-specific contract.
Year opened: 2000
Number of schools: 1

Demographics and student achievement:

» *Grades served:* K–5
» *Enrollment:* 474 students
» 60.5% Hispanic
» 36.7% Black
» 1.7% Asian
» 0.8% American Indian or Alaska Native
» 0.2% Other

» 85.5% Low-income
» 7.3%* Special education (data for tested students in grades 3–5 only)
» 4%* English language learners

% Students Proficient or Above on State Standardized Tests (Grade 5)

	Math	*Reading*
All students	*78%* school*	**53%* school**
	57% NYC Geographic District 4*	**42%* NYC Geographic District 4**
	67% New York State*	**58%* New York State**
Low-income students	*78%* school*	**54%* school**
	56% NYC Geographic District 4*	**41%* NYC Geographic District 4**
	57% New York State*	**45%* New York State**

Sources: Office of Information and Reporting Services, 2012a, 2012b, 2012d; SUNY Charter Schools Institute, 2013.

---

2. Avalon School, St. Paul, MN
www.avalonschool.org/

Mechanism for teacher voice: Teacher co-op
Year opened: 2001
Number of schools: 1
Demographics and student achievement:

» *Grades served:* 7–12
» *Enrollment:* 183 students
» 71.0% White
» 13.1% Black
» 8.2% Asian
» 4.9% Hispanic
» 2.7% American Indian or Alaska Native

» 32.2% Low-income

» 31.1% Special education
» 1.1% English language learners

% Students Proficient or Above on State Standardized Tests (All Grades)

	Math	*Reading*
All students	41.0% school	58.1% school
	42.1% St. Paul Public School District	37.1% St. Paul Public School District
	60.2% Minnesota	57.6% Minnesota
Low-income students	33.3% school	39.1% school
	31.7% St. Paul Public School District	25.5% St. Paul Public School District
	41.5% Minnesota	38.8% Minnesota

Source: Minnesota Department of Education, n.d.

3. Green Dot Public Schools, Los Angeles, CA
www.greendot.org/

Mechanism for teacher voice: Unionized by design; founder Steve Barr envisioned the network as unionized from the start. Teachers at Green Dot schools are represented by the Asociación de Maestros Unidos (AMU), a union specifically for teachers in the Green Dot network that is affiliated with the California Teacher Association (CTA) and the NEA. There is one contract for all schools in the network, but the contract leaves a number of issues open, to be decided at each campus.

Year opened: 2000

Number of schools: 19 middle and high schools, including independent start-up charter schools as well as "turnarounds," district schools that Green Dot has converted to charter schools.

Demographics and student achievement for Ánimo Leadership Charter High School:

» *Grades served:* 9–12
» *Enrollment:* 616 students
» 98.9% Hispanic
» 0.8% Other
» 0.2% White
» 0.2% Black

» 92.5% Low-income
» 4.4%* Special education
» 18.4%* English language learners

Academic Performance Index (API) (All Grades)

All students	*811 school*
	749 Los Angeles Unified School District
	790 California
Low-income students	*810 school*
	731 Los Angeles Unified School District
	743 California

Sources: California Department of Education, 2013a, 2013c, 2013f, n.d.-a.

4. IDEAL School, Milwaukee, WI
www5.milwaukee.k12.wi.us/school/ideal/

Mechanism for teacher voice: Teacher co-op. The school is also unionized by state law. Teachers at IDEAL are part of the Milwaukee Teachers' Education Association (MTEA), the local district union, affiliated with the Wisconsin Education Association Council (WEAC) and NEA. Teachers at IDEAL are part of the district contract, but they have a memorandum of understanding allowing them to use a different teacher evaluation system. The status of teacher unions in Wisconsin moving forward is unclear. In 2011, Wisconsin restricted collective bargaining to the issue of wages for most public employees; however, as of 2013, legal challenges to the law continued.

Year opened: 2001
Number of schools: 1
Demographics and student achievement:

» *Grades served:* K–8
» *Enrollment:* 228 students
» 43.0% Hispanic
» 40.4% White
» 9.2% Black
» 4.8% Asian
» 2.6% American Indian or Alaska Native
»
» 71.5% Low-income
» 16.2% Special education
» 8.3% English language learners

% Students Proficient or Above on State Standardized Tests (All Grades)

	Math	*Reading*
All students	**27.7% school**	**24.4% school**
	20.5% Milwaukee Public Schools	**15.0% Milwaukee Public Schools**
	48.1% Wisconsin	**36.2% Wisconsin**

Low-income students	18.8% school	15% school
	16.4% Milwaukee Public Schools	11.0% Milwaukee Public Schools
	30.5% Wisconsin	20.9% Wisconsin

Sources: Wisconsin Department of Public Instruction, 2013, n.d.

5. Minnesota New Country School, Henderson, MN
www.newcountryschool.com/

Mechanism for teacher voice: Teacher co-op
Year opened: 1994
Number of schools: 1
Demographics and student achievement:
»   *Grades served:* 6–12 (expanding to K–12)
»   *Enrollment:* 111 students
»   87.4% White
»   6.3% Hispanic
»   3.6% Black
»   1.8% American Indian or Alaska Native
»   0.9% Asian

»   38.7% Low-income
»   34.2% Special education
»   0.0% English language learners

% Students Proficient or Above on State Standardized Tests (All Grades)

	Math	*Reading*
All students	28.8% school	**54.0% school**
	44.2% Le Sueur-Henderson School District	**46.5% Le Sueur-Henderson School District**
	60.2% Minnesota	**57.6% Minnesota**
Low-income students	26.3% school	*46.7% school*
	32.9% Le Sueur-Henderson School District	*33.9% Le Sueur-Henderson School District*
	41.5% Minnesota	*38.8% Minnesota*

Source: Minnesota Department of Education, n.d.

6. Springfield Ball Charter School, Springfield, IL
www.sps186.org/schools/ballcharter/

Mechanism for teacher voice: Unionized by teacher vote. Teachers at Springfield Ball are represented by Springfield Ball Charter School Education Association, a school-specific union that is affiliated with the Illinois Education Association (IEA) and NEA. Springfield Ball teachers have a site-specific contract.

Year opened: 1999

Number of schools: 1

Demographics and student achievement:

» *Grades served:* K–8
» *Enrollment:* 378 students
» 45.1% White
» 42.2% Black
» 3.7% Hispanic
» 0.3% Asian
» 0.3% Native Hawaiian or Alaska Native
» 8.5% Other

» 53.6% Low-income
» 16.4% Special education
» 0.5% English language learners

% Students Proficient or Above on State Standardized Tests (Grade 8)

	Math	Reading
All students	50.0% school	63.9% school
	46.9% Springfield School District	48.7% Springfield School District
	58.9% Illinois	59.8% Illinois
Low-income students	46.6% school	46.7% school
	36.1% Springfield School District	35.5% Springfield School District
	44.4% Illinois	44.8% Illinois

Source: Illinois State Board of Education, 2013.

Charter Schools with Teacher Voice and Intentional Student Diversity

7. City Neighbors, Baltimore, MD
www.cityneighborsfoundation.org/

Mechanism for teacher voice: Collaborative culture. The schools are also unionized by state law. Teachers at City Neighbors schools are part of the Baltimore Teachers Union (BTU), the district union, which is affiliated with AFT. City Neighbors teachers are part of the district contract.

Mechanism for student diversity: Intentional location in a diverse neighborhood

Year opened: 2005

Number of schools: 3 schools, spanning elementary, middle, and high school grades—City Neighbors Charter School, City Neighbors High School, and City Neighbors Hamilton.

Demographics and student achievement for City Neighbors Charter School:

» Grades served: K–8
» Enrollment: 216 students
» 53.7% Black
» 42.1% White
» 4.2% Not reported

» 41.6% Low-income
» 24.3% Special education

Per Maryland State Department of Education, data on English language learners are too small to report (fewer than 20 students in category).

% Students Proficient or Above on State Standardized Tests (All Grades)

	Math	*Reading*
All students	**64.9% school**	*87.8% school*
	58.8% Baltimore City Public Schools	*67.9% Baltimore City Public Schools*
	78.2% Maryland	*84.9% Maryland*
Low-income students	53.9% school	*84.1% school*
	56.8% Baltimore City Public Schools	*65.7% Baltimore City Public Schools*
	66.2% Maryland	*75.5% Maryland*

Sources: Maryland State Department of Education, 2013a, 2013b, 2013c, 2013d, 2013e.

---

8. High Tech High, San Diego, CA
www.hightechhigh.org/

Mechanism for teacher voice: Collaborative culture
Mechanism for student diversity: Lottery weighted by zip code, seeking an even distribution of students from across San Diego
Year opened: 2000
Number of schools: 12 elementary, middle, and high schools
Demographics and student achievement for the Gary and Jerri-Ann Jacobs High Tech High:
»   Grades served: 9–12
»   Enrollment: 578 students
»   41.3% Hispanic
»   33.0% White
»   13.3% Asian
»   10.6% Black
»   1.0% American Indian or Alaska native
»   0.5% Native Hawaiian or Other Pacific Islander
»   0.2% Other

»   45.3% Low-income
»   10.9%* Special education
»   9.8%* English language learners

Academic Performance Index (API) (All Grades)

All students	*807 school*
	810 San Diego Unified School District
	790 California
Low-income students	*777 school*
	764 San Diego Unified School District
	743 California

Sources: California Department of Education, 2013b, 2013d, 2013f, n.d.-b.

---

9. Morris Jeff Community School, New Orleans, LA
www.morrisjeffschool.org/

Mechanism for teacher voice: Unionized by teacher vote. Teachers at Morris Jeff are represented by the Morris Jeff Association of Educators, a school-specific union that is affiliated with the Louisiana Association of Educators (LEA) and NEA. The union was formed in 2013, and as of 2014 teachers were beginning the collective bargaining process. Morris Jeff teachers will have a site-specific contract.

Mechanism for student diversity: Two-thirds of pre-K seats are available to low-income students free of charge, while one-third are open to families paying pre-K tuition. (All other grades have no tuition, but Louisiana only funds pre-K for low-income families.) The school also uses targeted recruitment and intentional location in a diverse neighborhood.

Year opened: 2010

Number of schools: 1

Demographics and student achievement:

» *Grades served:* pre-K–4 (growing to pre-K–8)
» *Enrollment:* 302 students

Note: Due to student privacy concerns, Louisiana does not release *exact* demographic data.

» ≥49.7% Black
» ≥36.4% White
» ≥3.3% Hispanic
» <3.3% Asian
» <3.3% American Indian or Alaska Native
» <3.3% Native Hawaiian or Other Pacific Islander
» <3.3% Other

» 60.9% Low-income
» <5% English language learners

Data on special education students were not available.

% Students Proficient or Above on State Standardized Tests (Grade 4)

	Math	*Reading*
All students	*83% school*	*95% school*
	63% Recovery School District-New Orleans	*65% Recovery School District-New Orleans*
	71% Louisiana	*77% Louisiana*

Note: Data on low-income students were not available.

Sources: Louisiana Department of Education, 2013a, 2013b.

Charter Schools with Intentional Student Diversity

10. Blackstone Valley Prep Mayoral Academy,
Cumberland and Lincoln, RI
www.blackstonevalleyprep.org/

Mechanism for student diversity: Lottery weighted by income; intentional regional location, enrolling from both lower- and higher-income communities

Year opened: 2009

Number of schools: 3 schools: 2 elementary and 1 middle. A high school is planned to open in fall 2014.

Demographics and student achievement for Blackstone Valley Prep Elementary School 1:
- » *Grades served:* K–4
- » *Enrollment:* 327 students
- » 43.1% White
- » 42.2% Hispanic
- » 7.3% Black
- » 2.8% Asian
- » 0.3% American Indian or Alaska Native
- » 4.3% Other

- » 63.9% Low-income
- » 9.8% Special education
- » 11.0% English language learners

% Students Proficient or Above on State Standardized Tests (Grade 3)

	Math	Reading
All students	80% school	79% school
	73% **Cumberland School District**	87% Cumberland School District
	60% **Rhode Island**	70% Rhode Island
Low-income students	72% school	75% school
	55% **Cumberland School District**	74% **Cumberland School District**
	44% **Rhode Island**	57% **Rhode Island**

Sources: New England Common Assessment Program, 2012a, 2012b; Rhode Island Department of Elementary and Secondary Education Information Services, n.d.

11. Capital City Public Charter School, Washington, DC
www.ccpcs.org/

Mechanism for student diversity: Targeted recruitment; intentional location in a diverse neighborhood
Year opened: 2000
Number of schools: 1
Demographics and student achievement:
- » *Grades served:* pre-K–12
- » *Enrollment:* 636* students
- » 47%* Hispanic
- » 35%* Black
- » 13%* White
- » 5%* Asian

» 62%* Low-income
» 17%* Special education
» 21%* English language learners

% Students Proficient or Above on State Standardized Tests (All Grades)

	Math	*Reading*
All students	51.2% school	*60.8% school*
	49.5% DC Public Schools (noncharter)	*47.4% DC Public Schools (noncharter)*
	53.0% all DC district and charter schools	*49.5% all DC district and charter schools*
Low-income students	44.6% school	*56.5% school*
	40.4% DC Public Schools (noncharter)	*37.6% DC Public Schools (noncharter)*
	46.2% all DC district and charter schools	*42.0% all DC district and charter schools*

Sources: District of Columbia Public Schools, 2013; District of Columbia Office of the State Superintendent of Education, 2013; Friends of Choice in Urban Schools, n.d.; Capital City Public Charter School, 2012.

---

12. Community Roots Charter School, Brooklyn, NY
www.communityroots.org/

Mechanism for student diversity: Lottery weighted by geography, reserving seats for residents of nearby public housing complexes; intentional location in a diverse neighborhood
Year opened: 2006
Number of schools: 1 school on two campuses (elementary and middle)
Demographics and student achievement:
» *Grades served:* K–6 (growing to K–8)
» *Enrollment:* 352 students
» 42.6% White
» 37.5% Black
» 10.5% Hispanic
» 3.1% Asian
» 6.3% Other

» 26.8%* Low-income
» 20.4%* Special education (data for tested students in grades 3–5 only)
» 1%* English language learners

% Students Proficient or Above on State Standardized Tests (Grade 5)

	Math	Reading
All students	66%* school	72%* school
	61%* NYC Geographic District 13	52%* NYC Geographic District 13
	67%* New York State	58%* New York State
Low-income students	53%* school	53%* school
	57%* NYC Geographic District 13	47%* NYC Geographic District 13
	57%* New York State	45%* New York State

Sources: Office of Information and Reporting Services, 2012a, 2012c, 2012e

13. DSST Public Schools, Denver, CO
dsstpublicschools.org/

Mechanism for student diversity: Lotteries weighted by income or geography (varies by campus)
Year opened: 2004
Number of schools: 7 middle and high schools
Demographics and student achievement for DSST: Stapleton High School:
»   *Grades served:* 9–12
»   *Enrollment:* 508 students
»   34.8% Hispanic
»   27.6% White
»   26.2% Black
»   3.0% Asian
»   0.8% American Indian or Alaska Native

»   7.7% Other
»   45.3% Low-income
»   3.0% Special education
»   9.5% English language learners

% Students Proficient or Above on State Standardized Tests (Grades 9 & 10)

	Math	Reading
All students	74.3% school	88.5% school
	25.7% Denver Public Schools	54.6% Denver Public Schools
	36.5% Colorado	68.7% Colorado

Low-income students	*67.1% school*	*83.6% school*
	16.4% Denver Public Schools	*44.9% Denver Public Schools*
	18.5% Colorado	*52.0% Colorado*

Source: Colorado Department of Education, 2013b.

14. E. L. Haynes Public Charter School, Washington, DC
www.elhaynes.org/

Mechanism for student diversity: Targeted recruitment; intentional location in a diverse neighborhood
Year opened: 2004
Number of schools: 1 school across 2 campuses
Demographics and student achievement:
»   *Grades served:* pre-K–9* (growing to pre-K–12)
»   *Enrollment:* 800* students
»   53%* Black
»   31%* Hispanic
»   14%* White
»   2%* Asian
»   1%* Other

»   59%* Low-income
»   17%* Special education
»   22%* English language learners

% Students Proficient or Above on State Standardized Tests (All Grades)

	Math	*Reading*
All students	*60.1% school*	*59.9% school*
	49.5% DC Public Schools (non-charter)	*47.4% DC Public Schools (non-charter)*
	53.0% all DC district and charter schools	*49.5% all DC district and charter schools*
Low-income students	*55.9% school*	*53.8% school*
	40.4% DC Public Schools (non-charter)	*37.6% DC Public Schools (non-charter)*
	46.2% all DC district and charter schools	*42.0% all DC district and charter schools*

Sources: District of Columbia Public Schools, 2013; District of Columbia Office of the State Superintendent of Education, 2013; Friends of Choice in Urban Schools, n.d.; E. L. Haynes Public Charter School, 2012.

15. Larchmont Charter School, Los Angeles, CA
www.larchmontcharter.org/

Mechanism for student diversity: Lottery weighted by income; targeted recruitment; intentional location in a diverse neighborhood
Year opened: 2005
Number of schools: 1 school spread across 4 campuses.
Demographics and student achievement:
» *Grades served:* K–9 (growing to K–12)
» *Enrollment:* 679 students
» 46.1% White
» 22.7% Hispanic
» 22.1% Asian
» 8.2% Black
» 0.4% American Indian or Alaska Native
» 0.4% Other

» 39.0% Low-income
» 9.4%* Special education
» 8.9%* English language learners

Academic Performance Index (API) (All Grades)

All students	*909 school*
	749 Los Angeles Unified School District
	790 California
Low-income students	*860 school*
	731 Los Angeles Unified School District
	743 California

Sources: California Department of Education, 2013a, 2013e, 2013f, n.d.-c.

References

Abdulkadiroglu, A., Angrist, J. Cohodes, S., Dynarski, S., Fullerton, J. Kane, T., & Pathak, P. (2009). *Informing the debate: Comparing Boston's charter, pilot, and traditional schools.* Boston, MA: Boston Foundation.

Ackerman, S. (2013, August 19). States continue increasing or eliminating caps on charter schools. *redefineED.* Retrieved from www.redefinedonline.org/2013/08/states-continue-increasing-or-eliminating-caps-on-charter-schools/

Alliance College-Ready Public Schools. (n.d.). About us: Overview. Retrieved October 23, 2013, from www.laalliance.org/apps/pages/index.jsp?uREC_ID=46278&type=d&pREC_ID=214223

Amber Charter School. (2011, January 14). Grants. Retrieved from www.ambercharter.org/resources/awards/grants-awarded

Amber Charter School. (2012, November 14). *By-laws of Amber Charter School.* Retrieved from www.ambercharter.org/www/ambercharter/site/hosting/Board%20Meetings/By-Laws%20of%20Amber%20Charter%20School%20as%20of%2011.14.12.pdf

Amber Charter School & United Federation of Teachers (UFT). (2010). *Amber Charter School and UFT collective bargaining agreement, September 1, 2010–August 31, 2012.* (Available from Amber Charter School, 220 E. 106th S., New York, NY 10029)

Anderson, A. B., & DeCesare, D. (2006, September 18). *Opening closed doors: Lessons from Colorado's first independent charter school.* Denver, CO: Augenblick, Palaich and Associates, Donnell-Kay Foundation, and Piton Foundation.

Anderson, J., Hollinger, D., & Conaty, J. (1992). *Poverty and achievement: Re-examining the relationship between school poverty and student achievement—an examination of eighth-grade student achievement using the National Educational Longitudinal Study of 1988.* Washington, DC: U.S. Department of Education.

Anderson, N. (2010a, January 30). Education secretary calls Katrina good for New Orleans schools. *The Washington Post.* Retrieved from articles.washingtonpost.com/2010-01-30/news/36899661_1_recovery-school-district-paul-g-vallas-paul-pastorek

Anderson, N. (2010b, February 4). Charter schools becoming less racially diverse, study finds. *The Washington Post,* p. A7.

Anrig, G. (2013). *Beyond the education wars: Evidence that collaboration builds effective schools.* New York, NY: Century Foundation Press. Retrieved from tcf.org/bookstore/detail/beyond-the-education-wars

Antonio, A. L., Chang, M. J., Hakuta, K., Kenny, D. A., Levin, S., & Milem, J. F. (2004). Effects of racial diversity on complex thinking in college students. *Psychological Science, 15*(8), 507–510.

Armor, D. (1995). *Forced justice: School desegregation and the law.* New York, NY: Oxford University Press.

Arroyo, C. (2008). *The funding gap.* Washington, DC: Education Trust.

ASPIRA Inc. of Pennsylvania. (n.d.) *About us.* Retrieved November 22, 2013, from aspirapa.org/about-us/#our-mission/

ASPIRA VOCES, Philadelphia ACSE. (2013, August 21). *ASPIRA "Back to School" rally* [Video]. Retrieved from aspiravoces.org/post/58912554483/a-week-before-they-returned-to-school-aspira

Aspire Public Schools. (2013). Approach: Results. Retrieved March 11, 2014, from aspirepublicschools.org/approach/results/

Associated Press. (2011, February 13). Students call for preservation of 1955 sit-in site. *The Star Democrat.* Retrieved from www.stardem.com/article_568509b2-99c0-54fe-951d-5fb263d685b3.html

Aud, S., Fox, M. A., & KewalRamani, A. (2010, July). *Status and trends in the education of racial and ethnic groups.* Washington, DC: U.S. Department of Education, Institute of Education Sciences, National Center for Education Statistics.

Aud, S., Hussar, W., Johnson, F., Kena, G., Roth, E., Manning, E., . . . Zhang, J. (2012, May). *The condition of education 2012.* Washington, DC: U.S. Department of Education, Institute of Education Sciences, National Center for Education Statistics.

Avalon School. (2013, October 4). Avalon wins national award! Retrieved from www.avalonschool.org/2013/10/avalon-wins-national-award/

Bailey, M., Harr, J., & Cooper, B. S. (2008). *The start-up of religious charter schools: Implications for privatization and choice in U.S. education.* New York, NY: National Center for the Study of Privatization in Education.

Balfanz, R., & Legters, N. (2004, September). *Locating the dropout crisis.* Baltimore, MD: Center for Research on the Education of Students Placed At Risk, Johns Hopkins University.

Ball Foundation. (2012). History of education initiatives. Retrieved from www.ballfoundation.org/ei/history.html

Bank Street College of Education. (n.d.). 2013 alumni award winners. Retrieved October 5, 2013, from bankstreet.edu/alumni/graduate-school-alumni/2013-alumni-award-winners/

Barnes, G., Crowe, E., & Schaefer, B. (2007). *The cost of teacher turnover in five school districts: A pilot study.* Washington, DC: National Commission on Teaching and America's Future.

Basford, L. (2010). From mainstream to East African charter: Cultural and religious experiences of Somali youth in U.S. schools. *Journal of School Choice, 4*(4), 485–509.

Basile, M. (2010, July 5). *False impression: How a widely cited study vastly overstates the benefits of charter schools.* Washington, DC: The Century Foundation and Economic Policy Institute.

Bayer, H. (2013, October 11). Is school segregation still a problem? [Web log post]. *StudentsFirst.* Retrieved from www.studentsfirst.org/blog/entry/is-school-segregation-still-a-problem

Beauprez, J. (2002, September 8). High-tech charter school set for Stapleton. *The Denver Post,* special section, p. K-05. Retrieved from LexisNexis Academic database.

Beck, M. (2013, January 7). Ball Charter parents object to proposed middle-school cutback. *The State Journal-Register.* Retrieved from www.sj-r.com/breaking/x1665858848/Ball-Charter-parents-object-to-proposed-middle-school-cutback

Berends, M., & Peñaloza, R. (2010). Increasing racial isolation and test score gaps in mathematics: A 30-year perspective. *Teachers College Record, 112*(4), 978–1007.

Betts, J. R., & Tang, E. Y. (2011, October). *The effects of charter schools on student achievement: A meta-analysis of the literature.* Seattle: National Charter School Research Project, Center on Reinventing Public Education, University of Washington, Bothell.

Bifulco, R., Cobb, C. D., & Bell, C. (2009). Can interdistrict choice boost student achievement? The case of Connecticut's interdistrict magnet school program. *Educational Evaluation and Policy Analysis, 31*(4), 323–345.

Bifulco, R., & Ladd, H. F. (2006). Institutional change and coproduction of public services: The effect of charter schools on parental involvement. *Journal of Public Administration Research and Theory, 16*(4), 553–576.

Bifulco, R., & Ladd, H. F. (2007). School choice, racial segregation, and test-score gaps: Evidence from North Carolina's charter school program. *Journal of Policy Analysis and Management, 26*(1), 31–56.

Bitterman, A., Gray, L., Goldring, R., & Broughman, S. (2013, August). *Characteristics of public and private elementary and secondary schools in the United States: Results from the 2011–12 Schools and Staffing Survey.* Washington, DC: U.S. Department of Education, Institute of Education Sciences, National Center for Education Statistics.

Blackburn, B. (2011, April 6). New Jersey Governor Chris Christie calls his state's teachers union "political thugs." *ABC News.* Retrieved from abcnews.go.com/Politics/jersey-governor-chris-christie-calls-teachers-union-political/story?id=13310446

Blumgart, J. (2013, June 27). Back to school for labor. *The American Prospect.* Retrieved from prospect.org/article/back-school-labor

Borman, G. D., & Dowling, M. (2010). Schools and inequality: A multilevel analysis of Coleman's Equality of Educational Opportunity data. *Teachers College Record, 112*(5), 1201–1246.

Bowie, L. (2011, March 16). KIPP, teachers union reach 10-year agreement. *The Baltimore Sun.* Retrieved from articles.baltimoresun.com/2011-03-16/news/bs-md-ci-kipp-union-agreement-20110316_1_kipp-teachers-marietta-english-baltimore-teachers-union

Brewer, D. J., & Ahn, J. (2010). What do we know about teachers in charter schools? In J. R. Betts & P. T. Hill (Eds.), *Taking measure of charter schools: Better assessments, better policymaking, better schools.* Lanham, MD: Rowman & Littlefield Education.

Brewer, D. J., Rees, D. I., & Argys, L. M. (1995). Detracking America's schools: The reform without cost? *Phi Delta Kappan 77*(3), 210–212, 214–215.

Brief of Amicus Curiae Pacific Legal Foundation, et al., Meredith v. Jefferson County Board of Education 551 U.S. 701 (2007) (No. 05-915).

Brief of Amicus Curiae United States, Parents Involved in Community Schools v. Seattle School District No. 1, 551 U.S. 701 (2007) (No 05-908).

Brief of Amicus Curiae 553 Social Scientists, Parents Involved v. Seattle School District 551 U.S. 701 (2007) (No. 05-908).

Brill, S. (2011). *Class warfare: Inside the fight to fix America's schools.* New York, NY: Simon & Schuster.

Brinson, D., Boast, L., Hassel, B. C., & Kingsland, N. (2012, January). *New Orleans-style education reform: A guide for cities. Lessons learned, 2004–2010.* New Orleans, LA: New Schools for New Orleans. Retrieved from www.newschoolsforneworleans.org/documents/03012012NOLAstylereform.pdf

The Broad Foundation: Education. (n.d.). Mission and overview. Retrieved November 21, 2013, from broadeducation.org/about/overview.html

Brooks, D. (2009, May 8). The Harlem miracle. *New York Times,* p. A31.

Brown, E. (2013, February 6). D.C. charter school enrollment outpaces that of DCPS. *The Washington Post.* Retrieved from articles.washingtonpost.com/2013-02-06/local/36942662_1_charter-school-enrollment-enrollment-figures-school-closures

Brown v. Board of Education, 347 U.S. 483 (1954).

Bryk, A. S., Sebring, P. B., Allensworth, E., Luppescu, S., & Easton, J. Q. (2010). *Organizing schools for improvement: Lessons from Chicago.* Chicago, IL: University of Chicago Press.

Budde, R. (1988). *Education by charter: Restructuring school districts.* Andover, MA: Regional Laboratory for Educational Improvement of the Northeast & Islands.

Burian-Fitzgerald, M. (2005). *Average teacher salaries and returns to experience in charter schools* (Occasional Paper No. 101). New York, NY: National Center for the Study of Privatization in Education.

Burian-Fitzgerald, M., & Harris, D. (2004). *Teacher recruitment and teacher quality? Are charter schools different?* (Policy Report No. 20). East Lansing: Education Policy Center, Michigan State University.

Burns, M. (2010, November 28). Are charter schools a choice for segregation? (includes an interview with Erica Frankenberg and Gary Miron by *Miller-McCune*). *Pacific Standard.* Retrieved from www.psmag.com/culture-society/are-charter-schools-a-choice-for-segregation-25575/

Burris, C. C., Wiley, E. W., Welner, K. G., & Murphy, J. (2008). Accountability, rigor, and detracking: Achievement effects of embracing a challenging curriculum as a universal good for all students. *Teachers College Record, 110*(3), 571–608.

Bushaw, W. J., & Lopez, S. J. (2013). Which way do we go? The 45th annual PDK/Gallup poll of the public's attitudes toward the public schools. *Phi Delta Kappan, 95*(1), 9–25.

California Department of Education. (2013a, September 19). 2012–13 Accountability Progress Reporting (APR). Local Educational Agency (LEA) report. Growth API. Los Angeles Unified. Retrieved November 1, 2013, from api.cde.ca.gov/Acnt2013/2013GrowthDstApi.aspx?allcds=1964733

California Department of Education. (2013b, September 19). *2012–13 Accountability Progress Reporting* (APR). Local Educational Agency (LEA) report. Growth API. San Diego Unified. Retrieved November 1, 2013, from api.cde.ca.gov/Acnt2013/2013GrowthDstApi.aspx?cYear=&allcds=3768338&cChoice=2013GDst2

California Department of Education. (2013c, September 19). *2012–13 Accountability Progress Reporting (APR). School report—API growth and targets met. Animo Leadership High.* Retrieved November 1, 2013, from api.cde.ca.gov/

Acnt2013/2013GrowthSch.aspx?allcds=19647091996313

California Department of Education. (2013d, September 19). *2012–13 Account-ability Progress Reporting (APR). School report—API growth and targets met. High Tech High.* Retrieved November 1, 2013, from api.cde.ca.gov/Acnt2013/2013GrowthSch.aspx?allcds=37683383731247

California Department of Education. (2013e, September 19). *2012–13 Account-ability Progress Reporting (APR). School report—API growth and targets met. Larchmont Charter.* Retrieved November 1, 2013, from api.cde.ca.gov/Acnt2013/2013GrowthSch.aspx?allcds=19-64733-0108928

California Department of Education. (2013f, September 19). *2012–13 Accountabil-ity Progress Reporting (APR). State report—growth API.* Retrieved November 1, 2013, from api.cde.ca.gov/Acnt2013/2013GrthStAPI.aspx

California Department of Education. (n.d.-a) *Executive Summary School Accountabil-ity Report Card, 2011–12, for Animo Leadership Charter High School.* Retrieved from www.greendot.org/uploaded/uploads/SARC/SARC_LEA.pdf

California Department of Education. (n.d.-b) *Executive Summary School Accountabil-ity Report Card, 2011–12, for High Tech High.* Retrieved from www.hightech-high.org/schools/SARC/2011-12/finalSARCHighTechHigh1112English.pdf

California Department of Education. (n.d.-c) *Executive Summary School Accountabil-ity Report Card, 2011–12, for Larchmont Charter School.* Retrieved from www.larchmontcharter.org/_literature_120975/11-12_LCS_SARC

Cannata, M. (2008). *Teacher qualifications and work environments across school types.* Tempe, AZ: Education Policy Research Unit, Education Public Interest Center.

Capital City Public Charter School. (2012). *Capital City Public Charter School An-nual Report, 2011–2012.* Retrieved from www.dcpcsb.org/data/files/annual_reports%202011-12/2011-2012_annual_report_(5w4)(capitacitypcs).pdf

Capital City Public Charter School. (n.d.) About. Retrieved February 13, 2014, from www.ccpcs.org/about/

Carini, R. M. (2002). Teachers unions and student achievement. In A. Molnar (Ed.), *School reform proposals: The research evidence* (pp. 197–215). Greenwich, CT: In-formation Age.

Carini, R. M. (2008). Is collective bargaining detrimental to student achievement? Evidence from a national study. *Journal of Collective Negotiations, 32*(3), 215–235.

Carr, S., & Barr, S. (2012, April 3). Q&A with Steve Barr: Lessons from charter schools in L.A. and New Orleans. *The Hechinger Report.* Retrieved from hech-ingerreport.org/content/qa-with-steve-barr-lessons-from-charter-schools-in-l-a-and-new-orleans_8236/

Casey, L. (2006). The educational value of democratic voice: A defense of collective bargaining in American education. In J. Hannaway & A. J. Rotherham (Eds.), *Collective bargaining in education: Negotiating change in today's schools* (pp. 181–201). Cambridge, MA: Harvard Education Press.

Casey, L. (2009, April 6). Testimony of Leo Casey, before New York City Council Education Committee. *United Federation of Teachers.* Retrieved from www.uft.org/testimony/testimony-charter-schools

Cashin, S. (2004). *The failures of integration: How race and class are undermining the American Dream.* New York, NY: PublicAffairs.

Center for Research on Education Outcomes at Stanford University (CREDO) (2009). *Multiple choice: Charter performance in 16 states.* Stanford, CA: Author.

Center for Research on Education Outcomes at Stanford University (CREDO). (2013a, February 28). *Charter school performance in Massachusetts.* Stanford, CA: Author.

Center for Research on Education Outcomes at Stanford University (CREDO). (2013b, August 8). *Charter school performance in Louisiana.* Stanford, CA: Author.

Cesar Chavez Public Charter Schools for Public Policy. (n.d.). Mission|Vision |Approach|Values. Retrieved August 27, 2013, from www.chavezschools.org/apps/pages/index.jsp?uREC_ID=124179&type=d&pREC_ID=246049&hideMenu=1

Charter School Growth Fund. (n.d.). Overview. Retrieved October 23, 2013, from chartergrowthfund.org/who-we-are/overview/

Chiappetta, J. (2012, November 30). The diverse schools dilemma: Book review [Web log post]. *BVP Musings.* Retrieved from bvprep.blogspot.com/2012/11/the-diverse-schools-dilemma-book-review.html

Chingos, M. M., & Peterson, P. E. (2011). It's easier to pick a good teacher than to train one: Familiar and new results on the correlates of teacher effectiveness. *Economics of Education Review, 30,* 449–465.

City Neighbors Charter School. (n.d.). Recognitions. Retrieved October 5, 2013, from www.cityneighbors.org/?q=Recognitions

Clotfelter, C. T., Ladd, H. F., & Vigdor, J. L. (2013, January 16). *Racial and economic diversity in North Carolina's schools: An update* (Sanford Working Paper No. SAN13-01). Durham, NC: Sanford School of Public Policy, Duke University.

Cohodes, S. R., Setren, E. M., Walters, C. D., Angrist, J. D., & Pathak, P. A. (2013). *Charter school demand and effectiveness: A Boston update.* Boston, MA: The Boston Foundation and NewSchools Venture Fund.

Coleman, J. S., Campbell, E. Q., Hobson, C. J., McPartland, J., Mood, A. M., Weinfeld, F. D., & York, R. L. (1966). *Equality of educational opportunity.* Washington, DC: U.S. Department of Health, Education, and Welfare, Office of Education, National Center for Education Statistics.

CollegeBoard Advocacy & EducationCounsel. (2009, November). *Access and diversity toolkit: A resource for higher education professionals.* Washington, DC: Authors.

Colorado Department of Education. (2012). *School performance framework 2012: DSST: Cole.* Retrieved from cedar2.cde.state.co.us/documents/SPF2012/0880%20-%202223%20-%201%20Year.pdf

Colorado Department of Education. (2013a). *School performance framework 2012–2013: SPF rating and indicator summary report.* Retrieved from spf.dpsk12.org/documents/current/1SPF_summary_traditional.pdf

Colorado Department of Education. (2013b). *The SchoolView Data Center.* Retrieved from www.schoolview.org/performance.asp

Comfort v. Lynn School Committee, 283 F. Supp. 2d 328, 357 (D. Mass. 2003).

Cookson, P. W., & Berger, K. (2002). *Expect miracles: Charter schools and the politics of hope and despair.* Boulder, CO: Westview Press.

Corson, R. (1998, July). Le Sueur-Henderson: Minnesota New Country School. *The American Prospect,* p. 56. Retrieved from prospect.org/node/189089

Cowen, J. M., & Winters, M. A. (2013). Do charters retain teachers differently? Evidence from elementary schools in Florida. *Education Finance and Policy,* 8(1), 14–42.

Crain, R. L., & Mahard, R. (1977). *Desegregation and Black achievement.* Santa Monica, CA: Rand Corporation.

Cramer, P. (2013, November 6). After restructuring its charter school, UFT reassures families. *Chalkbeat: New York.* Retrieved from ny.chalkbeat.org/2013/11/06/after-restructuring-its-charter-school-uft-reassures-families/

Cremata, E., Davis, D., Cickey, K., Lawyer, K., Negassi, Y., Raymond, M. E., & Woodworth, J. L. (2013). *National charter school study 2013.* Stanford, CA: Center for Research on Education Outcomes at Stanford University.

Cromida, R. (2012, May 16). High-needs enrollment targets could challenge some charters. *Chalkbeat: New York.* Retrieved from ny.chalkbeat.org/2012/05/16/high-needs-enrollment-targets-could-challenge-some-charters/

Dann, T. (2012, June 13). Family [Web log post]. *Great Big Blog.* Washington, DC: 50CAN. Retrieved from www.50can.org/what-we-do/blog/family

Darling-Hammond, L. (1997, November). *Doing what matters most: Investing in quality teaching.* New York, NY: National Commission on Teaching and America's Future.

Di Carlo, M. (2013, July 1). A few points about the new CREDO charter school analysis [Web log post]. *Shanker Blog.* Retrieved from shankerblog.org/?p=8579

Dillon, S. (2010, August 5). Education department deals out big awards. *New York Times.* Retrieved from www.nytimes.com/2010/08/05/education/05grants.html?_r=0

Dinkes, R., Cataldi, E. F., & Lin-Kelly, W. (2007 December). *Indicators of school crime and safety: 2007.* Washington, DC: U.S. Department of Education, Institute of Education Sciences, National Center for Education Statistics, and U.S. Department of Justice, Office of Justice Programs, Bureau of Justice Statistics.

Dinkes, R., Cataldi, E. F., & Lin-Kelly, W. (2008, December). *Indicators of school crime and safety: 2008.* Washington, DC: U.S. Department of Education, Institute of Education Sciences, National Center for Education Statistics, and U.S. Department of Justice, Office of Justice Programs, Bureau of Justice Statistics.

District of Columbia Office of the State Superintendent of Education. (2013, July 30). *2013 DC Comprehensive Assessment System Results.* Retrieved from osse.dc.gov/sites/default/files/dc/sites/osse/publication/attachments/OSSE%20Presentation%202013%20DC%20CAS%20Results%20(Statewide).pdf

District of Columbia Public Charter School Board. (2012). Latin American Montessori Bilingual PCS: 2012 school performance report. Retrieved from www.dcpubliccharter.com/data/images/093-lamb_es11-12.pdf

District of Columbia Public Schools. (2013, July). *DC CAS 2013 Results.* Retrieved from dcps.dc.gov/DCPS/Files/downloads/ABOUT%20DCPS/Announcements/2013%20DC%20CAS%20Presentation-Final.pdf

DSST Public Schools. (n.d.). Stapleton High School. Retrieved February 13, 2014, from dsstpublicschools.org/campuses/dsst-stapleton-high-school/

Duncan, A. (2009a, March 10). *Secretary of Education Arne Duncan is interviewed on CNN's "The Situation Room."* CQ Transcriptions, LLC. [Television transcript]. Retrieved from political-transcript-wire.vlex.com/vid/arne-duncan-interviewed-cnn-situation-66289658.

Duncan, A. (2009b, March 11). *The Charlie Rose Show: Education secretary wants to challenge status quo/[Interviewer: Charlie Rose].* CQ Transcriptions, LLC. [Television transcript]. Retrieved from LexisNexis Academic database.

Duncan, A. (2009c, April 30). *Partners in truth-telling: Secretary Arne Duncan's remarks to the Education Writers Association.* Washington, DC: U.S. Department of Education. Retrieved from www.ed.gov/news/speeches/partners-truth-telling

Duncan, A. (2009d, June 22). *Turning around the bottom five percent: Secretary Arne Duncan's remarks at the National Alliance for Public Charter Schools Conference* [Transcript]. Washington, DC: U.S. Department of Education. Retrieved from www2.ed.gov/news/speeches/2009/06/06222009.html

Dyslin, A. (2012, June 4). Local charter schools' enrollment steady. *The Mankato Free Press.* Retrieved from LexisNexis Academic database.

E. L. Haynes Public Charter School. (2012). *E. L. Haynes Public Charter School Annual Report: Georgia Avenue Campus, School Year 2011-2012.* Retrieved from www.dcpcsb.org/data/files/annual_reports%202011-12/2011-2012_annual_report_(pt1)(914)(elhaynespcs).pdf

E. L. Haynes Public Charter School. (n.d.). Awards and accomplishments. Retrieved February 13, 2014, from www.elhaynes.org/celebrate-awards.php

Eaton, S. (2006). *The children in room E4: American education on trial.* Chapel Hill, NC: Algonquin Books of Chapel Hill.

Eckes, S. E., & Trotter, A. E. (2007). Are charter schools using recruitment strategies to increase student body diversity? *Education and Urban Society, 40,* 62–90.

Education Commission of the States. (2013). School or student preference. *ECS state notes.* Retrieved April 29, 2014, from mb2.ecs.org/reports/Report.aspx?id=79

Education Evolving. (n.d.). *National inventory of schools with collective teacher autonomy.* Retrieved September 11, 2013, from www.educationevolving.org/teachers/inventory/table

Education Evolving & Widmeyer Communications. (2014, February). *Summary of research findings to inform campaign planning.* (Available from Widmeyer Communications, 301 E. 57th St., New York, NY 10022)

Expeditionary Learning Schools. (2009, February 3). President Barak Obama, First Lady Michelle Obama, and Education Secretary Arne Duncan visit Capital City Public Charter School; President Obama's second visit to an Expeditionary Learning school [Press release].*Business Wire.* Retrieved from www.businesswire.com/news/home/20090203006817/en/President-BaracK%E2%80%93Obama-Lady-Michelle-Obama-Education#.U1-uY_ldW1V

Fanning, P. (2009, March 4). City Neighbors students take over a courtroom [Web log post]. InsideEd, at the *Baltimore Sun.* Retrieved from weblogs.baltimoresun.com/news/education/blog/2009/03/baltimore_schools_1.html

Farkas, S., Johnson, J., & Duffett, A. (2003). *Stand by me: What teachers really think about unions, merit pay and other professional matters.* New York, NY: Public Agenda.

Farris-Berg, K., & Dirkswager, E. (2013). *Trusting teachers with school success: What happens when teachers call the shots.* Lanham, MD: Rowman & Littlefield Education.

Fertig, B. (2013, February 25). Teachers union's own charter school gets scathing report. *WNYC SchoolBook*. Retrieved from www.wnyc.org/story/301871-teachers-unions-own-charter-school-gets-scathing-report/

Fine, S. (2009, August 9). Schools need teachers like me. I just can't stay. *The Washington Post*. Retrieved from www.washingtonpost.com/wp-dyn/content/article/2009/08/07/AR2009080702046.html

Fischer, C. S., Hour, M., Jankowski, M. S., Lucas, S. R., Sidler, A., & Voss, K. (1996). *Inequality by design: Cracking the bell curve myth*. Princeton, NJ: Princeton University Press.

Fisher v. University of Texas at Austin et al., 113 S.Ct. 2411 (2013).

Fiske, E. B. (1989, January 4). Lessons. *New York Times*, p. B10.

Forbes, S. (2009, April 3). He still has the slows. *Forbes Magazine*. Retrieved from www.forbes.com/global/2009/0413/009-bernanke-restaurants-economy-fact-comment.html

Forman, J., Jr. (2005). The secret history of school choice: How progressives got there first. *Georgetown Law Journal, 93*, 1287–1319.

Frankenberg, E., & Siegel-Hawley, G. (2009). *Equity overlooked: Charter schools and civil rights policy*. Los Angeles, CA: The Civil Rights Project.

Frankenberg, E., Siegel-Hawley, G., & Orfield, G. (2010, May 13). Civil Rights Project's response to re-analysis of charter school study. *Education Next*. Retrieved from educationnext.org/civil-rights-projects-response-to-re-analysis-of-charter-school-study/

Frankenberg, E., Siegel-Hawley, G., & Wang, J. (2010). *Choice without equity: Charter school segregation and the need for civil rights standards*. Los Angeles, CA: The Civil Rights Project.

Freeman, R. B., & Medoff, J. L. (1984). *What do unions do?* New York, NY: Basic Books.

Friends of Choice in Urban Schools. (n.d.). *Data center: School by school performance dashboard*. Retrieved November 1, 2013, from focusdc.org/data

Fuentes, A. (2012, December 7). When teachers leave, students lose out. *Huff Post Education*. Retrieved from www.huffingtonpost.com/teach-plus/when-teachers-leave-stude_b_2259799.html

Fuller, B., & Elmore, R. F. (Eds.). (1996). *Who chooses? Who loses? Culture, institutions, and the unequal effects of school choice*. New York, NY: Teachers College Press.

Garcia, D. R. (2008). The impact of school choice on racial segregation in charter schools. *Educational Policy, 22*(6), 805–829.

Garcia, D. R. (2010). Charter schools challenging traditional notions of segregation. In C. A. Lubienski & P. C. Weitzel (Eds.), *The Charter School Experiment* (pp. 121–146). Cambridge, MA: Harvard Education Press.

Giordano, D. (2010, September 21). Education's "inconvenient truth"? *Philadelphia Enquirer*. Retrieved from articles.philly.com/2010-09-21/news/24999503_1_public-schools-michelle-rhee-educations

Glazerman, S., Protik, A., Teh, B., Bruch, J., & Max, J. (2013). *Transfer incentives for high-performing teachers: Final results from a multisite experiment*. Washington, DC: U.S. Department of Education, Institute of Education Sciences, National Center for Education Evaluation and Regional Assistance.

Gleason, P., Clark, M., Tuttle, C. C., & Dwoyer, E. (2010, June). *The evaluation of charter school impacts: Final report.* Washington, DC: U.S. Department of Education, Institute of Education Sciences, National Center for Education Evaluation and Regional Assistance.

Goenner, J. N. (1996). Charter schools: The revitalization of public education. *Phi Delta Kappan, 78*(1), 32–36.

Goldring, R., Gray, L., Bitterman, A., & Broughman, S. (2013, August). *Characteristics of public and private elementary and secondary school teachers in the United States: Results from the 2011–12 Schools and Staffing Survey: First look.* Washington, DC: U.S. Department of Education, Institute of Education Sciences, National Center for Education Statistics.

Goldstein, D. (2011, June 2). Integration and the "no excuses" charter school movement [Web log post]. *Wonkblog, The Washington Post.* Retrieved from www.washingtonpost.com/blogs/wonkblog/post/integration-and-the-no-excuses-charter-school-movement/2011/06/02/AGmKLRHH_blog.html

Gootman, E. (2009, January 12). State weighs approval of school dedicated to Hebrew. *New York Times,* p. A17.

The great charter tryout: Are New Orleans's schools a model for the nation—or a cautionary tale? (2013, September 20). *Newsweek.* Retrieved from mag.newsweek.com/2013/09/20/post-katrina-the-great-new-orleans-charter-tryout.html

Green, E. (2008, April 22). UFT Charter School leader will leave after clash with teacher. *New York Sun.* Retrieved from www.nysun.com/new-york/uft-charter-school-leader-will-leave-after-clash/75087/

Green, E. L. (2010, October 11). City teachers protest this week's vote on new contract. *The Baltimore Sun.* Retrieved from articles.baltimoresun.com/2010-10-11/news/bs-ci-teacher-contract-protests-20101011_1_vote-on-new-contract-baltimore-teachers-union-city-teachers-protest

Green, M. F. (1989). *Minorities on campus: A handbook for enhancing diversity.* Washington, DC: American Council on Education.

Green Dot Public Schools. (n.d.). Results. Retrieved November 14, 2013, from www.greendot.org/page.cfm?p=1650

Green Dot Public Schools & Asociación de Maestros Unidos/CTA/NEA. (2013). *Agreement between Green Dot Public Schools, a California not-for-profit corporation and the Asociación de Maestros Unidos/CTA/NEA. Effective through June 30, 2016.* Retrieved from www.amuanimo.org/uploads/2/7/5/1/27516771/amu_cba_-_2013-2014_28unsigned29.pdf

Green Woods Charter School. (2013). FAQs. Retrieved November 19, 2013, from www.greenwoodscharter.org/about-greenwoodscharter/faqs.asp#breakfast

Greenhouse, S., & Medina, J. (2009, January 14). Teachers at 2 charter schools plan to join union, despite notion of incompatibility. *New York Times,* p. A30.

Gross, B., & DeArmond, M. (2010). *Parallel patterns: Teacher attrition in charter vs. district schools.* Seattle: National Charter School Research Project, University of Washington.

Guarino, C., Santibañez, L., Daley, G., & Brewer, D. (2004). *A review of the research literature on teacher recruitment and retention.* Santa Monica, CA: RAND Corporation.

Guernsey, L., & Harmon, S. (2013). America's most amazing schools. *Ladies Home*

Journal. Retrieved from www.lhj.com/relationships/family/school/most-amazing-schools/?page=9

Guggenheim, D. (Writer/Director). (2010). *Waiting for Superman* [Motion picture]. United States: Paramount Vantage.

Gyurko, J. (2008, February). *The grinding battle with circumstance: Charter schools and the potential of school-based collective bargaining.* Unpublished manuscript, Program in Politics and Education, Teachers College, Columbia University, New York, NY.

Hanushek, E. A., Kain, J. F., & Rivkin, S. G. (2002). Why public schools lose teachers. *The Journal of Human Resources, 39*(2), 326–354.

Hanushek, E. A., Kain, J. F., & Rivkin, S. G. (2009). New evidence about *Brown v. Board of Education:* The complex effects of school racial composition on achievement. *Journal of Labor Economics, 27*(3), 349–383.

Hanushek, E. A., & Rivkin, S. G. (2007). Pay, working conditions, and teacher quality. *The Future of Children, 17*(1), 69–86.

Hanushek, E. A., & Rivkin, S. G. (2010). *Constrained job matching: Does teacher job search harm disadvantaged urban schools?* (NBER Working Paper No. 15816). Cambridge, MA: National Bureau of Economic Research.

Hardy, L. (2001). High Tech High. *The American School Board Journal, 188*(7), 12–15.

Harris, D. (2007). High-flying schools, student disadvantage, and the logic of NCLB. *American Journal of Education, 113*(3), 367–394.

Harris, D. (2014). *The role of city quality of life in attracting human capital to charter schools: A national analysis* [Unpublished working paper]. New Orleans, LA: Education Research Alliance for New Orleans.

Hart, B., & Risley, T. (1995). *Meaningful differences in the everyday experience of young American children.* Baltimore, MD: Brookes.

Hawkins, B. (2011, August 8). Ted Kolderie, nationally honored education innovator, explains why school change is so hard. *MinnPost.* Retrieved from www.minnpost.com/learning-curve/2011/08/ted-kolderie-nationally-honored-education-innovator-explains-why-school-chang

Herszenhorn, D. M. (2003, September 16). Teachers barter with work rules. *New York Times,* p. A1.

Hess, F. M. (2011, Fall). Our achievement-gap mania. *National Affairs, 9,* 113–129.

High Tech High. (n.d.). Results. Retrieved October 5, 2013, from www.hightechhigh.org/about/results.php

Hill, P. T., Rainey, L., & Rotherham, A. J. (2006, October). *The future of charter schools and teachers unions: Results of a symposium.* Seattle, WA: National Charter School Research Project, Center on Reinventing Public Education.

Holme, J. J., & Wells, A. S. (2008). School choice beyond district borders: Lessons for the reauthorization of NCLB from interdistrict desegregation and open enrollment plans. In R. D. Kahlenberg (Ed.), *Improving on No Child Left Behind: Getting education reform back on track* (pp. 139–216). New York, NY: Century Foundation Press.

Hope Community Academy. (n.d.). Our school. Retrieved March 8, 2013, from www.hope-school.org/school.html

Horne, J. (2012, October 23). NEA donates $250,000 to anti-charter-school campaign. *The Seattle Times.* Retrieved from blogs.seattletimes.com/politicsnorthwest/2012/10/23/nea-donates-250000-to-anti-charter-school-campaign/

Hoxby, C. M. (2000, August). *Peer effects in the classroom: Learning from gender and race variation.* (NBER Working Paper No. 7867). Cambridge, MA: National Bureau of Economic Research.

Hoxby, C. M., Murarka, S., & Kang, J. (2009, September). *How New York City's charter schools affect achievement.* Cambridge, MA: The New York City Charter Schools Evaluation Project.

Huerta, L. A., & d'Entremont, C. (2010). Charter school finance: Seeking institutional legitimacy in a marketplace of resources. In C. A. Lubienski & P. C. Weitzel (Eds.), *The charter school experiment* (pp. 121–146). Cambridge, MA: Harvard Education Press.

IDEAL School/Milwaukee Public Schools. (2013, September 5). IDEAL named Wisconsin School of Recognition for 7th straight year. Retrieved November 14, 2013, from www5.milwaukee.k12.wi.us/school/ideal/2013/09/05/ideal-named-wisconsin-school-of-recognition-for-7th-straight-year/

Illinois Network of Charter Schools. (n.d.). 2012 Charter Excellence Awards. Retrieved November 14, 2013, from incschools.org/school_supports/conference/2012_charter_excellence_awards/

Illinois State Board of Education. (2013). *Springfield Ball Charter School: 2013 Illinois school report card.* Retrieved from webprod.isbe.net/ereportcard/publicsite/getReport.aspx?year=2013&code=510841860201C_e.pdf

Ingersoll, R. M. (2001a). Teacher turnover and teacher shortages: An organizational analysis. *American Educational Research Journal, 38*(3), 499–534.

Ingersoll, R. M. (2001b). *Teacher turnover, teacher shortages, and the organization of schools.* Seattle: Center for the Study of Teaching and Policy, University of Washington.

Ingersoll, R. M. (2003). *Who controls teachers' work?* Cambridge, MA: Harvard University Press.

Ingersoll, R. M. (2007). Short on power, long on responsibility. *Educational Leadership, 65*(1), 20–25.

Institute on Race and Poverty. (2012, January). *Update of "Failed promises: Assessing charter schools in the Twin Cities."* Minneapolis: University of Minnesota Law School.

Isenberg, E., Max, J., Gleason, P., Potamites, L., Santillano, R., Hock, H., & Hansen, M. (2013, November). *Access to effective teaching for disadvantaged students.* Washington, DC: U.S. Department of Education, Institute of Education Sciences, National Center for Education Evaluation and Regional Assistance.

Jacob, B. A. (2007). The challenges of staffing urban schools with effective teachers. *The Future of Children, 17*(1), 129–153

Jennings, J. (Eduwonkette). (2009, January 7). The Boston pilot/charter school study: Some good news, and some cautions [Web log post]. *Eduwonkette blog. Education Week.* Retrieved from blogs.edweek.org/edweek/eduwonkette/2009/01/the_boston_pilotcharter_school.html

Jerald, C. D., & Ingersoll, R. (2002, August). *All talk no action: Putting an end to out-of-field teaching.* Washington, DC: Education Trust.

Jindal, B. (2013, September 14). New Orleans is leading the way in education re-form. *The Times-Picayune.* Retrieved from www.nola.com/opinions/index. ssf/2013/09/louisiana_is_leading_the_way_i.html

Johnson, D. W., & Johnson, R. T. (1994). *Learning together and alone: Cooperative, competitive and individualistic learning.* Boston: Allyn & Bacon.

Kahlenberg, R. D. (2001). *All together now: Creating middle-class schools through pub-lic school choice.* Washington, DC: Brookings Institution Press.

Kahlenberg, R. D. (2006, November). *A new way on school integration* (Issue brief). New York, NY: The Century Foundation.

Kahlenberg, R. (2007a, August 19). Americanization 101. *New York Times.* Retrieved from www.nytimes.com/2007/08/19/opinion/ nyregionopinions/19QUkahlenberg.html

Kahlenberg, R. D. (2007b). *Tough liberal: Albert Shanker and the battles over schools, unions, race and democracy.* New York, NY: Columbia University Press.

Kahlenberg, R. D. (2012). From all walks of life: New hope for school integration. *American Educator, 36*(4), 2–40.

Kahlenberg, R. D. (2013, August 9). *A report to the Little Rock School District on us-ing student socioeconomic status in the inter-district remedy for Little Rock School District v. Pulaski County Special School District.* Retrieved from posting.arktimes. com/images/blogimages/2013/08/13/1376421004-kahlenberg.pdf

Kahlenberg, R. D., & Potter, H. (2012, May). *Diverse charter schools: Can racial and socioeconomic integration promote better outcomes for students?* Washington, DC: The Century Foundation and the Poverty and Race Research Action Council.

Kain, E. (2011, September 29). 80% of Michigan charter schools are for-profits. *Forbes.* Retrieved from www.forbes.com/sites/erikkain/2011/09/29/80-of-michigan-charter-schools-are-for-profits/print/

Kelly, M. (1996, December 22). Charter schools take from the *pluribus* to destroy the *unum.* In A. Shanker, Where we stand: Dangerous minds. [Advertisement.] *New York Times.*

KIPP. (2012a). *KIPP: 2012 report card.* Retrieved from www.kipp.org/reportcard

KIPP. (2012b). *The promise of college completion: KIPP's early successes and chal-lenges, 2012 alumni data update.* Retrieved from www.kipp.org/files/ dmfile/2012AlumniDataUpdate2.pdf

KIPP. (2013). About KIPP. Retrieved November 21, 2013, from www.kipp.org/ about-kipp

KIPP's good work: Are the charter schools a success due to better kids? Or better teaching? (2010, June 27). *Houston Chronicle.* Retrieved from www.chron.com/ disp/story.mpl/editorial/7083660.html

Kirp, D. L. (2013). *Improbable scholars: The rebirth of a great American school system and a strategy for America's schools.* New York, NY: Oxford University Press.

Klein, J. (2010, September 24). Waiting for the teachers' union. *Huff Post IMPACT.* Retrieved from www.huffingtonpost.com/joel-klein/waiting-for-the-teachers-_b_738629.html

Kolderie, T. (1990, November). *Beyond choice to new public schools.* Washington, DC: Progressive Policy Institute.

Koumpilova, M. (2011, June 30). Bankruptcy, court defeat spell the end for TiZA. *Pioneer Press.* Retrieved from www.twincities.com/ci_18385236

Kowal, J., Hassel, B. C., & Hassel, E. A. (2008, November). *Financial incentives for hard-to-staff positions: Cross-sector lessons for public education*. Washington, DC: Center for American Progress.

Kurtz, B. (2011, December 9). Why should we care about integrating schools? [Web log post]. *Good.is*. Retrieved from www.good.is/posts/why-should-we-care-about-integrated-schools

Kurtz, B., & Gottlieb, A. (2006, March 5). Integrated schools can excel. *The Denver Post*, p. E-01. Retrieved from LexisNexis Academic database.

Lake, R. J. (2004, September). *Seeds of change in the Big Apple: Chartering schools in New York City*. Washington, DC: Progressive Policy Institute.

Larchmont Charter School. (n.d.) School profiles. Retrieved October 5, 2013, from www.larchmontcharter.org/school-profiles

Lee, V., & Smith, J. B. (1996). Collective responsibility for learning and its effects on gains and achievement and engagement for early secondary students. *American Journal of Education, 104*(2), 103–147.

The lens: Morris Jeff charter school board embraces new teachers union. (2013, May 17). *FOX 8 WVUE New Orleans*. Retrieved from www.fox8live.com/story/22281543/morris-jeff-charter-school-board-embraces-new-teachers-union

Lessons from New Orleans [Editorial]. (2011, October 16). *New York Times*, p. SR10.

Lilly Family School of Philanthropy. (2013). *Million dollar list: Scaling philanthropy*. Indianapolis, IN: Indiana University. Retrieved October 23, 2013, from www.milliondollarlist.org/

Lingenfelter, J. (2013, September 1). Morris Jeff makes history as first International Baccalaureate World School in Louisiana. Retrieved from blog.nola.com/new_orleans/2013/09/morris_jeff_in_mid-city_makes.html

Lord, M. (2003, August). Freedom of choice. [Living well parenting special.] *Essence, 34*(4), 178. Retrieved from LexisNexis Academic database.

Louisiana Department of Education. (2012). *Spring 2012 iLEAP criterion-referenced test state/district/school achievement level summary report—Grade 3: All testers*. Retrieved from www.louisianabelieves.com/docs/test-results/ileap-grade-3-state-district-school-achievement-level-summary-report-2012.pdf?sfvrsn=2

Louisiana Department of Education. (2013a). *Multiple statistics by site for public elementary/secondary students—February 2013*. Retrieved November 1, 2013, from www.louisianabelieves.com/resources/library/data-center

Louisiana Department of Education. (2013b). *Spring 2013 LEAP criterion-referenced test state/district/school achievement level summary report—Grade 4: All testers*. Retrieved from www.louisianabelieves.com/docs/test-results/leap-grade-4-state-district-school-achievement-level-summary-report-2013.pdf?sfvrsn=2

Lovenheim, M. F. (2009). The effect of teachers' unions on education production: Evidence from union election certifications in three midwestern states. *Journal of Labor Economics, 27*(4), 525–587.

Lubienski, C., & Lubienski, S. T. (2006, January). *Charter, private, public schools and academic achievement: New evidence from NAEP mathematics data*. New York, NY: National Center for the Study of Privatization in Education, Teachers College, Columbia University.

Lynch, L. M. (2000). Trends in and consequences of investments in children. In S. H. Danziger & J. Waldfogel. (Eds.), *Securing the future: Investing in children from birth to college* (pp. 19–46). New York, NY: Russell Sage Foundation.

Ma, J. S., & Kurlaender, M. (2005). The future of race-conscious policies in K–12 public schools: Support from recent legal opinions and social science research. In J. Boger & G. Orfield (Eds.), *School resegregation: Must the south turn back?* (pp. 239–260). Chapel Hill: University of North Carolina Press.

Malloy, C. L., & Wohlstetter, P. (2003). Working conditions in charter schools: What's the appeal for teachers? *Education and Urban Society, 35*(2), 219–241.

Mantil, A., Perkins, A. G., & Aberger, S. (2012). The challenge of high-poverty schools: How feasible is socioeconomic school integration? In R. D. Kahlenberg (Ed.), *The future of school integration: Socioeconomic diversity as an education reform strategy* (pp. 155–222). New York, NY: Century Foundation Press.

Marable, M. (2002). *The great wells of democracy: The meaning of race in American life*. Cambridge, MA: BasicCivitas.

Marin, P. (2000). The educational possibility of multi-racial/multi-ethnic college classrooms. In *Does diversity make a difference? Three research studies on diversity in college classrooms* (pp. 61–68). Washington, DC: American Council on Education & American Association of University Professors.

Maryland State Department of Education. (2013a). *School improvement in Maryland. How did our performance compare to the district and state? City Neighbors Charter School. 2013 Mathematics*. Retrieved November 1, 2013, from www.mdk12.org/data/MSA/CompareDistState.aspx?Nav=20.2:1.2:2.22:5.3:3.7:10.30:11.0326:15.99#dataTable

Maryland State Department of Education. (2013b). *School improvement in Maryland. How did our performance compare to the district and state? City Neighbors Charter School. 2013 Reading*. Retrieved November 1, 2013, from www.mdk12.org/data/MSA/CompareDistState.aspx?Nav=1.2:2.22:5.3:3.7:20.1:10.30:11.0326:15.99#dataTable

Maryland State Department of Education. (2013c, May 28). *Baltimore City—City Neighbors Charter School. Demographics. Students receiving special services. Elementary*. Retrieved November 11, 2013, from mdreportcard.org/SpecialServices.aspx?PV=36:E:30:0326:3:N:0:14:1:1:1:1:1:1:3

Maryland State Department of Education. (2013d, May 28). *Baltimore City—City Neighbors Charter School. Demographics. Students receiving special services. Middle*. Retrieved November 1, 2013, from mdreportcard.org/SpecialServices.aspx?PV=36:M:30:0326:3:N:0:14:1:1:1:1:1:1:3

Maryland State Department of Education. (2013e, October 30). *Baltimore City—City Neighbors Charter School. Demographics*. Retrieved November 1, 2013, from mdreportcard.org/Demographics.aspx?K=300326&WDATA=School#ENROLLMENTgrade3all

Massachusetts Teachers Association Center for Education Policy and Practice. (2009). *Charter school success or selective out-migration of low-achievers? Effects of enrollment management on student achievement*. Boston, MA: Author.

Mathews, J. (1998). *Class struggle: What's wrong (and right) with America's best public high schools*. New York, NY: Times Books.

Mathews, J. (2009a, November 17). Don't save bad schools—terminate them. *The Washington Post.* Retrieved from voices.washingtonpost.com/class-struggle/2009/11/dont_save_bad_schools--termina.html

Mathews, J. (2009b). *Work hard. Be nice: How two inspired teachers created the most promising schools in America.* Chapel Hill, NC: Algonquin Books.

Mathews, J., & Blum, J. (2003, June 20). School facilities run gamut of haves and have-nots; some boosted by private funds; others struggle. *The Washington Post,* p. A11. Retrieved from LexisNexis Academic database.

Maxwell, L. A. (2010, June 29). Study finds no clear edge for charter schools. *Education Week.* Retrieved from www.edweek.org/ew/articles/2010/06/29/36ies.h29.html

McConahay, J. (1981). Reducing racial prejudice in desegregated schools. In W. Hawley (Ed.), *Effective school desegregation: Equity, quality, and feasibility* (pp. 35–53). Beverly Hills, CA: Sage.

McGlothlin, H., & Killen, M. (2005). Children's perceptions of intergroup and intragroup similarity and the role of social experience. *Journal of Applied Developmental Psychology, 26,* 680–698.

Mead, J. F., & Green, P. C. (2012, February). *Chartering equity: Using charter school legislation and policy to advance equal educational opportunity.* Boulder: National Education Policy Center, School of Education, University of Colorado–Boulder.

Meier, D. (2002). *In schools we trust.* Boston: Beacon Press.

Meredith v. Jefferson County Board of Education, 551 U.S. 701 (2007).

Mickelson, R. A., & Bottia, M. (2010). Integrated education and mathematics outcomes: A synthesis of social science research. *North Carolina Law Review, 87,* 993–1089.

Milliken v. Bradley, 414 U.S. 717, 783 (1974) (Marshall, J., dissenting).

Minnesota Department of Education. (n.d.) *Data center.* Retrieved November 1, 2013, from education.state.mn.us/MDE/Data/index.html

Miron, G., & Applegate, B. (2007). *Teacher attrition in charter schools.* Tempe: Education Policy Research Unit, Arizona State University.

Miron, G., & Urschel, J. L. (2010). *Equal or fair? A study of revenues and expenditures in American charter schools.* Boulder and Tempe: Education and the Public Interest Center University of Colorado–Boulder and Education Policy Research Unit.

Miron, G., & Urschel, J. L. (2012, July). *Understanding and improving full-time virtual schools: A study of student characteristics, school finance, and school performance in schools operated by K12 Inc.* Boulder, CO: National Education Policy Center, School of Education, University of Colorado–Boulder.

Miron, G., Urschel, J. L., Mathis, W. J., & Tornquist, E. (2010). *Schools without diversity: Education management organizations, charter schools, and the demographic stratification of the American school system.* Boulder and Tempe: Education and the Public Interest Center and Education Policy Research Unit, Arizona State University.

Miron, G., Urschel, J. L., & Saxton, N. (2011, March). *What makes KIPP work? A study of student characteristics, attrition, and school finance.* New York, NY, and Kalamazoo, MI: National Center for the Study of Privatization in Education,

Columbia University, and the Study Group on Education Management Organizations, Western Michigan University.

Moe, T. M. (2011). *Special interest: Teachers unions and America's public schools.* Washington, DC: Brookings Institution.

Monahan, R. (2013, October 26). Top 16 NYC charter school executives earn more than Chancellor Dennis Walcott. *New York Daily News.* Retrieved from www. nydailynews.com/new-york/education/top-16-nyc-charter-school-execs-out-earn-chancellor-dennis-walcott-article-1.1497717

Mulgrew, M. (2010, April 22). Fairness for all. *Huffington Post.* Retrieved from www.huffingtonpost.com/michael-mulgrew/fairness-for-all_b_548553. html?view=screen

Mulvey, J. D., Cooper, B. X., & Maloney, A. (2010). *Blurring the lines: Charter, public, private and religious schools coming together.* Charlotte, NC: Information Age.

Nathan, J. (1996). Charter schools: Creating hope and opportunity for American education. San Francisco, CA: Jossey-Bass.

Nathan, J. (2008, February 18). Parents: yes and no to American freedom. *Minnpost.com.* Retrieved from www.minnpost.com/from_our_partners/2008/02/27/1008/hometownsourcecom_

Nathan, J. (2010, June 22). *The civil rights heritage of public charter schools.* Washington, DC: National Alliance for Public Charter Schools.

National Alliance for Public Charter Schools (NAPCS). (2008, October 20). *Teacher leadership in public charter schools: A statement by the National Alliance for Public Charter Schools.* Retrieved from www.publiccharters.org/wp-content/uploads/2014/01/Teacher_Leadership_in_Public_Charter_Schools_20110402T222340.pdf

National Alliance for Public Charter Schools (NAPCS). (2011). *Unionized charter schools: Data from 2009–10.* Retrieved from www.publiccharters.org/wp-content/uploads/2014/01/NAPCS-Unionized-Charter-Schools-Dashboard-Details_20111103T104815.pdf

National Alliance for Public Charter Schools (NAPCS). (2013a). *A growing movement: America's largest charter school communities* (8th annual ed.). Washington, DC: Author.

National Alliance for Public Charter Schools (NAPCS). (2013b). *Measuring up to the model: A tool for comparing state charter school laws.* Retrieved from www.public-charters.org/get-the-facts/law-database/

National Alliance for Public Charter Schools (NAPCS). (2013c). *The Public Charter Schools Dashboard.* Retrieved from dashboard.publiccharters.org/dashboard/home

National Alliance for Public Charter Schools (NAPCS). (2014, February). *Estimated number of public charter schools and students, 2013–2014.* Washington, DC: Author.

National Assessment for Educational Progress (NAEP). (2011). *NAEP Data Explorer.* Retrieved from nces.ed.gov/nationsreportcard/naepdata/

National Association of Charter School Authorizers. (2012, November 28). *A call for quality: National charter school authorizers group says more failing schools must close for reform to fully succeed.* Retrieved from www.qualitycharters.org/assets/files/images/stories/Final_OML_Press_Materials11.28.12.15.pdf?q=images/

stories/Final_OML_Press_Materials11.28.12.15.pdf

National Coalition on School Diversity. (2011, March). *Federal funded charter schools should foster diversity.* Washington, DC: Author.

National Commission on Teaching and America's Future. (2007). *Policy brief: The high cost of teacher turnover.* Washington, DC: Author.

National Education Policy Center. (2013, August 22). New Orleans charter school study: Comparing incomparables, repeated errors, and small differences [Press Release]. Retrieved from nepc.colorado.edu/newsletter/2013/08/review-credo-2013-NOLA

New England Common Assessment Program. (2012a). Fall 2012 beginning of grade 3 NECAP tests: Blackstone Valley Prep. Retrieved from reporting.measuredprogress.org/NECAPpublicRI/select.aspx

New England Common Assessment Program. (2012b). Fall 2012 beginning of grade 3 NECAP tests: District Results. Cumberland. Retrieved from reporting.measuredprogress.org/NECAPpublicRI/select.aspx

New York State Education Department. (2013). *The New York State report card 2011–12: Amber Charter School.* Albany, NY: Author. Retrieved from reportcards.nysed.gov/files/2011-12/RC-2012-310400860806.pdf

Newton, X. A., Rivero, R., Fuller, B., & Dauter, L. (2011). *Teacher stability and turnover in Los Angeles: The influence of teacher and school characteristics* (Los Angeles School Infrastructure Project Working Paper). Berkeley, CA: Policy Analysis for California Education.

Nichols-Barrer, I., Gill, B. P., Gleason, P., & Tuttle, C. C. (2012, September). *Student selection, attrition, and replacement in KIPP middle schools* [updated edition]. Princeton, NJ: Mathematica Policy Research. Retrieved from www.mathematica-mpr.com/publications/PDFs/education/KIPP_middle_schools_wp.pdf

Nnamdi, K., & Petrilli, M. (2012, December 12). Changing city, gentrifying schools. *The Kojo Nnamdi Show* [Transcript of radio broadcast]. Retrieved from thekojonnamdishow.org/shows/2012-12-12/changing-city-gentrifying-schools/transcript

Obama, B. (2009, February 3). Remarks following a visit to Capital City Public Charter School. *Public Papers of the Presidents: Barack Obama, 2009 (in two books). Book 1—January 20 to June 30, 2009* (pp. 40-41). Retrieved from www.gpo.gov/fdsys/pkg/PPP-2009-book1/pdf/PPP-2009-book1.pdf

Office of Information and Reporting Services. (2012a). *The New York State Report Card, 2011–12.* Albany, NY: New York State Education Department. Retrieved from reportcards.nysed.gov/statewide/2012statewideRC.pdf

Office of Information and Reporting Services. (2012b). *The New York State Report Card, 2011–12: Amber Charter School.* Albany, NY: New York State Education Department. Retrieved from reportcards.nysed.gov/files/2011-12/RC-2012-310400860806.pdf

Office of Information and Reporting Services. (2012c). *The New York State Report Card, 2011–12: Community Roots Charter School.* Albany, NY: New York State Education Department. Retrieved from reportcards.nysed.gov/files/2011-12/RC-2012-331300860893.pdf

Office of Information and Reporting Services. (2012d). *The New York State Re-*

port Card, 2011–12: New York City Geographic District #4. Albany, NY: New York State Education Department. Retrieved from reportcards.nysed.gov/files/2011-12/RC-2012-310400010000.pdf

Office of Information and Reporting Services. (2012e). *The New York State Report Card, 2011–12: New York City Geographic District #13.* Albany, NY: New York State Education Department. Retrieved from reportcards.nysed.gov/files/2011-12/RC-2012-331300010000.pdf

Oldberg, A., & Podgursky, M. J. (2011, June). *Charting a new course to retirement: How charter schools handle teacher pensions.* Washington, DC: Thomas B. Fordham Institute.

Orfield, G. (1978). *Must we bus? Segregated schools and national policy.* Washington, DC: Brookings Institution Press.

Orfield, G., & Frankenberg, E. (Eds.). (2013). *Educational delusions? Why choice can deepend inequality and how to make schools fair.* Berkeley and Los Angeles: University of California Press.

Orfield, M., & Luce, T. F. (2013 October). *Charter schools in the Twin Cities: 2013 update.* Minneapolis: Institute on Metropolitan Opportunity, University of Minnesota Law School.

Organisation for Economic Co-operation and Development (OECD). (2007). *PISA 2006: Science competencies for tomorrow's world* (Vol. 1). Paris, France: Author.

Ormsby, D. (2012, June 1). Chicago Charter School Board rejects Youth Connection Leader Academy closure. *The Illinois Observer.* Retrieved from www.illinoisobserver.net/2012/06/01/chicago-charter-school-board-rejects-youth-connection-leader-academy-closure/

Otterman, S. (2010a, June 8). The choosiest of the charters [Web log post]. *City Room. New York Times.* Retrieved from cityroom.blogs.nytimes.com/2010/06/08/the-choosiest-of-the-charters/?_r=0

Otterman, S. (2010b, October 13). Lauded Harlem schools have their own problems. *New York Times,* p. A20.

P.S. 67 Charles A. Dorsey. (2012). History of P.S. 067. Retrieved October 5, 2013, from www.ps67.net/site_res_view_template.aspx?id=e387507d-4088-4b21-9e22-8cae2196b82b

Palardy, G. J. (2013). High school socioeconomic segregation and student attainment. *American Educational Research Journal, 50*(4), 714–754.

Pallas, A. (2009, May 8). Just how gullible is David Brooks? *Chalkbeat: New York.* Retrieved from ny.chalkbeat.org/2009/05/08/just-how-gullible-is-david-brooks/

Parents Involved in Community Schools v. Seattle School District No. 1, 551 U.S. 701 (2007).

Partnership for 21st Century Skills. (n.d.) Our mission. Retrieved November 15, 2013, from www.p21.org/about-us/our-mission

Perry, L. B., & McConney, A. (2010). Does the SES of the school matter? An examination of socioeconomic status and student achievement using PISA 2003. *Teachers College Record, 112*(4), 1137–1162.

Petrilli, M. J. (2012). *The diverse schools dilemma: A parent's guide to socioeconomically mixed public schools.* Washington, DC: Thomas B. Fordham Institute.

Pettigrew, T. F., & Tropp, L. R. (2006). A meta-analytic test of intergroup contact theory. *Journal of Personality and Social Psychology, 90*(5), 751–83.

Phillips, K. J. R., Rodosky, R. J., Muñoz, M. A., & Larsen, E. S. (2009). Integrated schools, integrated futures? A case study of school desegregation in Jefferson County, Kentucky. In C. E. Smrekar, & E. B. Goldring (Eds.), *From the courtroom to the classroom: The shifting landscape of school desegregation* (pp. 239–70). Cambridge, MA: Harvard Education Press.

Podgursky, M., & Ballou, D. (2001, August). *Personnel policy in charter schools.* Washington, DC: Thomas B. Fordham Foundation.

Pondiscio, R. (2013). "No excuses" kids go to college: Will high-flying charters see their low-income students graduate? *Education Next, 13*(2), 8–14.

Ponza, M., Gleason, P., Hulsey, L., & Moore, Q. (2009, February). *Who picks up the tab? Reducing payment errors in school nutrition programs.* Princeton, NJ: Mathematica Policy Research.

Potter, H. (2013, May). Boosting achievement by pursuing diversity. *Educational Leadership, 70*(8), 38–43.

Price, H. B. (1999, December 8). Urban education: A radical plan. *Education Week, 19*(15), 29, 44. Retrieved from www.edweek.org/ew/articles/1999/12/08/15price.h19.html

Price, M. (2011, November). *Are charter school unions worth the bargain?* Seattle, WA: Center on Reinventing Public Education.

Provenzo, E. F., Jr., & McCloskey, G. N. (1981 October). Catholic and federal Indian education in the late 19th century: Opposed colonial models. *Journal of American Indian Education, 21*(1). Retrieved March 7, 2013, from jaie.asu.edu/v21/V21S1opp.html

Public Impact. (2008, January). *Boosting performance and containing costs through Mayoral Academies.* Chapel Hill, NC: Author.

Radcliffe, J. (2011, April 28). KIPP college grad rates draw both praise and concern. *Houston Chronicle.* Retrieved from www.chron.com/news/houston-texas/article/KIPP-college-grad-rates-draw-both-praise-and-1692194.php

Ravitch, D. (2011, October 18). Why "miracle schools" aren't really miracles. *The Washington Post.* Retrieved from www.washingtonpost.com/blogs/answer-sheet/post/ravitch-why-miracle-schools-arent-really-miracles/2011/10/18/gIQAM62RuL_blog.html

Ravitch, D. (2013). *Reign of error: The hoax of the privatization movement and the danger to America's public schools.* New York, NY: Knopf.

Reardon, S. F. (2009, November). *Review of "How New York City's charter schools affect achievement."* Boulder and Tempe: Education and the Public Interest Center, University of Colorado at Boulder, and Education Policy Research Unit, Arizona State University.

Reichgott Junge, E. (2005, August 7–9). *Chartering 2.0 Leadership Summit, Mackinac Island, MI: Proceedings document.* Washington, DC: National Alliance for Public Charter Schools.

Reichgott Junge, E. (2012). *Zero chance of passage.* Edina, MN: Beaver's Pond Press.

Rhode Island Department of Education (RIDE). (2013a). RIDE releases 2013 school classifications. Retrieved from www.ride.ri.gov/InsideRIDE/AdditionalInformation/News/ViewArticle/tabid/408/ArticleId/74/RIDE-Releases-

2013-School-Classifications.aspx

Rhode Island Department of Education (RIDE). (2013b). *2013 school classification summary.* Retrieved from www.ride.ri.gov/Portals/0/Uploads/Documents/ Information-and-Accountability-User-Friendly-Data/Accountability/2013-school-classification-summary.pdf

Rhode Island Department of Elementary and Secondary Education Information Services (n.d.). *Creating aggregate report.* Retrieved November 1, 2013, from www. eride.ri.gov/reports/reports.asp

Rich, M. (2013, August 27). At charter schools, short careers by choice. *New York Times,* p. A1.

Rimer, S. (2009, January 10). Immigrants in charter schools seeking the best of two worlds. *New York Times,* p. A1.

Riordan, R., Roche, B., Goldhammer, H., & Stephen, D. (1999). *Seeing the future: A planning guide for high schools.* Providence, RI: The Big Picture Company.

Ritter, G., Jensen, N., Kisida, B., & McGee, J. (2010). A closer look at charter schools and segregation: Flawed comparisons lead to overstated conclusions. *Education Next, 10*(3), 69–73.

Roach, R. (2003, June 19). Class-based affirmative action. *Diverse Issues in Higher Education.* Retrieved from diverseeducation.com/article/3029/#

Robles, Y. (2011, July 13). Mogul John Malone to donate $7 million to Denver School of Science and Technology. *The Denver Post.* Retrieved from www.denverpost.com/ci_18465843

Roda, A., & Wells, A. S. (2013). School choice policies and racial segregation: Where White parents' good intentions, anxiety, and privilege collide. *American Journal of Education, 119*(2), 261–293.

Ronfeldt, M., Lankford, H., Loeb, S., & Wyckoff, J. (2011, June). *How teacher turnover harms student achievement* (NBER Working Paper No. 17176). Cambridge, MA: National Bureau of Economic Research.

Rose, L. C., & Gallup, A. M. (2003). Urban dwellers on urban schools. *Phi Delta Kappan, 84*(5), 408-409.

Rothstein, R. (2000). Equalizing education resources on behalf of disadvantaged children. In R. D. Kahlenberg (Ed.), *A notion at risk: Preserving public education as an engine for social mobility* (pp. 79–85). New York, NY: Century Foundation Press.

Rui, N. (2009). Four decades of research on the effects of detracking reform: Where do we stand?—A systematic review of the evidence. *Journal of Evidence Based Medicine, 2*(3), 164–183.

Rumberger, R. W. (2003). The causes and consequences of student mobility. *Journal of Negro Education, 72*(1), 6–21.

Rumberger, R. W., & Palardy, G. J. (2005). Does segregation still matter? The impact of student composition on academic achievement in high school. *Teachers College Record, 107*(9), 1999–2045.

Rusk, D. (2002, July 5). Classmates count: A study of the interrelationship between socioeconomic background and standardized test scores of 4th grade pupils in the Madison-Dane County Public Schools. Retrieved from www.schoolinfosystem.org/archives/Unifiedfinalreport.pdf

Russo, A. (2010a). Charters and unions: What's the future for this unorthodox relationship? *Harvard Education Letter, 26*(1), 1–3, 6.

Russo, A. (2010b, August 5). CMSA: Pregnant charter teacher fired for organizing [Web log post]. *District 299: The Inside Scoop on CPS.* Retrieved from www.chicagonow.com/district-299-chicago-public-schools-blog/2010/08/cmsa-pregnant-charter-teacher-fired-for-organizing/

Rutland, A., Cameron, L., Bennett, L., & Ferrell, J. (2005). Interracial contact and racial constancy: A multi-site study of racial intergroup bias in 3–5 year old Anglo-British children. *Journal of Applied Developmental Psychology, 26,* 699–713.

Sackler, M. (Director). (2010). *The lottery* [Motion picture]. United States: Great Curve Films.

Sahm, C. (2013, September 11). The ugly war on co-locating city schools. *New York Post.* Retrieved from nypost.com/2013/09/11/the-ugly-war-on-co-locating-city-schools/

Salcido, I. (2000, March 3). Testimony of Irasema Salcido, Principal, Cesar Chavez Public Charter High School for Public Policy. *Hearings of the House Committee on Education and the Workforce.* Retrieved November 22, 2013, from archives.republicans.edlabor.house.gov/archive/hearings/106th/oi/charter3300/salcido.htm

Sanbonmatsu, L., Kling, J. R., Duncan, G. J., & Brooks-Gunn, J. (2006, January). *Neighborhoods and academic achievement: Results from the Moving to Opportunity Experiment* (NBER Working Paper No. 11909). Cambridge, MA: National Bureau of Economic Research.

Sawchuk, S. (2013, November 13). Transferring top teachers has benefits. *Education Week, 33*(12), 1, 13.

Scherer, R., Robin, J., Caillier, S., Daley, B., Hayman, P., McBain, L, & Riordan, R. (2008). Welcome. *Unboxed: A Journal of Adult Learning in Schools, 1*(1), 4–5.

School Structure Committee, Citizens League. (1988, November 17). *Chartered schools = choices for educators + quality for all students.* Minneapolis, MN: Citizens League.

Schwartz, H. (2010). *Housing policy is school policy: Economically integrative housing promotes academic success in Montgomery County, Maryland.* New York, NY: The Century Foundation.

Shanker, A. (1988a, January 10). Where we stand: Re-struc-ture. [Advertisement.] *New York Times.* Retrieved from locals.nysut.org/shanker/

Shanker, A. (1988b, March 31). *National Press Club speech.* Retrieved from www.reuther.wayne.edu/files/64.43.pdf

Shanker, A. (1988c, July 10). Where we stand: Convention plots new course, a charter for change. [Advertisement.] *New York Times.* Retrieved from locals.nysut.org/shanker/

Shanker, A. (1993, November 7). Where we stand: Goals not gimmicks. [Advertisement.] *New York Times.* Retrieved from locals.nysut.org/shanker/

Shanker, A. (1994, July 3). Where we stand: Noah Webster Academy. [Advertisement.] *New York Times.* Retrieved from locals.nysut.org/shanker/

Shanker, A. (1995, November 19). Where we stand: Parents under contract. [Advertisement.] *New York Times.* Retrieved from locals.nysut.org/shanker/

Shanker, A. (1996, March 3). Where we stand: Yellow journalism. [Advertisement.] *New York Times.* Retrieved from locals.nysut.org/shanker/

Sherry, A. (2006a, August 3). Charter shines through birth pangs. *Denver Post.* Retrieved from www.denverpost.com/ci_4128170

Sherry, A. (2006b, September 13). Charter overtakes school it replaced. *Denver Post.* Retrieved from www.denverpost.com/ci_4327408?IADID=Search-www.denverpost.com-www.denverpost.com

Sherry, A. (2007, March 13). New start at Cole ends this spring. *Denver Post.* Retrieved from www.denverpost.com/specialreports/ci_5421568

Sievers, S. (1996, February 19). Charter school: Education with a twist. *St. Louis Post-Dispatch*, p. 1. Retrieved from LexisNexis Academic database.

Smarick, A. (2010). The turnaround fallacy. *Education Next, 10*(1), 20–26.

Smith, R. (2010, April 13). Charter school pledges to "not coerce" unionizing teachers. *Washington City Paper.* Retrieved from www.washingtoncitypaper.com/blogs/citydesk/2010/04/13/charter-school-pledges-to-not-coerce-unionizing-teachers/

Snyder, T. D., & Dillow, S. A. (2010, April). *Digest of education statistics 2009.* Washington, DC: U.S. Department of Education, Institute of Education Sciences, National Center for Education Statistics.

A sobering charter report. (2009, July 8). *Philadelphia Inquirer.* Retrieved from articles.philly.com/2009-07-08/news/25288723_1_charter-schools-charter-movement-charter-report

Stuit, D. A., & Smith, T. M. (2012). Explaining the gap in charter and traditional public school teacher turnover rates. *Economics of Education Review, 31*(2), 268–279.

SUNY Charter Schools Institute. (2013, October 22). *SUNY authorized charter schools 2012–2013 comparative performance analysis: Amber Charter School.* New York: State University of New York.

Sykes, L. L. (2004, March 14). In seeking best education, some choose segregation. *Milwaukee Journal Sentinel*, A1.

Tamayo, J. R. (2009, August 11). The selflessness of teaching. *The Washington Post.* Retrieved from www.washingtonpost.com/wp-dyn/content/article/2009/08/10/AR2009081003018_pf.html

Teach for America. (2011). *Segregation in American schools and its impact on the achievement gap* [Video]. Retrieved from vimeo.com/19974401

TELL Maryland: Teaching, Empowering, Leading and Learning. (2013). [School summary comparison results for City Neighbors Charter elem middle]. Retrieved November 22, 2013, from www.tellmaryland.org/results/report/14/10849

Thernstrom, A., & Thernstrom, S. (2003). *No excuses: Closing the racial gap in learning.* New York, NY: Simon & Schuster.

Thomas, D. [Doug]. (2007, August). Co-op history. *EdVisions Cooperative.* Retrieved from edvisionscooperative.org/about/history

Thompson, J. (2013, August 8). Roland Fryer's "no excuses" excuses [Web log post]. *Alexander Russo's This Week in Education (Scholastic Administrator).* Retrieved from scholasticadministrator.typepad.com/thisweekineducation/2013/08/thompson.html

Torres, K. (2000, September 7). Teaching pioneers will get millions; Bill Gates Foundation will back two Minnesota education projects. *Saint Paul Pioneer Press*, p. 1A. Retrieved from LexisNexis Academic database.

Tough, P. (2006, November 26). What it takes to make a student. *New York Times.* Retrieved from www.nytimes.com/2006/11/26/magazine/26tough.html?_r=1&oref=slogin

Tough, P. (2008). *Whatever it takes: Geoffrey Canada's quest to change Harlem and America*. New York, NY: Houghton Mifflin.

Traub, J. (1999, April 4). In theory: A school of your own. *New York Times*, section 4A, p. 30, Column 1, education life supplement. Retrieved from LexisNexis Academic database.

Trotter, A. (2007, September 5). Mideast-themed schools raise curricular, church–state issues. *Education Week, 27*(2), 1, 13.

Turque, B. (2011a, July 15). 206 D.C. teachers fired for poor performance. *The Washington Post*. Retrieved from www.washingtonpost.com/local/education/206-low-performing-dc-teachers-fired/2011/07/15/gIQANEj5GI_story.html

Turque, B. (2011b, August 6). Huge achievement gaps persist in D.C. schools. *The Washington Post*. Retrieved from www.washingtonpost.com/local/education/huge-achievement-gaps-persist-in-dc-schools/2011/08/05/gIQAB7b2yI_story.html

Tuttle, C. C., Gill, B., Gleason, P., Knechtel, V., Nichols-Barrer, I., & Resch, A. (2013, February 27). *KIPP middle schools: Impacts on achievement and other outcomes. Final Report*. Washington, DC: Mathematica Policy Research.

Undermining a success story [Editorial]. (2009, August 15). *The Washington Post*. Retrieved from www.washingtonpost.com/wp-dyn/content/article/2009/08/14/AR2009081403106_pf.html

Unions consider charter schools of their own. (1996, September 22). *New York Times*, p. A14.

U.S. Census Bureau. (1991, June). *Current population reports. Poverty in the United States: 1988 and 1989*. Washington, DC: Author.

U.S. Census Bureau. (2010). POV01: Age and sex of all people, family members and unrelated individuals iterated by income-to-poverty ratio and race: 2009. *Current Population Survey, 2010 Annual social and economic supplement*. Retrieved from www.census.gov/hhes/www/cpstables/032010/pov/new01_200_01.htm

U.S. Census Bureau. (n.d.). Selected economic characteristics: 2008–2012 American Community Survey 5-year estimates. Lincoln town, Providence County, Rhode Island. *American FactFinder*. Retrieved April 29, 2014, from factfinder2.census.gov/faces/nav/jsf/pages/searchresults.xhtml?refresh=t#none

U.S. Census Bureau. (2013, June 27). Central Falls (city), Rhode Island. *State and County QuickFacts*. Retrieved November 14, 2013, from quickfacts.census.gov/qfd/states/44/4414140.html

U.S. Department of Education. (2008, June 17). U.S. Secretary of Education Spellings visits High Tech High in San Diego, delivers keynote address at Biotechnology Institute award banquet [Press release]. *US Fed News*. Retrieved from LexisNexis Academic database.

U.S. Department of Education. (2011, April). *Charter Schools Program, Title V, Part B of the ESEA, nonregulatory guidance*. Retrieved from www2.ed.gov/programs/charter/nonregulatory-guidance.doc

U.S. Department of Education. (2012a, March 6). Application for new awards; Charter Schools Program (CSP); grants for replication and expansion of high-quality charter schools. *Federal Register, 77*(44), 13304–13311.

U.S. Department of Education. (2012b, November 19). U.S. Department of Education releases early snapshot of School Improvement Grants data [Press release]. Retrieved from www.ed.gov/news/press-releases/us-department-education-releases-early-snapshot-school-improvement-grants-data

U.S. Department of Education. (2013, August 2). *National conference highlights federal grants to charter schools.* Retrieved www.ed.gov/oii-news/national-conference-highlights-federal-grants-charter-schools

U.S. Department of Education. (2014, January). *Charter Schools Program, Title V, Part B of the ESEA, nonregulatory guidance.* Retrieved from www2.ed.gov/programs/charter/fy14cspnonregguidance.doc

U.S. Department of Education, National Center for Education Statistics (NCES). (2008). Total number of public school teachers and percentage of public school teachers in a union or employees' association, by state: 1999–2000, 2003–04, and 2007–08. *Schools and Staffing Survey (SASS).* Retrieved from nces.ed.gov/surveys/sass/tables/sass0708_043_t1s.asp

U.S. Department of Education, National Center for Education Statistics (NCES). (2012a). Percentage distribution of public school districts, by type of agreement with teachers' associations or unions and selected public school district characteristics: 2011–12. *Schools and Staffing Survey (SASS).* Retrieved from nces.ed.gov/surveys/sass/tables/sass1112_2013311_d1n_007.asp

U.S. Department of Education, National Center for Education Statistics (NCES). (2012b). Search for public schools. *Common Core of Data.* Retrieved from nces.ed.gov/ccd/schoolsearch/index.asp

U.S. Department of Education, National Center for Education Statistics (NCES). (2012c). Table 44. Enrollment and percentage distribution of enrollment in public elementary and secondary schools, by race/ethnicity and region: Selected years, fall 1995 through fall 2021. *Digest of Education Statistics 2012.* Retrieved from nces.ed.gov/programs/digest/d12/tables/dt12_044.asp

U.S. Department of Education, National Center for Education Statistics (NCES). (2012d). Table 112. Number and percentage distribution of public school students eligible for free or reduced-price lunch, by school level, locale, and student race/ethnicity: 2010–11. *Digest of Education Statistics 2012.* Retrieved from nces.ed.gov/programs/digest/d12/tables/dt12_112.asp

U.S. Department of Labor, Bureau of Labor Statistics. (2012, January 23). *Union members—2012* [News release]. Retrieved from www.bls.gov/news.release/archives/union2_01232013.htm

U.S. Government Accountability Office. (2010, November). *Many challenges arise in educating students who change schools frequently.* Publication No. GAO-11-40. Retrieved November 25, 2013, from www.gao.gov/products/GAO-11-40?source=ra

U.S. Government Accountability Office. (2012, June). *Charter schools: Additional federal attention needed to help protect access for students with disabilities* (Publication No. GAO-12-543). Washington, DC: Author.

Vander Ark, T. (2009, May 6). Why charter schools matter. *Huffington Post.* Retrieved from www.huffingtonpost.com/tom-vander-ark/why-charter-schools-matte_b_197512.html

Vasagar, J., & Stratton, A. (2010, October 5). Geoffrey Canada warns Michael Gove teaching unions "kill" innovation. *The Guardian*. Retrieved from www.theguardian.com/politics/2010/oct/05/geoffrey-canada-education-unions

Vaznis, J. (2009, August 12). Charter schools lag in serving the neediest. *The Boston Globe*. Retrieved from www.boston.com/news/education/k_12/articles/2009/08/12/charter_schools_lag_in_serving_students_with_special_needs/

Visser, T. (2013, September 27). The forgotten promise of charter schools [Opinion]. *Washington Post*. Retrieved from articles.washingtonpost.com/2013-09-27/opinions/42457285_1_charter-school-movement-charter-schools-charter-movement

Walker, T. (2013, July 8). NEA steps up organizing efforts in non-union charter schools. *NEA Today*. Retrieved from neatoday.org/2013/07/08/nea-steps-up-organizing-efforts-in-non-union-charter-schools/

Walton Family Foundation. (2013a). *Market share demonstration sites*. Retrieved from www.waltonfamilyfoundation.org/educationreform/market-share-demonstration-sites

Walton Family Foundation. (2013b). *2012 grant report*. Retrieved from www.waltonfamilyfoundation.org/about/2012-grant-report/

Warerkar, T., & Blau, R. (2013, November 19). United Federation of Teachers charter schools are a tale of two cities. *New York Daily News*. Retrieved from www.nydailynews.com/new-york/bronx/uft-charters-tale-cities-article-1.1522676

Weingarten, R. (2006, December 17). What matters most: It's time to take the politics out of charter schools. [Advertisement.] *New York Times*. Retrieved from www.aft.org/pdfs/press/wmm_101509c.pdf

Weiss, A. (2008, May 29). Mega-donor throws clout behind Hebrew charter school. *The Jewish Daily Forward*. Retrieved from www.forward.com/articles/13482/

Weitzel, P. C., & Lubienski, C. A. (2010). Assessing the charter school experiment. In C. A. Lubienski & P. C. Weitzel (Eds.), *The charter school experiment* (pp. 219–230). Cambridge, MA: Harvard Education Press.

Wells, A. S. (1993). *Time to choose: America at the crossroads of school choice policy*. New York, NY: Hill & Wang.

Wells, A. S., & Crain, R. L. (1994). Perpetuation theory and the long-term effects of school desegregation. *Review of Educational Research, 64*(4), 531–555.

Welner, K. G. (2006). K–12 race-conscious student assignment policies: Law, social science, and diversity. *Review of Educational Research, 76*(3), 349–382.

WestEd. (2006, October). *Charter high schools closing the achievement gap: Innovations in education*. Jessup, MD: U.S. Department of Education.

Whitehurst, G. J. (2012, December). *The education choice and competition index: Background and results 2012*. Washington, DC: Brookings Institution.

Whitman, D. (2008). An appeal to authority: The new paternalism in urban schools. *Education Next, 8*(4), 53–58.

Willms, J. D. (2010). School composition and contextual effects on student outcomes. *Teachers College Record, 112*(4), 1008–1037.

Wisconsin Department of Public Instruction. (2013). *IDEAL | Milwaukee. School Report Card | 2012–2013*. Retrieved November 1, 2013, from apps2.dpi.wi.gov/reportcards/

Wisconsin Department of Public Instruction. (n.d.). *WISEdash: Wisconsin Information System for Education Data Dashboard*. Retrieved November 1, 2013, from wisedash.dpi.wi.gov/Dashboard/portalHome.jsp

Wohlstetter, P., Smith, J., & Farrell, C. C. (2013). *Choices and challenges: Charter school performance in perspective*. Cambridge, MA: Harvard Education Press.

Woodard, B. (2013, February 18). Charter school union dissolved by National Labor Relations Board. *DNAinfo Chicago*. Retrieved from www.dnainfo.com/chicago/20130218/rogers-park/chicago-math-science-academy-union-regroups-after-ruling

Woodworth, K. R., David, J. K., Guha, R., Wang, H., & Lopez-Torkos, A. (2008). *San Francisco Bay Area KIPP Schools: A study of early implementation and achievement, final report*. Eugene, OR: Center for Educational Policy and SRI International.

Yglesias, M. (2008, November 6). A charter for the Obamas? [Web log post]. *ThinkProgress*. Retrieved from thinkprogress.org/yglesias/2008/11/06/190443/a_charter_for_the_obamas/

Yglesias, M. (2011, June 2). Charter schools and low-SES students: Damned if they do and damned if they don't? [Web log post]. *Think Progress*. Retrieved from thinkprogress.org/yglesias/2011/06/02/234962/charter-schools-and-low-ses-students-damned-if-they-do-and-damned-if-they-don%E2%80%99t/

Zeehandelaar, D., & Winkler, A. M. (Eds.). (2013, August). *What parents want: Education preferences and trade-offs*. Washington, DC: Thomas B. Fordham Institute.

Zehr, M. A. (2010, November 10). Regular public schools start to mimic charters. *Education Week*. Retrieved from www.edweek.org/ew/articles/2010/11/10/11charter.h30.html

Zelinski, A. (2013, July 29). Senators' fact-finding mission on charter schools zeroes in on pros not cons. *The City Paper: Nashville's Online Source for Daily News*. Retrieved from nashvillecitypaper.com/content/city-news/senators-fact-finding-mission-charter-schools-zeroes-pros-not-cons

Zimmer, R., Gill, B., Booker, K., Lavertu, S., Sass, T. R., & Witte, J. (2009). *Charter schools in eight states: Effects on achievement, attainment, integration, and competition*. Santa Monica, CA: The RAND Corporation.

Index

SUBJECTS

About the Authors

Richard D. Kahlenberg has been called "the intellectual father of the economic integration movement" in K–12 schooling, and "arguably the nation's chief proponent of class-based affirmative action in higher education admissions" (Eaton, 2006, p. 347; Roach, 2003). He is the author of five books, including *Tough Liberal: Albert Shanker and the Battles Over Schools, Unions, Race and Democracy* (Columbia University Press, 2007); and *All Together Now: Creating Middle Class Schools Through Public School Choice* (Brookings Institution Press, 2001). In addition, Kahlenberg is the editor of ten Century Foundation books, including *The Future of School Integration: Socioeconomic Diversity as an Education Reform Strategy* (2012) and *Divided We Fail: Coming Together Through Public School Choice*. Kahlenberg's articles have been published in the *New York Times, The Washington Post, The Wall Street Journal, The New Republic*, and elsewhere. He is a graduate of Harvard College and Harvard Law School.

Halley Potter is a fellow at The Century Foundation, where she researches public policy solutions for addressing educational inequality. Her work focuses on school integration, charter schools, and college access. She is coauthor, with Richard D. Kahlenberg, of *Diverse Charter Schools: Can Racial and Socioeconomic Integration Promote Better Outcomes for Students?* (The Century Foundation, 2012). Before joining The Century Foundation, Halley taught at Two Rivers Public Charter School in northeast Washington, DC. She graduated summa cum laude from Yale University with a bachelor's degree in religious studies.